Writing for radio

MANCHESTER
UNIVERSITY PRESS

Writing for radio

VINCENT MCINERNEY

MANCHESTER UNIVERSITY PRESS
Manchester and New York

distributed exclusively in the USA by Palgrave

Published by Manchester University Press
Oxford Road, Manchester M13 9NR, UK
and Room 400, 175 Fifth Avenue, New York, NY 10010, USA
http://www.manchesteruniversitypress.co.uk

Distributed exclusively in the USA by
Palgrave, 175 Fifth Avenue, New York, NY 10010, USA

Distributed exclusively in Canada by
UBC Press, University of British Columbia, 2029 West Mall,
Vancouver, BC, Canada V6T 1Z2

British Library Cataloguing-in-Publication Data
A catalogue record for this book is available from the British Library

Library of Congress Cataloging-in-Publication Data applied for

ISBN 0 7190 5842 2 *hardback*
0 7190 5843 0 *paperback*

First published 2001

08 07 06 05 04 03 02 01 10 9 8 7 6 5 4 3 2 1

Typeset by Carnegie Publishing, Lancaster
Printed in Great Britain by Bell & Bain Ltd, Glasgow

Contents

'It's a funny thing, this Marconi business, isn't it?' said Mr Shaynor coughing heavily.

Rudyard Kipling, 'Wireless', *Traffics and Discoveries*

GEOFFREY: Oh surely you're not prejudiced against wireless, grandfather! Now, have you heard it?

GRANDFATHER: Ay. More than I want to hear again. Parson's gotten one ... and doctor and schoolmaster, and I've heard 'em all – leastways I've tried to! ... Parson tempted me first wi' his crystallised set ... Clapped some telephone things ower my lugs, and told me to listen. All I could hear was howling enough to deafen a body. He said summat was wrong with t'cat's whisker. 'Nay' I said. 'It's somebody treading on cat's tail, you ask me!' Doctor's wasn't much better, though he had electric lights on his, but I've heard cows at home make a tunelier noise ... Schoolmaster's set, though, was happen best of lot – never a sound from it!

F. Austin Hyde and W. G. S. Fifth, from *Wireless and Sich-Like*

'It's a shame.' said Leda

Every one of us agreed.

'We're the only school I know' said Leda, 'that hasn't got wireless laid on. Absolutely the only one. Why, it's as necessary as electricity, or even a water-supply. I've heard my cousins say so; they're both going in for wireless. They know all the different types of microphones; and they know all about ...' Leda stopped. 'Well, anyway, I'm sure it's necessary' she said

Ethel Talbot, *Listening-In!*

'Every broadcast is a moral act.'

J. Scupham, *Broadcasting and the Community*

For Susie, Vincent and Anna

Acknowledgements

I would like to thank: those members of the BBC, past and present, who have taught and supported me – especially Shaun MacLoughlin; Harry Stamper, actor (fifty-seven radio parts in three days), for his comments on radio dialogue and other insights; John Corner, Liverpool University, for his unswerving commitment to this project for so many years and his invaluable editorial suggestions; Tim O'Sullivan, De Montfort University, for helpful and pertinent comments; Andrew McCarthy and Gerard F. Tierney of Projectile Productions for corrections and incisive suggestions regarding the first manuscript draft; Matthew Frost and the staff at Manchester University Press, for their help and patience, and Diane Jones, for her help with copy editing. And finally, those who have given substance to this book – my students.

Foreword

In a hectic audio-visual culture, radio is a medium that can be deceptive in its qualities. Too easily, it can be defined in relation to what it lacks – sounds without images. But rather than being limited by their lack of visual accompaniment, the spoken words of radio are often thereby freed into a sharper focus and a more powerful resonance. The texture of a voice and the rhythm of a sentence coming to us straight out of the airwaves create something that cannot be got from the printed page and is rarely produced by television. Radio's words can inform, argue, entertain, disturb and shock in ways which draw on the core energies of a language and therefore of a culture. If radio is no longer quite so often listened to in living rooms, new settings for hearing speech programming have followed with its increasing portability and its use in cars. The internet, already carrying radio stations, might finally work to develop many of the 'radio arts' in new ways, rather than to diminish them.

Vincent McInerny has written a book that explores a wide range of radio language from the point of view of the writer's *craft*, the practical skills involved in assembling 'the right words in the right order'. Vincent has a long and successful career as a writer for radio and I can think of no better person to offer guidance in its basics. He has also taught writing for many years in different educational settings and as one of his former evening-class students, I am able to testify to the pleasure and improvement that his distinctive approach can bring. Radio is a wonderful medium for the nurturing of new scriptwriters. I hope that this book, with its clear advice and its many examples, helps keep up a good supply of aspiring talent.

John Corner, Professor of Communication Studies,
University of Liverpool

Preface

This textbook, to serve student readers and writers working alone, has been developed over the years as 'writing for radio' has become more and more an integral part of media studies; more and more a requested skill within media lectureships; and as more and more students and writers realise the benefits of beginning or expanding a career within radio. The recent wave of in-house radio stations within educational establishments has also sharpened the need for a book of this nature.

The volume has three elements. The first details a radio writing course that involves leading the student reader/writer through a process which provides a thorough grounding in all aspects of factual and imaginative radio writing – that is, writing for a medium which requires a 'non-visual' scripting format. Beginning with the single voice in narration, the course is structured to move on to two voices, then two voices plus narrator. Then the radio short story. This leads to dealing with script layout and presentation, in preparation for the writing of the radio play and drama-documentary. Then the radio talk, interview, documentary and feature. The radio adaptation and dramatisation, followed by the radio poem and then the radio advertisement. There is an Appendix at the end of the book containing numerous suggestions for storylines/plotlines that can be used for exercises, or to develop professional pieces of writing. Each full chapter contains at least one example taken from a broadcast radio script. These scripts, when it seems pertinent, will be discussed and analysed.

The second element of the book is a short historical and analytical examination of the more important radio genres, covering how they began and developed to the point at which they stand today.

The third element of the book is an examination of the nature of radio writing itself. When listening to a radio piece one of two things usually happens. Either what's being listened to produces pictures in the mind of the listener – or a stream of words without any visual images is heard. If a piece of radio writing does its work properly it should produce a stream of connected mindvisible images in the mind of the listener. But what is it about any particular piece of writing that generates these images? Does it require a particular vocabulary and particular syntactical structures? Is there a 'radio language'? If there is, then any piece of writing can be examined as to its suitability and probable success as radio while still on the page, and can then be recorded and listened to, in order to test that assumption. This means a new academic approach to radio is possible whereby any piece of prose, drama or verse can, theoretically, be assessed as good or bad radio on the page, and then tested by means of tape recording.

Radio scripts are notoriously difficult to come by. They are heard, pass and often never surface again. By using the method of analysis in the book, any piece of writing, from any literary genre, can be tested as radio. All writing is opened up for analysis and examination as possible radio.

So, while the main thrust of the volume is directed towards the student reader and the writer working alone – providing self-contained units that offer explanatory text, and ideas for possible development in all the major radio formats; the book and course have also been designed to facilitate the work of a busy lecturer requiring a comprehensive class text. There are numerous examples, short exercises and assignments that a lecturer could set from the page – reducing preparation and photocopying time to a minimum.

The book has been structured to be taught in two hour units that are run sequentially, although individual sessions can be omitted, transferred or linked to suit circumstances. The shorter exercises within the book are designed to be completed within any two hour class session – and then to be heard by the students within the class time. Just as a runner's abilities can only be gauged by entering races against other competitors, so students can only really gauge their strengths and weaknesses by hearing what they have written for radio being read out against the work of their peers. The longer exercises and projects could be set as assignments to be written and produced in the course, or used to provide the base for actual submissions to producers at radio stations.

Basic equipment for this course is the cassette recorder/simple editing facilities. The book and course attempt to offer a complete grounding in this most universal arm of the media at an extremely competitive and cost-effective rate compared with courses requiring film or video equipment. The course could run from one to three years depending on the depth and complexity of assignments set by an individual lecturer.

Although the book is built around radio, because all classically constructed writing works the same way, the book should be of use to all writers and on all writing courses in general.

All examples, extracts and whole works that are not credited to a specific author, or are 'Anonymous', are the work of the writer of this book; as are the Brecht and Uhland translations.

1 From the beginning: the philosophy of radio

On principle, it is quite wrong to try founding a theory on observable magnitudes alone. In reality ... it is the theory which decides what we can observe.

Einstein in conversation with C. Heisenberg, 1927.
Quoted in Otto Friedrich, *Before the Deluge*.

Into the street the piper stept,
Smiling first a little smile,
As if he knew what magic slept,
In his quiet pipe the while ...

Robert Browning (1812–89)
'The Pied Piper of Hamelin'

In many ways, radio has always seemed the friendliest of all the media – especially in terms of music. Music, perhaps, is the one art which transcends all barriers of race and class. Everyone responds to a beautiful melody.

But talk radio, too, offers its own, often underrated, attractions. Television may entertain, film visually impress, the theatre stimulate; but radio is more like the old friend who never fails to call after lunch; the comforting voice at night next to the bed; the cheery whistle of the postman in the early morning. These three images, set in the afternoon, the evening and at dawn, have been deliberately chosen because radio has now become, essentially, a day-time activity. But while our evenings are given over to the visual media, at most other times it is to radio that we turn.

Unlike television, radio demands nothing from us in terms of forced laughter or melodramatic sighs, but, instead, offers what we ourselves require. In times of happiness we can find the light comedy to accelerate our mood. In times of stress, its calm tones can provide a ready shoulder on which to lean. In times of loneliness, like the soldier's last cigarette, it can provide both food and fire; and a friend.

But how does it work? How can mere mechanical sound waves translate into the 'cloud-capp'd towers' and 'gorgeous palaces'; the 'solemn temples' and 'great globe itself' which we sometimes see in our minds when listening to radio?

To answer this, perhaps we should try to assess the intellectual and linguistic sources that generate radio's images. That is, if we investigate what aspect it is of the broadcast spoken word that produces instantly recognisable pictures into our minds, perhaps this, in turn, will lead us to understand how radio provides these representations.

The object of all radio writing, all talk radio, whether it be prose, drama or verse, is to produce an image, or set of images, in the mind of the listener. These images can be separate, or causally continuous, but should be vivid and precisely defined. In the best radio writing they will be automatically triggered by the words being spoken.

These immediate, mindvisible images, should, ideally, fit within the sensory experiences of the average listener as regards time and place, and be causally linked.

But how are they generated, and what is their linguistic history?

As language developed so did the storyteller. Before pictorial record, before writing, there would have been people who could command and hold an audience by what they said, and the way their material was expressed.

In family or tribal groups, certain individuals would have come to the fore because of their gifts as storytellers. They would have been those who, as they related an incident or described a character, simultaneously conjured up in the minds of their listeners vivid images of that which they were describing. The vocabulary they used, and the syntactical constructions they employed, immediately translated their verbal descriptions into mental images. Instinctively, they knew how to generate representative pictures and work an audience. Their direct artistic descendants are the best of today's radio writers. Their verbal descendants can be found in bars, buses and boats; and writing speeches for politicians and the heads of large corporations.

All first-class radio writers are masters of the graphic phrase, the striking simile, the apt metaphor – all of which immediately translate *pictorially*. These images then have to be placed accurately in a properly constructed narrative or plot to enhance and drive forward a particular work.

But what is the vocabulary of the immediate image? And can certain words in a certain order guarantee a series of mental pictures/picture sequences? And, if so, how?

Consider the following three descriptions which might be heard in a radio play, short story or documentary – describing a politician's gifts as a debater and speechmaker. He/she could

- 'talk a glass eye to sleep'
- 'talk the leg off a chair'
- 'talk the sole off a sea-boot'.

They are all immediately striking, but which of these do you 'see'? Which, as you read/hear it, becomes simultaneously mindvisible?

A nautical example to complement the third description above: 'Many vessels at that time were long, narrow and noted for their instability. The *Virtue*, for example, was the sort of sailing ship where ...

- 'a barrel rolled across the deck was enough to produce a ten degree list'
- 'the only way to keep her upright was for the skipper to make sure his hair was always parted in the middle'.

Now a final example, contrived to give true images in a causally continuous sequence:

> Below the waterline, the protruding shelf of the iceberg dug into the ship's side like a giant putty knife, opening the hull plates in a long, jagged wound and allowing thousands of tons of icy water to rush into the cargo and machinery spaces. The vessel gradually began to lose way – at the same time beginning to list, almost imperceptibly, to starboard. Suddenly there were orders and shouts from the boat-decks; and rockets bursting in the clear, cold, night sky. Then there was silence. Eventually, still encrusted by lights, and with faint strains of dance music echoing over the black freezing water, she settled by the stern and began to sink.

Which of the foregoing, if heard over the radio, would immediately produce a *true* picture in the listener's mind of what is being described?

Look again at the first three descriptions, dealing with the verbal abilities of the politician. He/she could

- 'talk a glass eye to sleep'
- 'talk the leg off a chair'
- 'talk the sole off a sea-boot'.

All three are immediate on the page – but do not come up simultaneously in the mind – do not give true immediate distinctive images. We cannot formulate, as part of our experience, a glass eye being talked to sleep, or a leg being talked off a chair. And while the image of a sole peeling back off a sea-boot does come up as something we can envisage, there is something inherently improbable about this being caused by someone talking in a repetitive, ingratiating, repulsive, meaningless fashion.

Similarly, with e. e. cummings's couplet about a politician:

> a politician is an arse upon
> which everyone has sat except a man.

Though striking on the page, this again does not work in terms of visual radio imagery. We may see an arse on the seat but to what, simultaneously with hearing it, can we visualise it being attached if not a human trunk? Far better the item by J. B. Morton ('Beachcomber') from *Captain Foulenough & Company* (1944):

Current rates

> A man the other day handed two shillings to a taxi-driver for a one and sixpenny fare, saying, 'Keep the change – or buy yourself a professional politician with it.'

Although sketchy in the extreme, this conjures up an immediate set of pictures as we read it.

Take the example about the listing of the ship: Many vessels at that time were long, narrow and noted for their instability. The *Virtue*, for example, was the sort of sailing ship where …

- 'a barrel rolled across the deck was enough to produce a ten degree list'
- 'the only way to keep her upright was for the skipper to make sure his hair was always parted in the middle'.

Again, hopefully, these are fanciful, amusing and striking images. But this time we can also mentally see a sort of cause and effect in what is being described. We can see the picture of someone rolling a barrel over the deck of a ship and the ship beginning to list. Or, in the second example, a man parting his hair to one side and the ship listing over with the weight of the extra hair.

We may *know* that the actions detailed cannot produce the results described, but we can still see in our minds what is being described as it is being described. Cause, with the use of a strong imagination, can produce a particular, if erroneous, effect.

We know a ship will list with an unequal transfer of weight, and this provides the impetus for the image – but a false image.

So, while there is a degree of *imaginative* truth in the second pair of examples, we are not yet producing a true effect.

Moving on to the third example:

> Below the waterline, the protruding shelf of the iceberg dug into the ship's side like a giant putty knife, opening the hull plates in a long, jagged wound and allowing thousands of tons of icy water to rush into the cargo and machinery spaces. The vessel gradually began to lose way – at the same time beginning to list, almost imperceptibly, to starboard. Suddenly there were orders and shouts from the boat-decks; and rockets bursting in the clear, cold, night sky. Then there was silence. Eventually, still encrusted by lights, and with faint strains of dance music echoing over the black freezing water, she settled by the stern and began to sink.

In this example there are no false steps. We may not have personally seen the sinking of a ship by its striking an iceberg. But through experience, books, film, discussion, we know the sequence of events and we have seen all the major incidents described in the extract happen in one form or another. A knife cutting through putty or butter, water rushing unstoppably, cries, whistles and rockets to signal distress ... All the various steps mentioned in the example are accessible in our experience and memories, and we can link them in a causal chain that we can immediately identify as true.

So here we have a complete, specific sequence that contains no false measures and which works unreservedly. And as well as the causal chain, we are presented with the vivid and immediate pictures of 'light-encrusted ship' lying slightly over to one side, and somehow we actually *hear* the strains of the dance band sounding faintly over the icy, dark ocean. True aural engagement has simultaneously given us a visual product. We have been bought over by skill, and by the writer's understanding of what to do and how to do it. But what did the writer understand – and how did he know what words would produce the desired effects?

Here are two passages quoted in Christopher Salmon's essay, 'Broadcasting, Speech and Writing':

> I want to tell you a tale – just one tale – out of many hundred sights and atrocities I saw. I myself was driving a milk stall, and round this milk stall was a screaming crowd of women with babies. I kept picking a few babies out and feeding them. One woman who was – I think she was – mad kept kissing my feet, hands and clothing. So I took the baby from her, and when I looked at the baby its face was black – it'd been dead for a few days. I couldn't convince her it was dead – so I pressed the lips open and poured the milk down its dead throat. The woman crooned, gibbered with delight. I gave her the baby back and she staggered off, and lay in the sun. And when I next looked she was dead with the baby in her arms, and so I put her with a stack of other dead bodies – two or three hundred dead, and I turned away.
>
> Anon., Broadcast by the BBC Home Service, May 1945

> The deceitful and dangerous experiment of the criminal quaestio, as it is emphatically styled, was admitted, rather than approved, in the jurisprudence of the Romans. They applied this sanguinary mode of examination only to servile bodies, whose sufferings were seldom weighed by those haughty republicans in the scale of justice or humanity; but they would never consent to violate the sacred person of a citizen till they possessed the clearest evidence of his guilt. The annals of tyranny, from the reign of Tiberius to that of Domitian, circumstantially relate the executions of many innocent victims; but, as long as the faintest remembrance was kept alive of the national freedom and honour, the last hours of a Roman were secure from the danger of ignominious torture.
>
> Edward Gibbon (1737–94)
> *The Decline and Fall of the Roman Empire* (1776–88)

The writer/speaker in the first of these pieces was an unknown inmate of Belsen Concentration Camp; the writer of the second piece was Edward Gibbon, historian and author of *The Decline and Fall of the Roman Empire.*

The two extracts are ostensibly about the same thing – the nature of arbitrary arrest and torture under totalitarian regimes. They are complementary pieces, not templates, for Gibbon remarks that the sacred person of the Roman citizen was not to be violated until there was clear evidence of guilt, while in Germany, under the Nazis, the question of innocence or guilt seems to have been one of the few things not required of a German citizen before arrest and torture.

As to the writing, with the Belsen piece everything is vivid, clear, immediately comprehensible. We are there with the speaker and the effects become immediately accessible as they are related. Pure radio. About the speaker in this first extract we know nothing.

Gibbon's own personal case has often been documented. From his rejection of his time at Magdalen College, 'the most idle and unprofitable of my whole life', to Beckford's 'your most ludicrous self-complacency ... tumid diction ... monotonous jingle of periods' and ending with Porson's remark about *Decline and Fall*, that 'there could not be a better exercise for a schoolboy than to turn a page of it into English'.

And while it might provide good copy for an English exercise, as good radio the Gibbon does not work.

Salmon, in his essay, observes that we have two men, each with something to communicate, writing in English. The question he asks is – if the advantage in using the language goes to one rather than the other, is this because one of them uses the language more skilfully than the other? He awards no prize, because he says that the two writers are 'pulling at English from different situations'. He goes on to say, 'What may be properly attempted with language in speech is different from what may properly be written.'

Salmon is on the right track, but this seems a partially invalid judgement as regards the anonymous Belsen extract. This not only *reads* graphically, clearly and beautifully, but it obviously broadcast the same way. It works both as prose and as speech. Considering it as a potential piece of radio, to read it is both to *hear* and to *see* the events described.

The Gibbon is a different matter. It reads well, in its own pretentious fashion, but could never be broadcast as an example of anything that is good radio. Why?

We have two pieces of writing that are both acceptable as prose pieces on a page, yet as soon as one is broadcast it ceases to hold or impress. Why?

The answer must lie in the language used. In the differences in the language used in the two extracts. But what are these differences?

Do they lie in the use of the nouns? The verbs? The syntax generally? And can a set of rules be formulated which will produce good radio? Is there a *radio language*? A language which all those who write the best radio use automatically – albeit perhaps unknowingly? A writing that immediately generates strong, coherent, mindvisible images?

Suppose a group of native people, who have had no contact at all with any aspect of Western civilisation, are walking through a dense rainforest along a narrow path. They come to a clearing, and in the middle of the clearing there is a new, fully chromed, motorcycle. What do they see?

One thing they do not see, as we understand it, is a motorcycle. So what do they see?

Now suppose it is we who are walking along the path and eventually reach the clearing. We stop and gaze at the motorcycle, identify it as a motorcycle, and continue walking across the clearing, and back into the forest on the other side of the clearing where the path begins again. We continue walking along the path and come to another clearing. Here, in the middle of this clearing, is a second motorcycle; perhaps an early machine built, say, in the year 1920. What conclusions would we draw? We would feel we have seen two objects that we have readily identified as motorcycles. The two pieces of machinery might be eighty years apart, and look almost totally different in design – but we would immediately recognise them both as motorcycles. How?

Or if we saw an Irish wolfhound and then a Chihuahua, we would know that both were dogs even though they were totally opposite in size and appearance. How?

We would know because we possess the *concepts* of motorcycleness and of dogginess. In our minds, through experience, we have formulated and carry a universal blueprint for both dogs and motorcycles, and when we see either of these things, no matter in what shape, condition or state, we know automatically that what we are looking at is either a motorcycle or a dog.

The Greek philosopher, Plato (*c.* 429–347 BC), referred to these universal blueprints in their pure state as *Forms*. Forms are the eternal reality of the imperfect examples we have and use in this world. We may see a potter, working at his wheel, throw a circular plate. Of course, it will not be completely circular – but its Form, the Form of the Plate in eternity, will be a perfect circle.

Forms of such things as plates and motorcycles came very low on Plato's list – and all Forms, even those of truth and beauty, were subordinate to the *Form of the Good*. The Form of the Good was the summit of all philosophical knowledge.

Socrates (*c.* 470–399 BC), through the mouth of Plato, told his listeners that the Form of the Good lay beyond all definition. It has been said that there is a touch of mysticism in Socrates's refusal to put into language the meaning of the 'Good'. There may also have been a touch of ignorance.

Plato felt that the Forms were the ultimate reality, that through them we are in touch with eternity. But the way to the stars was hard. And he explained himself by asking his listeners to imagine a line drawn vertically, and divided so that the top portion is longer than the bottom. The top portion represents the eternal world of the Forms; the bottom portion the world of appearances and opinions. Then both parts of the line are divided yet again into two sections. So we have a vertical line divided into four sections which, beginning at the bottom section and working upwards, we will call A, B, C and D.

Beginning at the bottom section, A. Here, Plato tells us, we find all works of art; images which copy things that are already images – the everyday things of our world of appearances. In this bottom section of the line we might find a painting or photograph of a motorcycle. Section B of the line contains the world of sensible appearances – our everyday world. The world in which we find the objects known as motorcycles, objects which we can then represent in paintings or photographs. But these motorcycles in section B are only rust-prone, failed M-O-T, illegal, untaxed copies of the true reality of the motorcycle, which lies in the world of the Forms.

We then move to the top portion of the line which, as stated, is again divided into two sections – C and D. In section C we find mathematics, in which Plato felt the proofs were abstract and universal (that the three angles of a triangle will always equal 180 degrees, even though no human being can experience and measure all triangles). The angles will never move slightly out of shape, as the potter's plate might, nor will they rust, as might the motorcycle, but will always be enduringly true and can be used to work out the design of the motorcycle. And through the universality and enduring truths of mathematics Plato felt we could finally contemplate section D, the world of the Forms – which Plato called Dialectic. The world where we struggle to understand the Forms in themselves, and the world where we might find the perfect motorcycle – and from where we gain our concept of a motorcycle. That no one should go away dissatisfied, or feeling short-changed, Plato said he felt that this knowledge without experience was because the soul remembered visions that it had had in a previous disembodied existence. Others, less fanciful, approached the problem with more caution.

The philosopher John Locke (1632–1704) called the Forms *ideas* and felt that there were two types of *idea* – two types of thing from which we form our concepts, both of which come from experience. He called these *Ideas of Sensation* and *Ideas of Reflection*. Ideas of Sensation come through the five outer senses of sight, sound, touch, smell and taste, and provide us with our concepts of the physical world. Ideas of Reflection come from the inner senses and provide our ideas of love, hate, pleasure and pain – from which we draw ideas about our inner life. Locke maintained that all our concepts are drawn from these two kinds of ideas of experience.

David Hume (1711–76) went further, making a distinction between *ideas* and *impressions*. His use of these words was as follows. If you see a red spot – you have red *impression*; but if you close your eyes and imagine a red spot you have an *idea* of red. But if you have never seen red you can have no idea of red. And the same applies to the inner senses. If a person has had no experience of pain – he or she cannot imagine pain. So if we hear the words 'there was a red spot' on the radio we can see the red spot but only because we already have a concept (sense impression) of red.

There is, of course, a fallacy here. We can have concepts/ideas of things which we have never seen and which have never existed. Imagine hearing the following in sequence on the radio: 'A donkey. A blue donkey. A blue donkey wearing a gold crown. A blue donkey wearing a gold crown and spectacles. A blue donkey wearing a gold crown and spectacles and holding a glass of gin. A blue donkey wearing a gold crown and spectacles, carrying a glass of gin and riding a red hyena.' There is not one of these separate ideas we cannot imagine in our minds – but what we imagine as the finished concept has never physically existed. So how can we imagine that which we have not seen?

Locke overcame this barrier by splitting ideas into simple and complex ideas. The *simple ideas* in our example would be blue, donkey, gold, crown, spectacles, glass, gin, red, hyena. The final *complex idea* is generated in our minds by putting together all the simple ideas – the blue donkey wearing a gold crown and spectacles, carrying the glass of gin and riding the red hyena. Through the individual elements (the simple ideas) we can arrive at, and see, the complex idea – even if it is something completely outside our experience.

So, in the case of the motorcycle, by referring internally to the blueprint we have built up of motorcycles, we can identify that which carries a whiff of motorcycleness in it – no matter in what bastardised form. As long as the handlebars, petrol tank, gear chain, two wheels (or something resembling them) are there and organised in a certain way – then we know that what we are looking at is a motorcycle.

Look again at the Belsen extract used by Salmon. It is full of simple ideas and concepts.

> I want to tell you a tale – just one tale – out of many hundred sights and atrocities I saw. I myself was driving a milk stall, and round this milk stall was a screaming crowd of women with babies. I kept picking a few babies out and feeding them. One woman who was – I think she was – mad kept kissing my feet, hands and clothing. So I took the baby, from her, and when I looked at the baby its face was black – it'd been dead for a few days. I couldn't convince her it was dead – so I pressed the lips open and poured the milk down its dead throat. The woman crooned, gibbered with delight. I gave her the baby back and she staggered off, and lay in the sun. And when I next looked she was dead with the baby in her arms, and so I put her with a stack of other dead bodies – two or three hundred dead, and I turned away.

In the first three lines we have 'a tale', 'milk', 'stall', 'crowd', 'women', 'babies'. Simple noun-based ideas and concepts which we can remove from the text and, by joining them together, form a perfectly comprehensible and series of mental images that must be intelligible to almost everyone on the planet. 'In my tale I am driving a milk stall, around which is a crowd of women with babies.' The rest of the first three lines, 'many hundred sights', 'atrocities', adds colour and emotion, and builds up atmosphere.

Now the first lines of Gibbon:

> The deceitful and dangerous experiment of the criminal quaestio, as it is emphatically styled, was admitted, rather than approved,

> in the jurisprudence of the Romans. They applied this sanguinary mode of examination only to servile bodies ...

Broadcast on the radio, we would hear mellifluous and pleasing verbal sounds, probably delivered in a voice especially imported into the studio at some expense to the licence payer, but we would see virtually nothing in terms of immediate mindvisible images. Information is there, but the pictures are missing.

If, then, there is a radio language – a language which automatically produces immediate mindvisible images – then this language seems to demand readily identifiable concepts based upon simple ideas and contained within a strong, causally continuative narrative.

Consider the following three examples of pairs of complementary texts. First we have two accounts of a party. The party in Dickens's *David Copperfield* and the party that Pierre attends near the beginning of Tolstoy's *War and Peace*. Tolstoy was very impressed by Dickens, especially *David Copperfield*, translating it himself. And the use of the windows in the two extracts seems to contain echoes. Dostoevsky, too, fell under the spell of Dickens; indeed, Dickens had an enormous influence on them both. Edmund Wilson, in his essay, 'Dickens: The Two Scrooges', commented, 'it is difficult for British pundits to see in him the great artist and social critic he was ... The literary men from Oxford and Cambridge ... snubbingly let him alone. The Bloomsbury that talked about Dostoevsky ignored Dostoevsky's master, Dickens.' Read the two accounts, imagining you are hearing them read on the radio.

Charles Dickens (1812–70) *David Copperfield* (1849/50) Chapter XXIV

> Mrs. Crupp then said what she would recommend would be this. A pair of hot roast fowls – from the pastry-cook's; a dish of stewed beef, with vegetables – from the pastry-cook's; two little corner things as a raised pie and a dish of kidneys – from the pastry-cook's; a tart, and (if I liked) a shape of jelly – from the pastry-cook's. This, Mrs Crupp said, would leave her at full liberty to concentrate her mind on the potatoes, and to serve up the cheese and celery as she could wish to see it done.
>
> I acted on Mrs. Crupp's opinion, and gave the order at the pastry-cook's myself. Walking along the Strand, afterwards, and observing a hard mottled substance in the window of a ham and

beef shop, which resembled marble, but was labelled 'Mock Turtle', I went in and bought a slab of it, which I have since seen reason to believe would have sufficed fifteen people. This preparation, Mrs. Crupp, after some difficulty, consented to warm up; and it shrunk so much in a liquid state, that we found it what Steerforth called 'rather tight fit' for four.

These preparations happily completed, I bought a little dessert in Covent Garden Market, and gave a rather extensive order at a retail wine-merchant's in that vicinity. When I came home in the afternoon, and saw the bottles drawn up in a square on the pantry-floor, they looked so numerous (though there were two missing, which made Mrs. Crupp very uncomfortable), that I was absolutely frightened at them.

One of Steerforth's friends was named Grainger, and the other Markham. They were both very gay and lively fellows; Grainger, something older than Steerforth; Markham, youthful-looking, and I should say not more than twenty. I observed that the latter always spoke of himself indefinitely, as 'a man', and seldom or never in the first person singular.

'A man might get on very well here, Mr. Copperfield,' said Markham – meaning himself.

'It's not a bad situation,' said I, 'and the rooms are really commodious.'

'I hope you have both brought appetites with you?' said Steerforth.

'Upon my honour,' returned Markham, 'town seems to sharpen a man's appetite. A man is hungry all day long. A man is perpetually eating.'

Being a little embarrassed at first, and feeling much too young to preside, I made Steerforth take the head of the table when dinner was announced, and seated myself opposite to him. Everything was very good; we did not spare the wine; and he exerted himself so brilliantly to make the thing pass off well, that there was no pause in our festivity. I was not quite such good company during dinner, as I could have wished to be, for my chair was opposite the door, and my attention was distracted by observing that the handy young man went out of the room very often, and that his shadow always presented itself, immediately afterwards, on the wall of the entry, with a bottle at his mouth. The 'young gal' likewise occasioned me some uneasiness: not so much as neglecting to wash the plates, as by breaking them. For being of an inquisitive disposition, and unable to confine herself (as her positive instructions were) to the pantry, she was constantly peering in at us, and constantly imagining herself detected; in which belief, she several times retired upon the plates (with which she had carefully paved the floor), and did a great deal of destruction.

These, however, were small drawbacks, and easily forgotten when the cloth was cleared, and the dessert put on the table; at which period of the entertainment the handy young man was discovered to be speechless. Giving him private directions to seek the society of Mrs. Crupp, and to remove the 'young gal' to the basement also, I abandoned myself to enjoyment.

I began by being singularly cheerful and light-hearted; all sorts of half-forgotten things to talk about, came rushing into my mind, and made me hold forth in a most unwonted manner. I laughed heartily at my own jokes, and everybody else's; called Steerforth to order for not passing the wine; made several engagements to go to Oxford; announced that I meant to have a dinner party exactly like that, once a week until further notice; and madly took so much snuff out of Grainger's box, that I was obliged to go into the pantry, and have a private fit of sneezing ten minutes long. I went on, by passing the wine faster and faster yet, and continually starting up with a corkscrew to open more wine before any was needed. I proposed Steerforth's health. I said he was my dearest friend, the protector of my boyhood and the companion of my prime. I said I was delighted to propose his health. I said I owed him more obligations than I could ever repay, and held him in a higher admiration than I could ever express. I finished by saying, 'I'll give you Steerforth! God bless him! Hurrah!' We gave him three times three, and another, and a good one to finish with. I broke my glass in going round the table to shake hands with him, and I said (in two words) 'Steerforth you'retheguidingstarofmyex-istence.' I went on, by finding suddenly that somebody was in the middle of a song. Markham was the singer, and he sang 'When the heart of a man is depressed with care.' He said, when he had sung it, he would give us 'Woman!' I took objection to that, and I couldn't allow it. I said it was not a respectful way of proposing the toast, and I would never permit that toast to be drunk in my house otherwise than as 'The Ladies!'

I was very high with him, mainly I think because I saw Steerforth and Grainger laughing at me – or at him – or at both of us. He said a man was not to be dictated to. I said a man was. He said a man was not to be insulted, then.

I said he was right there – never under my roof where the Lares were sacred, and the laws of hospitality paramount. He said it was no derogation from a man's dignity to confess that I was a devilish good fellow. I instantly proposed his health.

Somebody was smoking. We were all smoking. I was smoking, and trying to suppress a rising tendency to shudder. Steerforth had made a speech about me, in the course of which I had been affected almost to tears.

I returned thanks, hoped the present company, would dine with me tomorrow and the day after – each day at five o'clock, that we might enjoy the pleasure of conversation and society through a long evening. I felt called upon to propose an individual. I would give them my aunt. Miss Betsy Trotwood, the best of her sex!

Somebody was leaning out of my bed-room window, refreshing his forehead against the cool stone of the parapet, and feeling the air upon his face. It was myself. I was addressing myself as 'Copperfield,' and saying, 'Why did you try to smoke? You might have known you couldn't do it.' Now, somebody was unsteadily contemplating his features in the looking-glass. That was I too. I was very pale in the looking-glass; my eyes had a vacant appearance; and my hair – only my hair, nothing else – looked drunk.

Somebody said to me, 'Let us go to the theatre, Copperfield.' There was no bed-room before me, but again the jingling table covered with glasses; the lamp; Grainger on my right hand, Markham on my left, and Steerforth opposite – all sitting in a mist, and a long way off. The theatre? To be sure. The very thing. Come along! But they must excuse me if I saw everybody out first, and turned the lamp off – in case of fire.

Owing to some confusion in the dark, the door was gone. I was feeling for it in the window-curtains, when Steerforth laughing, took me by the arm and led me out. We went down-stairs, one behind another. Near the bottom, somebody fell, and rolled down. Somebody else said it was Copperfield. I was angry at that false report, until, finding myself on my back in the passage, I began to think there might be some foundation for it.

Turning from Dickens, the writer referred to by Taine as 'The Master of all Hearts', to Tolstoy, the writer known as 'A serene god' – though his private life hardly bears this out.

Leo Tolstoy (1828–1910) *War and Peace* (1865–69)
Chapter IX

It was past one o'clock when Pierre left his friend. It was a cloudless, northern, summer night. Pierre took an open cab intending to drive straight home. But the nearer he drew to the house the more he felt the impossibility of going to sleep on such a night. It was light enough to see a long way in the deserted street and it seemed more like morning or evening than night. On the way Pierre remembered that Anatole Kuragin was expecting the usual set for cards that evening, after which there was generally a drinking bout, finishing with visits of a kind Pierre was very fond of.

'I should like to go to Kuragin's,' thought he.

But he immediately recalled his promise to Prince Andrew not to go there. Then, as happens to people of weak character, he desired so passionately once more to enjoy that dissipation he was so accustomed to, that he decided to go. The thought immediately occurred to him that his promise to Prince Andrew was of no account, because before he gave it he had already promised Prince Anatole to come to his gathering; 'besides,' thought he, 'all such "words of honour" are conventional things with no definite meaning, especially if one considers that by to-morrow one may be dead, or something so extraordinary may happen to one that honour and dishonour will be all the same!' Pierre often indulged in reflections of this sort, nullifying all his decisions and intentions. He went to Kuragin's.

Reaching the large house near the Horse Guards' barracks, in which Anatole lived, Pierre entered the lighted porch, ascended the stairs, and went in at the open door. There was no one in the ante-room; empty bottles, cloaks, and over-shoes were lying about; there was a smell of alcohol, and sounds of voices and shouting in the distance.

Cards and supper were over, but the visitors had not yet dispersed. Pierre threw off his cloak and entered the first room, in which were the remains of supper. A footman, thinking no one saw him, was drinking on the sly what was left in the glasses. From the third room came sounds of laughter, the shouting of familiar voices, the growling of a bear, and general commotion. Some eight or nine young men were crowding anxiously round an open window. Three others were romping with a young bear, one pulling him by the chain and trying to set him at the others.

'I bet a hundred on Stevens!' shouted one.

'Mind, no holding on!' cried another.

'I bet on Dolokhov!' cried a third. 'Kuragin, you part our hands.'*

'There, leave Bruin alone; here's a bet on.'

'At one draught, or he loses!' shouted a fourth.

'Jacob, bring a bottle!' shouted the host, a tall handsome fellow who stood in the midst of the group, without a coat, and with his fine linen shirt unfastened in front. 'Wait a bit, you fellows ... Here is Petya! Good man!' cried he, addressing Pierre.

Another voice, from a man of medium height with clear blue eyes, particularly striking among all these drunken voices by its sober ring, cried from the window: 'Come here; part the bets!' This was Dolokhov, an officer of the Semenov regiment, a notorious gambler and duellist, who was living with Anatole. Pierre smiled, looking about him merrily.

'I don't understand. What's it all about?'

'Wait a bit, he is not drunk yet! A bottle here,' said Anatole, and taking a glass from the table he went up to Pierre.

'First of all you must drink!'

Pierre drank one glass after another looking from under his brows at the tipsy guests who were again crowding round the window and listening to their chatter. Anatole kept on refilling Pierre's glass while explaining that Dolokhov was betting with Stevens, an English naval officer, that he would drink a bottle of rum sitting on the outer sloping ledge of the third-floor window with his legs hanging out.

'Go on, you must drink it all,' said Anatole, giving Pierre the last glass, 'or I won't let you go!'

'No, I won't,' said Pierre, pushing Anatole aside, and he went up to the window.

Dolokhov was holding the Englishman's hand and clearly and distinctly repeating the terms of the bet, addressing himself particularly to Anatole and Pierre.

Dolokhov was of medium height, with curly hair and light blue eyes. He was about five-and-twenty. Like all infantry officers he wore no moustache, so that his mouth, the most striking feature of his face, was clearly seen. The lines of that mouth were remarkably finely curved. The middle of the upper lip formed a sharp

---

* The Russian custom was to shake hands on a bet and for some third person, acting as a witness, to separate the hands.

wedge and closed firmly on the firm lower one, and something like two distinct smiles played continually round the two corners of the mouth; this, together with the resolute, insolent intelligence of his eyes, produced an effect which made it impossible not to notice his face. Dolokhov was a man of small means and no connexions. Yet though Anatole spent tens of thousands of rubles, Dolokhov lived with him and had placed himself on such a footing that all who knew them, including Anatole himself, respected him more than they did Anatole. Dolokhov could play all games and nearly always won. However much he drank he never lost his clear-headedness. Both Kuragin and Dolokhov were at that time notorious among the rakes and scapegraces of Petersburg.

The bottle of rum was brought. The window frame which prevented any one from sitting on the outer sill, was being forced out by two footmen, who were evidently flurried and intimidated by the directions and shouts of the gentlemen around.

Anatole with his swaggering air strode up to the window. He wanted to smash something. Pushing away the footmen he tugged at the frame, but could not move it. He smashed a pane.

'You have a try, Hercules,' said he, turning to Pierre.

Pierre seized the crossbeam, tugged, and wrenched the oak frame out with a crash.

'Take it right out, or they'll think I'm holding on,' said Dolokhov.

'Is the Englishman bragging ... Eh? Is it all right?' said Anatole.

'First rate,' said Pierre, looking at Dolokhov, who with a bottle of rum in his hand was approaching the window, from which the light of the sky, the dawn merging with the afterglow of sunset, was visible.

Dolokhov, the bottle of rum still in his hand, jumped onto the window-sill. 'Listen!' cried he, standing there and addressing those in the room. All were silent.

'I bet fifty imperials' – he spoke French that the Englishman might understand him, but he did not speak it very well – 'I bet fifty imperials, or do you wish to make it a hundred?' added he, addressing the Englishman.

'No, fifty,' replied the latter.

'All right. Fifty imperials ... that I will drink a whole bottle of rum without taking it from my mouth, sitting outside the window on this spot' (he stooped and pointed to the sloping ledge outside the window), 'and without holding on to anything. Is that right?'

'Quite right,' said the Englishman.

Anatole turned to the Englishman and taking him by one of the buttons of his coat and looking down at him – the Englishman was short – began repeating the terms of the wager to him in English.

'Wait!' cried Dolokhov, hammering with the bottle on the window-sill to attract attention. 'Wait a bit, Kuragin. Listen! If any one else does the same, I will pay him a hundred imperials. Do you understand?'

The Englishman nodded, but gave no indication whether he intended to accept this challenge or not. Anatole did not release him, and though he kept nodding to show that he understood, Anatole went on translating Dolokhov's words into English. A thin young lad, an hussar of the Life Guards, who had been losing that evening, climbed on the window-sill, leaned over, and looked down.

'Oh! Oh! Oh!' he muttered, looking down from the window at the stones of the pavement.

'Shut up!' cried Dolokhov, pushing him away from the window. The lad jumped awkwardly back into the room, tripping over his spurs.

Placing the bottle on the window-sill where he could reach it easily, Dolokhov climbed carefully and slowly through the window and lowered his legs. Pressing against both sides of the window, he adjusted himself on his seat, lowered his hands, moved a little to the right and then to the left and took up the bottle. Anatole brought two candles and placed them on the window-sill, though it was already quite light. Dolokhov's back in his white shirt, and his curly head, were lit up from both sides. Every one crowded to the window, the Englishman in front. Pierre stood smiling but silent. One man, older than the others present, suddenly pushed forward with a scared and angry look and wanted to seize hold of Dolokhov's shirt.

'I say, this is folly! He'll be killed,' said this more sensible man. Anatole stopped him. 'Don't touch him! You'll startle him and then he'll be killed. Eh? ... What then? ... Eh?'

Dolokhov turned round, and again holding on with both hands, arranged himself on his seat. 'If any one comes meddling again,' said he, emitting the words separately through his thin compressed lips, 'I will throw him down there. Now then!'

Saying this he again turned round, dropped his hands, took the bottle and lifted it to his lips, threw back his head, and raised his free hand to balance himself. One of the footmen, who had stooped to pick up some broken glass, remained in that position without taking his eyes from the window and from Dolokhov's back. Anatole stood erect with staring eyes. The Englishman looked on sideways, pursing up his lips. The man who had wished to stop the affair ran to a corner of the room and threw himself on a sofa with his face to the wall. Pierre hid his face, from which a faint smile forgot to fade though his features now expressed horror and fear. All were still. Pierre took his hand from his eyes, Dolokhov still sat in the same position, only his head was thrown further back till his curly hair touched his shirt collar, and the hand holding the bottle was lifted higher and higher and trembled with the effort. The bottle was emptying perceptibly and rising still higher and his head tilting yet further back. 'Why is it so long?' thought Pierre. It seemed to him that more than half an hour had elapsed. Suddenly Dolokhov made a backward movement with his spine, and his arm trembled nervously; this was sufficient to cause his whole body to slip as he sat on the sloping ledge. As he began slipping down, his head and arm wavered still more with the strain. One hand moved as if to clutch the window-sill, but refrained from touching it. Pierre again covered his eyes and thought he would never open them again. Suddenly he was aware of a stir all around. He looked up: Dolokhov was standing on the window-sill with a pale but radiant face.

'It's empty!'

He threw the bottle to the Englishman, who caught it neatly. Dolokhov jumped down. He smelt strongly of rum.

'Well done! ... Fine fellow! ... There's a bet for you! ... Devil take you!' came from different sides.

The Englishman took out his purse and began counting out the money. Dolokhov stood frowning and did not speak. Pierre jumped upon the window-sill.

'Gentlemen, who wishes to bet with me? I'll do the same thing!' he suddenly cried. 'Even without a bet, there! Tell them to bring me a bottle. I'll do it ... Bring a bottle!'

'Let him do it, let him do it,' said Dolokhov, smiling.

'What next? Have you gone mad? ... No one would let you! ... Why, you go giddy even on a staircase,' exclaimed several voices.

'I'll drink it! Let's have a bottle of rum!' shouted Pierre, banging the table with a determined and drunken gesture and preparing to climb out of the window.

They seized him by his arms; but he was so strong that every one who touched him was sent flying.

'No, you'll never manage him that way,' said Anatole. 'Wait a bit and I'll get round him ... Listen! I'll take your bet to-morrow, but now we are all going to —'s.'

'Come on then,' cried Pierre. 'Come on! ... And we'll take Bruin with us.'

And he caught the bear, took it in his arms, lifted it from the ground, and began dancing round the room with it.

Trans. Louise and Almyer Maude, OUP, 1941

Read again the foregoing accounts. As you do so, try to hear the way they would read, and, as you read, ask yourself if you find that pictures of what is on the page are appearing in your mind. If you do hear/see simultaneously, then what you are reading will work as good radio.

After re-reading the Dickens and Tolstoy extracts, ask yourself which did you hear/see better? Ask yourself why you think this was. Record both these extracts on to cassette. Close your eyes. Play back. Listen to them as radio. Which now comes across as more compelling? Which produces the more mindvisible effects? Were you right in your own assessment of which would transfer better to radio? Where, if anywhere, does either fail as radio? Could the texts be edited down to simple mindvisible ideas/concepts and re-recorded? Try this. Which text is easier to handle as an editing task? Why?

The above were both fictional accounts. Now a fictional and a factual account, both, like the Salmon extracts, commenting on the nature of the totalitarian regime.

The fictional account is from George Orwell's *Nineteen Eighty-Four* – a projection of what he saw for the future of Britain. The factual material is from an account left by the actor Wolfgang Langhoff of an incident during his time in captivity in the concentration camp at Lichtenburg Castle.

In the extract from *Nineteen Eighty-Four*, Winston Smith has been captured, in London, by the Thought Police in the shape of O'Brien. He is in the throes of being persuaded to become a good citizen. He has been beaten, tortured, has rolled on the floor in his own 'blood and vomit' and has betrayed everyone and everything except 'Julia', his lover.

George Orwell (1903–50) *Nineteen Eighty-Four* (1949)

There was a heavy tramp of boots in the passage. The steel door swung open with a clang. O'Brien walked into the cell. Behind

him were the waxen-faced officer and the black-uniformed guards.
'Get up,' said O'Brien. 'Come here.'

Winston stood opposite him. O'Brien took Winston's shoulders between his strong hands and looked at him closely.

'You have had thoughts of deceiving me,' he said. 'That was stupid. Stand up straighter. Look me in the face.'

He paused, and went on in a gentler tone:

'You are improving. Intellectually there is very little wrong with you. It is only emotionally that you have failed to make progress. Tell me, Winston – and remember, no lies: you know that I am always able to detect a lie – tell me, what are your true feelings towards Big Brother?'

'I hate him.'

'You hate him. Good. Then the time has come for you to take the last step. You must love Big Brother. It is not enough to obey him: you must love him.'

He released Winston with a little push towards the guards.

'Room 101,' he said.

At each stage of his imprisonment he had known, or seemed to know, whereabouts he was in the windowless building. Possibly there were slight differences in the air pressure. The cells where the guards had beaten him were below ground level. The room where he had been interrogated by O'Brien was high up near the roof. This place was many metres underground, as deep down as it was possible to go. It was bigger than most of the cells he had been in. But he hardly noticed his surroundings. All he noticed was that there were two small tables straight in front of him, each covered with green baize. One was only a metre or two from him, the other was further away, near the door. He was strapped upright in a chair, so tightly that he could move nothing, not even his head. A sort of pad gripped his head from behind, forcing him to look straight in front of him.

For a moment he was alone, then the door opened and O'Brien came in.

'You asked me once,' said O'Brien, 'what was in Room 101. I told you that you knew the answer already. Everyone knows it. The thing that is in Room 101 is the worst thing in the world.'

The door opened again. A guard came in, carrying something made of wire, a box or basket of some kind. He set it down on the further table. Because of the position in which O'Brien was standing, Winston could not see what the thing was.

'The worst thing in the world,' said O'Brien, 'varies from individual to individual. It may be burial alive, or death by fire, or drowning, or by impalement, or fifty other deaths. There are times where it is some quite trivial thing, not even fatal.'

He had moved a little to one side, so that Winston had a better view of the thing on the table. It was an oblong wire cage with a handle on top for carrying it by. Fixed to the front of it was something that looked like a fencing mask, with the concave side outwards. Although it was three or four metres away from him, he could see that the cage was divided lengthways into two compartments, and that there was some kind of creature in each. They were rats.

'In your case,' said O'Brien, 'the worst thing in the world happens to be rats.'

A sort of premonitory tremor, a fear of he was not certain what, passed through Winston as soon as he caught his first glimpse of the cage. But at this moment the meaning of the mask-like attachment in front of it suddenly sank into him. His bowels turned to water.

'You can't do that!' he cried out in a high cracked voice. 'You couldn't, you couldn't! It's impossible.'

'Do you remember,' said O'Brien, 'the moment of panic that used to occur in your dreams? There was a wall of blackness in front of you, and a roaring sound in your ears. There was something terrible on the other side of the wall. You knew that you knew what it was, but you dared not drag it into the open. It was rats that were on the other side of the wall.'

'O'Brien!' said Winston, making an effort to control his voice. 'You know this is not necessary. What is it that you want me to do?'

O'Brien made no direct answer. When he spoke it was in the schoolmasterish manner that he sometimes affected. He looked thoughtfully into the distance, as though he were addressing an audience somewhere behind Winston's back.

'By itself,' he said, 'pain is not always enough. There are occasions when a human being will stand out against pain, even to the point of death. But for everyone there is something unendurable – something that cannot be contemplated. Courage and cowardice are not involved. If you are falling from a height it is not cowardly to clutch at a rope. If you have come up from deep water it is not cowardly to fill your lungs with air. It is merely an instinct which cannot be destroyed. It is the same with the rats. For you, they are unendurable. They are a form of pressure that you cannot withstand, even if you wished to. You will do what is required of you.'

'But what is it, what is it? How can I do it if I don't know what it is?'

O'Brien picked up the cage and brought it across to the nearer table. He set it down carefully on the baize cloth. Winston could hear the blood singing in his ears. He had the feeling of sitting in utter loneliness. He was in the middle of a great empty plain, a flat desert drenched with sunlight, across which all sounds came to him out of immense distances. Yet the cage with the rats was not two metres away from him. They were enormous rats. They were at the age when a rat's muzzle grows blunt and fierce and his fur brown instead of grey.

'The rat,' said O'Brien, still addressing his invisible audience, 'although a rodent, is carnivorous. You are aware of that. You will have heard of the things that happen in the poor quarters of this town. In some streets a woman dare not leave her baby alone in the house, even for five minutes. The rats are certain to attack it. Within quite a small time they will strip it to the bones. They also attack sick or dying people. They show astonishing intelligence in knowing when a human being is helpless.'

There was an outburst of squeals from the cage. It seemed to reach Winston from far away. The rats were fighting; they were trying to get at each other through the partition. He heard also a deep groan of despair. That, too, seemed to come from outside himself.

O'Brien picked up the cage, and, as he did so, pressed something in it. There was a sharp click. Winston made a frantic effort to tear himself loose from the chair. It was hopeless; every part of him, even his head, was held immovably. O'Brien moved the cage nearer. It was less than a metre from Winston's face.

'I have pressed the first lever,' said O'Brien. 'You understand the construction of this cage. The mask will fit over your head, leaving no exit. When I press this other lever, the door of the cage will slide up. These starving brutes will shoot out of it like bullets. Have you ever seen a rat leap through the air? They will leap on to your face and bore straight into it. Sometimes they attack the eyes first. Sometimes they burrow through the cheeks and devour the tongue.'

The cage was nearer; it was closing in. Winston heard a succession of shrill cries which appeared to be occurring in the air above his head. But he fought furiously against his panic. To think, to think, even with a split second left – to think was the only hope. Suddenly the foul musty odour of the brutes struck his nostrils. There was a violent convulsion of nausea inside him, and he almost lost consciousness. Everything had gone black. For an instant he was insane, a screaming animal. Yet he came out of the blackness clutching an idea. There was one and only one way to save himself. He must interpose another human being, the *body* of another human being, between himself and the rats.

The circle of the mask was large enough now to shut out the vision of anything else. The wire door was a couple of hand-spans from his face. The rats knew what was coming now. One of them was leaping up and down, the other, an old scaly grandfather of the sewers, stood up, with his pink hands against the bars, and fiercely sniffed the air. Winston could see the whiskers and the yellow teeth. Again the black panic took hold of him. He was blind, helpless, mindless.

'It was a common punishment in Imperial China,' said O'Brien didactically as ever.

The mask was closing on his face. The wire brushed his cheek. And then – no, it was not relief, only hope, a tiny fragment of hope. Too late, perhaps too late. But he had suddenly understood that in the whole world there was just *one* person to whom he could transfer his punishment – *one* body that he could thrust between himself and the rats. And he was shouting frantically, over and over.

'Do it to Julia! Do it to Julia! Not me! Julia! I don't care what you do to her. Tear her face off, strip her to the bones. Not me! Julia! Not me!'

He was falling backwards, into enormous depths, away from the rats. He was still strapped in the chair, but he had fallen through the floor, through the walls of the building, through the earth, through the oceans, through the atmosphere, into outer space, into the gulfs between the stars – always away, away, away from the rats. He was light-years distant, but O'Brien was still standing at his side. There was still the cold touch of a wire against his cheek. But through the darkness that enveloped him he heard another metallic click, and knew that the cage door had clicked shut and not open.

And the factual account:

Wolfgang Langhoff *Rubber Truncheon*

'Heil Hitler!'

This is the story of a man who would not say 'Heil Hitler!' He was a member of a religious sect, the 'Community of Devout Bible-Readers'. God had forbidden him to greet with the Hitler-salute. His name was Frank or Franke. He was a kind of engineer. Since God had forbidden him to honour Hitler, no earthly power could force him to do so. The 'Devout Bible-Readers' were fanatics and implicitly obeyed the inner voice. They said to everyone, whether he wanted to listen or not: 'Hitler has founded his Reich on blood!' And since they were among the forty thousand men who would be allowed after the New Flood to enter Paradise on Earth, it was easy for them to endure pain and privation and the poverty of their earthly existence.

This is why he was brought to Lichtenburg Castle and became our fellow-sufferer. He spoke little, but looked kindly at everyone. He had thin, wavy, fair hair above a smooth forehead, large blue eyes, rosy cheeks, an effeminate mouth, and a rather small round chin. He was about forty years of age. Untiringly he swept the cell and the corridor, fetched water, and made himself useful to everybody.

But he never raised his arm to salute, he never said: 'Heil Hitler!'

When the guard noticed it the first time, he called him back.

'Why didn't you salute?'

'Because God has forbidden it!'

The guard did not trust his ears. He glared at him in amazement.

'Are you making fun of me?'

'No.'

'To what division do you belong?'

'Division III.'

In the evening they fetched him and put him into the dark-cell for a whole week. When he returned, his eyes were blood-shot.

'Be sensible,' the comrades said to him. 'What does this bit of "Heil Hitler!" matter! Do as we do, with your tongue in your cheek!'

He shook his head. The next day he was found out again. This time he spent a fortnight in the dark-cell.

We could scarcely recognise him when he came out. But he did not raise his arm to salute.

Now fat Zimmermann took it on himself to teach him. Accompanied by five S.S.-men Franke was led down to the little courtyard.

'Up with your arm! Up with your arm!'

The Commander looked on.

'Up with your arm!'

They fell on him. He rolled down into the ice-covered pools.

'Arm up! Heil Hitler! Heil Hitler! Get a move on!'

This went on until he lay there unconscious. His blood froze on the hard ground.

We implored him. In vain. His face became set, with a childish, obstinate expression. He would not salute. We felt desperate.

Now he was separated from us and put into the cells of the habitual criminals. He was given the same uniform as they. Day after day he had to run along with the latrine boxes. His hands were bloody from the strain. He spent his life between arrest, blows, and latrine-duty.

We nodded kindly to him when we saw him. We whispered to him. We stretched out our arms to show him the salute.

The S.S.-men had bets on him. After many weeks he joined us again.

On entering the corridor he met an S.S.-man. His right arm rose awkwardly. His hand, crusted with blood, stretched out. He whispered:

'Heil Hitler!'

Trans. Lilo Linke

Finally, parts of two fantastic accounts:

William Blake (1757–1827) *A Memorable Fancy*

An Angel came to me and said: 'O pitiable foolish young man! O horrible! O dreadful state! consider the hot burning dungeon thou art preparing for thyself to all eternity, to which thou art going in such career.'

I said: 'Perhaps you will be willing to shew me my eternal lot, & we will contemplate together upon it, and see whether your lot or mine is most desirable.'

So he took me thro' a stable & thro' a church & down into the church vault, at the end of which was a mill: thro' the mill we went, and came to a cave: down the winding cavern we groped our tedious way, till a void boundless as a nether sky appear'd beneath us, & we held by the roots of trees and hung over this immensity; but I said: 'if you please, we will commit ourselves to this void, and see whether providence is here also: if you will not, I will:' but he answer'd: 'do not presume, O young man, but as we here remain, behold thy lot which will soon appear when the darkness passes away.'

So I remain'd with him, sitting in the twisted root of an oak; he was suspended in a fungus, which hung with the head downward into the deep.

By degrees we beheld the infinite Abyss, fiery as the smoke of a burning city; beneath us, at an immense distance, was the sun, black but shining; round it were fiery tracks on which revolv'd vast spiders, crawling after their prey, which flew, or rather swum, in the infinite deep, in the most terrific shapes of animals sprung from corruption; & the air was full of them, & seem'd composed of them: these are Devils, and are called Powers of the air. I now asked my companion which was my eternal lot? he said: 'between the black & white spiders.'

Peter Redgrove *Being Beauteous*

A spiderweb stretched between the trunks of the last two forest trees. The trees were loaded with snow, and the web loaded with the spider, which was smooth khaki, big as a football, with a black hourglass shaped across its heavy back, quivering a very little on the taut, almost invisible strands.

The web must have been spun since the last fall, for it was clean of snow, and glistening with adhesive as if it had just been extruded. Neither were there any husks in it, and had I not paused to recover my breath and admire the sparkling of the sun on the snow-plain beyond, I should never have seen the gigantic wheel-and-hub shadow thrust into the wood almost to my feet by the cold sun. I should have hung there like a cloudy stocking with a full cap of bushy black hair, before my cries had shaken off their last snow from the far reaches of the forest.

The spider clutched the very centre of its trap. As I stared, a claw reached from beneath the speckled haunch and seized as with tortoiseshell pliers the next coil of the spiral.

With a sudden revulsion, and not wishing to see its face, or have it bounding across the snow at me on terrier legs, I plucked my revolver from my pocket and fired. The spider exploded with a soft thud, and like a firework showered its gold and vermilion contents all over the wheel.

The sun broke on the shambles of wrinkling tissues; golden juice lashed away from it. Gobbets of amber gum, rags of crimson flesh, black plates thickly set with spines and thin brown sheets like mica cascaded past, frosting and shattering in the cold. Ginger, strawberry, and apricot: it was as though pots of various sorts of jam had been flung across a whitewashed wall. The bony forehead-piece studded with its eight eyes in sets of two, the size of walnuts and clear and unwinking as diamonds, glided over a hump of ruby tissue and sank into the snow. The whole mess started to steam and through the rolling clouds I glimpsed a portion of the coppercoloured jaws still munching.

Exercises (1)

Theory, prediction and observation are said to be the tests for accurate research. Read and comment on which piece from each of the pairs you think will make the better radio. Analyse why you think this is in terms of which of the pieces you feel have the more simple mindvisible concepts and ideas. Then, using a tape facility, record the various pairs of extracts. Listen, then state which you consider to be the better radio – and analyse why.

Can you edit the accounts to make good radio? Are there some extracts that will not edit into radio? What does this tell you?

From your own readings/research find pairs of complementary pieces of prose of about 450 words (about three minutes' broadcast time) and analyse on the page their potential as the type of writing which produces immediate mindvisible radio images. These pairs of texts can be reports of the same historical/political event from two different books with authors of widely varying style. Or of the same sporting event – football/cricket/tennis/boxing/hockey/matches from two different newspapers. Two reviews of the same CD/concert/exhibition from different magazines. Reports of a criminal trial. Or of any other incident – local, national, international.

Then record the pairs of reports, and re-analyse – comparing what you felt about them as possible radio on the page – to what images you actually saw in terms of radio images when you heard them read back from a cassette.

In this chapter we have tried to isolate what sort of writing works on radio – what sort of writing produces immediate, strong, mindvisible images. We have found it to be writing that contains simple ideas attached to universal concepts. The sort of writing that, as you read it on the page, you simultaneously hear being spoken and see the descriptions it contains generated in your mind.

'The man in the Mexican hat, standing by the patio door, whistled: – and the black dog ran excitedly across the white paving stones and into the house.'

Everyone hearing this sort of thing immediately sees it. This gives us an understanding of what sort of writing is peculiar to, and works best for, radio, but not why a writer should attempt to work in the medium.

2 Why radio?

A small boy was asked why he preferred radio to the visual media – 'Because the pictures are better' he replied.

Anon.

A control of the nation's broadcasting facilities has become the first target of the aspirant to power. The world has become familiar with the *pronunciamento* delivered while the revolutionaries still command little more than the station from which it was made.

J. Scupham, *Broadcasting and the Community*

In America there are more radio sets than people.

J. Scupham, *Broadcasting and the Community*

The above story about the small boy, although probably apocryphal and concocted for the occasion, has made the rounds for many years. But it is part of the uniqueness of radio that it can be said to have generated such a fable. And in the boy's answer is contained the reason why a writer should seriously consider beginning a career in the medium – because the pictures can be better.

We now have an idea of what words actually work to produce immediate mindvisible images. But how are sequences containing these words to be manipulated? How are these better pictures to be formed inside longer works – inside radio genres as different as plays, adaptations, short stories, poems and documentaries? And if we learn to devise and shape the writing necessary for sustaining such works what, then, are the prospects for selling the finished product within the market?

To address these points it might be best to split the question into two: (1) Are there *artistic advantages* in learning to write radio? (2) Is there a *professional advantage* within the media market in learning to write radio?

Artistic advantages of writing radio

When the curtain rises in the theatre, or the camera focuses on the opening set of a piece of television, or the lights go down in a cinema, immediately the audience has the visual prop of the scenery. This, plus the attitudes, accents and dress of the actors, or presenters, helps them identify the time, place and manner of what it is they are about to see. Dialogue has no immediate importance. Indeed, if what is in front of the audience is sufficiently compelling, dialogue need not exist at all: 'silent movies'.

Radio is the opposite. In radio, what the audience 'sees' will come solely through the writer's manipulation of sound; that is, by the use of narration and dialogue, the length of the pauses between the narration and dialogue, and the audio effects. These words, silences and sound effects will conjure up both the sense and the structure of the pictures the writer wishes to give the listener, and if these pictures are to be better, the words used in a script will have to make them so.

In radio news/journalism, for instance, the words have to set the scene as the visiting dignitary steps down from the plane on to the tarmac, but must also invest the proceedings with a suitable air of dignity as befits the occasion:

> REPORTER: She moves forward away from the plane, her dark robes swirling in the wind, and contrasting sharply against the silver of the wings and fuselage behind her. And now the President, leaning slightly on his stick, comes forward slowly, and stops, facing her. As they shake hands the cameramen move in to record this historic event.

In radio drama, the make of the car in which the villain escapes after the bank robbery:

> WITNESS X: They ran out and jumped into it ... One of them new Gremlins ... Light blue ... Rear offside light looked a bit bashed. Customised wheels ... wire spokes ... spoiler ... About two litre ... maybe two point five!

> SERGEANT Y: That will do for now, Sir. I'm not here to buy it.

In the radio feature, the ocean at sunset:

> NARRATOR: That evening, the ship having now settled down, we decided to stroll up for'd at sunset. The Indian Ocean was

> a soft, deep, emerald green. The sun a blood-red arc on the horizon. We stood leaning over the rails, watching the translucent sea-snakes being turned aside by the white collars of foam from the ship's bows. Suddenly, the last of the sun slipped away, the temperature dropped, the sea darkened over, and dusk folded us in.

Everything 'seen' in these three examples has to be given to the listener aurally. The listener, through the skill of the writer, has been provided with the wherewithal to become his or her own casting director, electrician, scenery builder, artistic director and stage manager. Just as the DNA molecule provides information for a complete person – so a good radio script should provide information for a complete world.

So here is the first reason, artistically, why the aspiring writer should come to radio. Because learning to write radio properly means learning the techniques of creating worlds without the aid of direct visual props. Of developing a facility to produce solid, well-structured, mindvisible scripts which rely solely on words.

Without a good script a radio director cannot produce a good programme. In television and film it is possible to make a partial success of a bad script – good scenery, sets, acting, camera work and direction can do this – but radio is a completely exposed position. In radio, if your material and technique fail, so will you.

In radio, there are no 'beautiful people' to look at; no panoramic film views in which 'Alps on Alps arise'; not even the price of an expensive theatre ticket to keep someone in their seat when faced with the usual load of insipid tripe. If, in radio, the listener's attention slips due to weaknesses and deficiencies in the script, there is nothing visual to bring it back. At which point, it's off with the receiver, on with the coat, and out for a walk.

Dr Johnson observed that when a man was to be hanged the next morning it concentrated his mind wonderfully; and those who write seriously for radio should have their minds permanently concentrated by the fact that, for them, oblivion is no further away than the 'off' button on the set.

In radio, basic grass-roots writing techniques must be mastered if any long-term progress is to be seen. It is learning to play the piano without the use of the 'colouring' pedal, though the effect is all the purer because of this.

However, it must be pointed out that even the best teacher in the world can do no more than provide technique – imagination is something that can neither be taught nor bought. Which is the reason the rich do not produce great works of art; having to rely instead on creative feats such as paddling across the Atlantic standing in a dustbin or hang-gliding over the Andes on a diesel-driven feather.

But technique can be a strong and effective weapon. Imagine a scene in a radio play where a radio writer wants the listener to know that one of the male characters is tall. An obvious way would be for the character in question to say in the course of some remark or other ...

CHARACTER X: ... As you can see I'm pretty tall, so I could watch from anywhere on the riverbank that day.

But by utilising radio technique the same character could simply remark ...

CHARACTER X: Here, let me hang up that coat ... (STRETCHES UPWARDS AND OFF MIKE) ... It's easier for me ... (COMING BACK ON MIKE) Yes, I was watching from the riverbank that day ...

In this second speech, without a mention of physical height, but by mentioning the hanging up of a coat, the listener gains the impression of a tall person. And as the character leans away from the microphone we will get a secondary impression of someone tall stretching up.

Age, too, could be dealt with in this manner:

CHARACTER X: You won't be old enough to remember the old money. But with a couple of shillingsworth of copper pennies in your pocket, there wasn't a wind on earth could lift you off your feet ... Even if I did lose one of mine on convoy duty ...

And from this speech we gain a mental picture of a disabled old seaman, with a sense of humour, who has seen war service.

This sort of technique needs practice – but will add an immediate and professional gloss on any work presented as an assignment before a tutor, or in a submission before a commissioning editor looking for something different.

A second artistic reason for learning to write radio is that once basic techniques are mastered, radio then offers unparalleled scope for writing something different. It allows truly innovative and imaginative concepts to be explored, and has to be acknowledged as a fundamental source of experimental writing.

It is the one form of media writing where the sky's the limit, even though the budget is firmly fixed. Where anything that can be imagined can be portrayed, requiring little in terms of resources. Spain can be evoked by a few chords struck on a guitar. A Roman arena by playing a tape 'mix' of a roaring football crowd over one of snarling lions. A listener can languish on the sands of Acapulco, or those of Mars. Where a cast of thousands or a ghost in a locked tomb are equally viable and equally cheap.

Then there is radio's facility for scene changing. In radio, it is possible to cut from the cabin of an aeroplane to that of a trapper in the Canadian wilds; from the depths of the ocean to the top of Mount Everest; from the heart of a South American rainforest to that of a patient on an operating table.

Some of the venues and cuts mentioned, if scripted for the visual media, would require a producer with a valium-coated, asbestos chequebook. But locations needing a multi-million pound budget in film, and unthinkable in terms of television, can be granted to a radio writer without anyone having to leave the studio console.

Finally, an important bonus of this 'no-locations-barred' facility within radio is that it offers the chance for a writer to prepare to learn the basics of film script construction.

To sum up, radio should be artistically attractive to the aspiring writer not only because it offers a platform to gain basic but enduring writing skills, but also because it offers a medium where writers can obtain locations in space and time that would cost a fortune to bring before a camera or mount upon a stage. Radio, therefore, enables a writer to work, without constraint, to the limits of his or her imagination – provided that the material involved is thought to be acceptable.

But even with these distinct artistic advantages, the questions still remain as to whether there is room within radio to place new work and, if so, what are the difficulties facing the aspiring radio writer as compared with someone working towards a commission in television, theatre or film.

Professional reasons for writing radio

Radio is always seeking fresh material. It is a dragon that must be fed.

And as new stations proliferate at international, national, community and college level, more and more food must be found. The chances of a new writer breaking into radio are good. It is almost impossible to get into theatre, television and film without help, and even should you manage it the prospects for a beginner are slim; but radio can be, for certain writers, a continuing and continuous employer.

Take the BBC. A cursory look at any week's scheduling in the *Radio Times* will show at a glance what can be stated as a fact – the BBC is the largest and most comprehensive presenter of talk radio in the world. And as most of that material is original it follows that there is a constant demand for new work.

It is part of BBC policy to seek out new writers. Producers in London and the regions are always hoping to discover a fresh talent in every script that arrives. Occasionally they find it.

But once it is found, what help can a new writer expect in developing this talent? Radio again scores heavily. Radio has a quieter, more intimate atmosphere. An account can be taken of both the writer and his/her work. Enduring friendships and working relationships are often formed between writers and producers that bring added depth and development to the work. Producers in radio generally tend to hold the positions they occupy because they love the work involved – because it is the quality and individuality of the writing which count.

This, unfortunately, does not happen as often in the visual media. Financial pressures and audience figures can take precedence over personal feelings. Television producers are usually on short-term contracts and are often seen as being simply 'As good as their last play ... documentary ... adaptation'. For this reason they will very understandably opt for writers with a proven 'track record'; that is, writers who have a record of produced work in that branch of the media and, often, in a specific genre within that branch. In radio, however, there is still a small percentage of full-time staff who can, will and are expected to look for the new and the different and who have the security to try and find and help to foster a new talent.

So here is the second reason 'Why radio?' Because in radio the new writer may find a more sympathetic attitude towards first efforts; and an ongoing source of professional help and advice during the absolutely critical first years.

Given these distinct and undeniable advantages, there are still writers who are loath to turn to radio or turn to it only as a last resort – after having had the same idea or script rejected from film or television. A reluctance that seems to stem from the fact that many writers see radio as very much the 'poor relation' of the media world, holding out neither the glamour of the big names nor the sort of audience and critical response that the visual media attract. It is worth remembering that many writers who later found great international fame, Orson Welles, for instance, began their careers in radio. That many extremely successful series and serials have been picked up and developed for television from radio. And that with the tying up of most of the major sports events by satellite television, Radio 5 now attracts an ever-expanding audience for sport, as does Radio 1 for new music. That the audience for an 'afternoon play' can be somewhere in the region of 250,000. A West End production would have to run for years to attract those sorts of numbers – and it is no mean thing for any writer to have an audience of a quarter of a million people for a first effort.

In conclusion, radio, first and foremost, can be seen as a school for writers, many of whom go on to reach the highest peaks of popular, critical or financial success. A school which, by virtue of the breadth of the curriculum and facilities for experiment, can accommodate everyone from the primary pupil to the postgraduate research fellow. A school where the careers of ex-pupils are closely observed and followed, and whose doors are usually permanently open for advice and support.

Although many of those elected into the highest political power seem to have conveniently forgotten it, the most important contact people we meet in our academic lives are our first teachers. Because from these we learn how to read – which makes possible all that follows – including entry to that same political power.

Equally, the most important contact person that an aspiring writer can meet is another sort of teacher – one who can pass on the skills necessary for basic structures and techniques – often across wide and varied fields of writing. The sort of teacher who may be found, sometimes, within the pure, clear, verbal world of radio.

Exercises (1)

After re-reading the foregoing text a short essay, 'What Radio Means To Me', could be attempted, using the following notes as guidance.

'What Radio Means To Me' gives the student/writer the opportunity and the incentive to *think* about radio, as opposed to simply taking it for granted as something that is automatically in the car, in the kitchen, in the supermarket, at the beach. A something that is 'switched on' when coming into the house or flat – and then forgotten about except as a sort of friendly background noise that fulfils the function of a second person, without making the same demands on time and concentration.

This essay will force the student/writer to focus on what programmes she or he listens to, and why. In a class situation, the completed essays could be read out individually, and from discussion the students learn both more about each other, about different tastes and approaches to radio, and about writing generally.

The writer at home should complete the exercise, record it on to cassette, then come back to it two or three days later and listen to it as objectively as possible. And then ask, 'If I heard this on the radio as a transmission would I want to listen to it?'

Prompts for 'What Radio Means To Me'

- When do you tend to listen to radio?
- What station do you naturally turn to? Why?
- Are there ever times when radio seems preferable to television? Why?
- Of which sort of programme would you like to hear more?
- What, if anything, turns you away from radio?
- How would you try to improve radio?

Short specimen answer: 'What Radio Means To Me'

NARRATOR: I like to listen to radio when I go to bed. I always put on Radio 5 because this brings me up to date on the sports scene and sometimes on this station there are good talks and discussions that seem geared to young people like myself. Occasionally I put it on earlier in the evening if there is a 'Five Live' football match on and if there is nothing much on television. The type of programme of which I'd like to hear more is one giving profiles of my favourite bands. The one thing I don't like is politics – just too boring. The way I'd go about improving radio is to ask people what 'they' want – and then put it on for them.

The above is obviously very factual, and contrived as an attempt from the point of view of a young student. In reality the piece should be more idiosyncratic and allow us to 'see' the writer as a person.

George Orwell (1940), writing about Dickens, says:

> When one reads any strongly individual piece of writing, one has the impression of seeing a face somewhere behind the page. It is not necessarily the face of the writer. I feel this very strongly with Swift, Defoe, with Fielding, Stendhal, Thackeray, Flaubert, though in several cases I do not know what these people looked like and do not want to know. What one sees is the face the writer *ought* to have. Well, in the case of Dickens I see a face that is not quite the face of Dickens's photographs, though it resembles it. It is the face of a man of about forty, with a small beard and high colour. He is laughing, with a touch of anger in his laughter, but no triumph, no malignity. It is the face of a man who is always fighting against something, but who fights in the open, and is not frightened, the face of a man who is *generously* angry.

In many ways this is what all writing for radio should incline towards – attempting to give the listener a picture of the face behind the voice behind the microphone. Building enough technique and ability for the listener to see both the writing and the writer. So that the listeners think and feel that the writer is as real as they are – notwithstanding any differences in viewpoint.

So, take 'What Radio Means To Me' again and attempt to give it a more 'real' face.

Revised specimen answer: 'What Radio Means To Me'

NARRATOR: Sometimes when I've been working really hard, or just had a bad day generally, I go to bed early, with a cup of coffee, and put on Radio 5. That way I can catch up on the sports, which mean a lot to me, as I'm really interested, especially in football. Sometimes, too, there are good talks and discussions – the sort that tell you what you want to know without preaching at you, and which seem geared to young people like myself.

To be honest, usually I prefer the television, but sometimes

> I like the quietness of radio and the fact that you can do other things while you listen ... even if it's only falling asleep while looking up at the ceiling. And unlike the television it doesn't sometimes seem to be watching you, staring at you from the corner of the room ... Somehow it's more 'user friendly'. It's good for music, too. Not as good as some of the commercial stations, and it could do with having more profiles of my favourite bands, but what's on is a good mixture. I suppose that if I were going to improve it I'd do it by asking people what 'they' want – and put it on for them.

In this second answer to 'What Radio Means To Me' certain additions have been made to the text, to make the whole scene more mindvisible and intimate: 'a cup of coffee', 'looking up at the ceiling', 'staring at you from the corner of the room'. These additions also give a far more pronounced mental picture of the writer as a distinct individual. Someone who, at the end of a long day, becomes just as tired as we do. Who doesn't like being 'preached at' ... who likes sports ... and someone who sometimes feels 'watched' by the television. All these points make up a distinct individual ... perhaps hazy in outline and features, but who exists for us as a real person.

With this in mind, try stamping individuality and a 'face' on this final set of exercises. To go back to the three earlier examples. First the 'news' item:

> REPORTER: She moves forward away from the plane, her dark robes swirling in the wind, and contrasting sharply against the silver of the wings and fuselage behind her. And now the President, leaning slightly on his stick, comes forward slowly, and stops, facing her. As they shake hands the cameramen move in to record this historic event.

In radio drama, the make of the car in which the villain escapes after the bank robbery:

> WITNESS X: They ran out and jumped into it ... One of them new Gremlins ... Light blue ... Rear offside light looked a bit bashed. Customised wheels ... wire spokes ... spoiler ... About two litre ... maybe two point five!
>
> SERGEANT Y: That will do for now, Sir. I'm not here to buy it.

In the radio feature, the ocean at sunset:

> NARRATOR: That evening, the ship having now settled down,

> we decided to stroll up for'd at sunset. The Indian Ocean was a soft, deep, emerald green. The sun a blood-red arc on the horizon. We stood leaning over the rails, watching the translucent sea-snakes being turned aside by the white collars of foam from the ship's bows. Suddenly, the last of the sun slipped away, the temperature dropped, the sea darkened over, and dusk folded us in.

In the first of the above examples, the arrival of the visiting dignitary, the idea was to show a reporter whose language was that of someone who was impressed by the political event unfolding and by the stature of those involved: '... her dark robes swirling in the wind', '... the silver of the wings and fuselage ...', '... the President, leaning slightly on his stick ...'.

Also of interest in this manufactured example is the fact that it is in the present tense – as are most radio news items. Mitchell V. Charnley observed in his 1948 book *News by Radio*, 'Radio news – because of its advantage of speed over the newspaper – has come to place heavy emphasis on the present tense. Most newspaper news is either in the past or future tense ... but a radio newscast is often able to report an event within minutes of its occurrence ... indeed, while it is still occurring.'

In the second example, the idea was to attempt to show behind the dialogue a drama writer who, in giving the police sergeant a jovial remark to calm the witness, gives us a picture of someone who believes that there is perhaps room for lightness of touch in even the heaviest of situations.

The third example was to show a writer/narrator who is so much moved by nature and the natural world that what is seen and felt must be expressed in as poetic terms as possible.

Exercises (2)

Now, utilising exactly the same layout as in these examples, prepare three fresh items in which you try to give an impression of the person writing the piece – the 'face' behind the voice behind the microphone:

- A 'radio news' item describing two captains tossing a coin at a major sporting event, or two players coming out for a Wimbledon tennis final.

- An exchange in 'radio drama' between a ticket inspector on a bus and a passenger who has not paid; or someone who has attempted to pay at a supermarket checkout with their partner's cheque card which they picked up at home by accident – their partner having left to fly to Australia.
- A 'radio feature' description of a ship arriving or leaving the quay; or a train leaving or arriving at a country or mainline station.

As a final example of writing which would ideally lend itself to radio, the following extract contains what might be referred to as 'underwriting', or sub-textual material.

It tells us about the character and work of its subject, Chekhov, without actually mentioning his life or writing. Yet within what is said, the character of Chekhov and the breadth of his work are revealed. This is not done in any savage ironic sense – such as that employed by Swift in his pamphlet relating to the state of Ireland, 'A Modest Proposal for preventing the Children of Poor People from being a Burden to their Parents or their Country' (by cooking them and using them as food for the landlords and the rich) but by giving what seems a simple account of events at Chekhov's funeral. It appears at first glance quite loose and light-hearted, but a deeper examination shows just how observant and tight and crowned with graphic, memorable description it is:

Maxim Gorky (1868–1936) 'Chekhov's Funeral'

> The coffin of the writer, so 'tenderly loved' by Moscow, was brought in a green wagon bearing the inscription 'OYSTERS' in big letters on the side. A section of the crowd which had gathered at the station to meet it followed the coffin of General Keller just arrived from Manchuria, and wondered why Chekhov was being carried to his grave to the music of a military band. When the mistake was discovered certain genial persons began laughing and sniggering. The coffin was followed by about a hundred people, not more. Two lawyers stand out in my memory, both in new boots and gaily patterned neckties, like bridegrooms. Walking behind them, I heard one of them … talking about the cleverness of dogs and the other … boasting of … his country cottage. And some lady, holding up a lace sunshade was assuring an old gentlemen in horn-rimmed spectacles.

> 'Oh, he was such a darling, and so witty ...'.
>
> The old gentleman coughed incredulously. It was a hot, dusty day. The procession was headed by a stout police officer on a stout white horse ...
>
> Trans. Ivy Litvinov

This is an extract whose simple ideas and universal concepts, 'green' ... 'van' ... 'OYSTERS' ... 'lawyers' ... 'neckties' ... 'stout police officer' ... 'stout white horse', immediately guarantee that the writing translates pictorially into the mind of the reader/listener. We hear nothing of Chekhov's character and way of life, but through the approach and tone of the writing, we sense he was everything that the people and events mentioned are not. By Gorky deliberately not telling us the why and wherefore of what Chekhov was, and what he wrote; and by the way the extract is structured, we know exactly what he was and what he wrote.

We also realise from the indignation implicit in Gorky's account that he considered Chekhov an important and unique talent, and not just someone who had taken to the pen because it was more romantic than finding a job. Or because it was 'well, you know, suggested by one's tutor over a cup of cocoa one evening'.

We understand Gorky's admiration as if he had chosen to give us an in-depth biography. We know that Chekhov would have had a sense of the ridiculous, had humility, was quiet in dress and demeanour, and would certainly have appreciated every minute of his own funeral.

Exercises (3)

Library/Internet search. Investigate the main/relevant facts of Chekhov's life, and build them into the Gorky funeral description – making the whole a seamless and informative radio talk. Record/play back/analyse/rewrite/re-record.

So what will make a piece of writing really come alive will be an individual voice. Good, telling descriptions, in simple ideas and universal concepts that immediately trigger mindvisible images in the listener. And a technique that offers the listener as much material as can be readily assimilated at one hearing without being either tedious or repetitive.

But be careful of becoming so engrossed in building up atmosphere that the result is the 'contrived' voice straining for effect and covered in the smoke of the study lamp. Such a voice appears as either a lack of technique, or affectation. To go back to a phrase used in 'What Radio Means To Me': 'And unlike the television it doesn't sometimes seem to be watching you, staring at you from a corner of the room.' This is a succinct and 'real person' observation; but if it were to be replaced by: 'And unlike the all-powerful television, that one-eyed, techno-monster symbol of the "Big Brother" society to which we are all now wedded, if not cloned from. How all of us have sometimes felt, as it crouches in the corner of the room, that it watches ... and watches ... and watches ...!!!' All that can be said to this is that there is a large and discriminating audience 'out there' which listens ... and listens ... and listens.

3 The medium is the message

> Who has two languages has two weapons.
>
> Anon.

> True ease in writing comes from art, not chance,
> As those move easiest who have learnt to dance.
> 'Tis not enough no harshness gives offence,
> The sound must be an echo of the sense.
>
> Pope

The object of this chapter is to try to 'think' in radio terms and to begin to construct complete self-sustaining works in the medium. Just as to use the language of another country properly it is important to be able to think in the language, so to use radio to its best advantage you have to 'think radio'.

This means that all the images that are presented to your mind have to be then re-presented to the listener in narration, dialogue, sound effects and silences. They will have to be carefully translated or 'recoded' to fit a new medium. This will take practice.

There is no substitute for practice. All the books that have ever been written about swimming will not help anybody who refuses to go into the pool.

Similarly, the only way to learn to write radio is by sitting at the machine and beginning. Then putting what you have written on to tape and listening carefully, and then re-writing.

Begin simply, with simple themes and ideas, perhaps by writing straightforward accounts in the first person, and then gradually introducing other voices.

In a class situation the above exercises, when completed, will be listened to/commented upon by the rest of the class. A writer working at home will write the exercise, use a radio cassette to record the exercise, listen to it carefully, re-write if necessary, and then re-record. Then answer as objectively as possible the questions on p. 48.

Exercises (1)

Below is a series of three exercises to introduce students/writers to the medium of radio and to some of its possibilities in prose and dialogue.

You have been given the chance to write three short (3–5 min.) 'fillers' for radio:

- The first, 'Leaving Home', is to be broadcast at five to eight in the morning.
- The second, 'Lunch Break', is to be broadcast at around mid-day.
- The third, 'Coming Home At Midnight', is to be broadcast shortly before the news at midnight.
- 'Leaving Home', to be written in the first person with no reported speech or sound effects.
- 'Lunch Break', to be written in the first person with reported speech from a second character. No sound effects.
- 'Coming Home At Midnight', to be written in the first person, with direct speech from a second person. No sound effects.

Example 1

'Leaving Home'

To be written in first person with no reported speech or sound effects.

Leaving home can be about many things. A person leaving a childhood home to be married. A young person going abroad for the first time – or going off to college. Someone running away in the middle of the night. A person emigrating. An animal that has been badly treated deciding to leave a house. Someone being buried from the family home. A baby leaving the womb. A ghost or spirit deciding to leave a house that it has haunted for years. One student wrote about faeces leaving the body, while on a residential writing course a student came into the session wearing a large metal casserole pot on his head through which he recited his script – he was a Martian 'Leaving Home' to travel to Earth.

As an introductory example, consider a woman deciding she no longer wishes to live in her old house. Her husband is dead; the children have left; the house is now too expensive to run. She has made the painful decision she must sell up.

The following could be the closing paragraph. The information contained in it will be given twice: once in a straightforward fashion and once more obliquely, using the sort of radio technique we discussed earlier. It will centre around her going out of the front door.

For film or television all that would be shown is the door opening from the outside or from the inside and the character involved either emerging or simply standing framed in the doorway. The house itself would, in terms of situation and state of repair, announce the probable financial status of the tenant or owner. There need be nothing said to identify the action and surroundings.

In radio all this has to be turned into dialogue or, should the door belong to a haunted house, with the accompanying sound effects of a key turning in rusty lock and creaking hinges.

The first way of treating this scene is as a piece of factual reportage, having the character announce something like:

> WOMAN: I walked down the hall and opened the door and saw it was raining. I walked down the path, opened the front gate and turned towards town and the estate agents. Looking back I saw how shabby the house looked.

This is accurate, with simple concepts/ideas and will serve the purpose, but it is a bit dry ... Far better and more effective, perhaps, to use something like the following:

> NARRATOR: I picked up my coat as I walked down the hall. I noticed the patch of damp had grown bigger and the plaster had started to peel. Once outside, I had to pull twice to engage the lock. The garden was as weed-choked as ever; the narrow concrete path cracked and crumbling. Turning up my collar against the rain, I headed wearily towards town and the estate agents.

In the second example the listener opens and passes through the front door *without hearing it mentioned*, and also gains an impression of a house that has damp and a broken door lock – and is therefore a bit run down. A picture of the untended garden and the prevailing weather is also given, which will hopefully engender an impression of melancholy, sadness, poverty and defeat. The ideas are all simple and all the concepts immediate.

In a class situation, after a set time to complete the exercise, each individual piece is read out by its writer. With the first, 'Leaving Home', the lecturer and members of the class should imagine they are at home preparing to leave for college/work when the piece comes on the radio. Trying to snatch breakfast, have a shower, sort out necessary books or equipment.

General questions to be asked are:

- Would you stop what you are doing to listen to it?
- What are felt to be the strengths and weaknesses of each individual piece?
- Some of the pieces will immediately be heard as being successful radio and some will not. Why is this?
- Is there anything that links the successful pieces, such as strength of imagery? Length of sentences? Percentage of description as opposed to pure reportage?
- Does the emotional content seem to have anything to do with the success or failure of a particular piece of writing?

The lecturer can then quickly go round each member of the class and ask which of the pieces were found to be most interesting. Usually there are two or three which instinctively attract the most attention from the students. Why?

The above questions can be posed after all the class exercises.

Examples 2 and 3, 'Lunch Break' and 'Coming Home At Midnight', are progressively more complex.

Example 2

'Lunch Break'

To be written in the first person with reported speech from a second character. No sound effects.

The student writer will describe the action in his/her own voice but add reported comment from a second person. The bulk of the story will be related in narrative, plus reported speech. This gives the student writer practice in working on the tensions that occur when two voices/separate personalities/characters are being used against each other in a script, and in having to construct a competent narrative structure around this.

> WOMAN: I glanced at the clock – three minutes to one. I clicked the mouse and began to shut down the computer. I stood up and moved across to the coat rack. I could feel Wilson's eyes on me all the time. How he'd like to see me go out of the door even a minute early. Then he'd really have something to tell the boss. 'Oh, Mr Richards, I thought you should know that Jane went off early again ... I don't know if you'd given her permission' ... I could just hear that whining voice of his. That particular day, though, I didn't care. I put on my Mac and scarf and simply walked past him. I closed the door and waited for a couple of seconds then opened it again. He already had the receiver in his hand, about to call Richards. He stared at me. 'By the way', I said, 'I've a doctor's appointment at half-one. Mr Richards gave me permission to go at half twelve, but I stayed to finish the Steglitz account. If you speak to him let him know, would you?' I smiled into his large blank eyes and left him holding the phone alongside his ear as if it were a shell through which he was listening for the sea.

In this example we get a sense of Wilson, but only hear his voice through the woman's idea of what he would say and how he would say it. What would make it more tense and dramatic would be to give Wilson his own voice:

> WOMAN: I glanced at the clock – three minutes to one. I clicked the mouse and began to shut down the computer. I stood up and moved across to the coat rack. I could feel Wilson's eyes

> on me all the time. How he'd like to see me go out of the door even a minute before one. Then he'd really have something to tell the boss, Richards. That day, though, I didn't care. I put on my Mac and scarf and simply walked past him. I put my hand on the door handle and as I did so he said, 'You know what time it is?' I closed the door and waited for a couple of seconds then opened it again. He immediately continued from where he had left off: 'What this firm expects is people who work for it, not self-seekers who work against it!' He already had the receiver in his hand about to call Richards. I faced him directly. 'I've a doctor's appointment at half-one,' I said. 'Mr Richards gave me permission to go off at half twelve, but I stayed to finish the Steglitz account. If you speak to him let him know, would you, that I did the extra time?' I smiled into his large blank eyes and left him still holding the phone alongside his ear as if it were a shell through which he was attempting to listen to the sea.

Here we not only get the sense of Wilson but his voice establishes him as a separate 'character' and he becomes a real living person who, by the addition of this small speech, dramatically 'interacts' with the narrator.

Example 3a

'Coming Home At Midnight'

To be written in the first person, with two characters speaking in reported speech within the narrative. No sound effects.

WOMAN: As the taxi pulled away Malcolm fell over. He raised an arm to me but I just stood and stared at him. I was throbbing with rage. As he slowly began to try to find his feet, I turned and began to walk off. Then I heard him stumbling after me. 'Kim,' he shouted in a thick, drunken, voice.

I wouldn't look back, just kept walking slowly in front of him. Although it was after midnight, the heat from that stifling July day was still in the pavement, and I kicked off my shoes. As I bent and picked them up I reflected on the events of the evening. We had been to the annual summer dinner thrown by my firm. It had been a fancy dress occasion, and as I walked I still dragged behind me the train from my Queen Elizabeth the First outfit. Malcolm had gone dressed as Sir Francis Drake, just back from playing bowls and beating the Spanish Armada. Suddenly overcome again with anger I turned to where he trudged along about ten paces behind me. 'You effing nutter!' I shouted. 'Throwing that stupid bowling ball at the Managing Director's legs. I'll be lucky to have a job tomorrow.' I half-ran back down to him and shook a fist under his nose.

'My Lady has not the best of humours, I trow,' he said to me in a thick, slurred voice.

'You bastard,' I said and pushed him in the middle of his chest. He staggered slowly and drunkenly back, and sat down heavily in the middle of the pavement. From there he waved a regal hand at me. I shook my head angrily from side to side, then walked the other hundred or so yards to the door of the house. Anxious to get in, and get myself under the shower, I began searching through my bag. 'That bloody key,' I muttered as I rooted through all the usual shit. Before I knew what was happening, Malcolm had arrived behind me and leaned over my shoulder, making a grab at my breasts. I swung round without thinking and hit him across the head with my bag. I thought he'd fall, with the weight of the half-bottle of vodka I always carry in it, but he just swayed like a boxer who has taken a tremendous punch.

'The key!' I shouted in his face. 'What have you done with the key, you bloody Sozzle-Pipe?'

He raised one finger at me and rolled back his eyes solemnly. 'My Lady …' he began and then stopped. He tried again, 'My lady …'. At this point I lost it and punched him in the face.

He stepped away from me and hit the door. It opened under his weight and he fell backwards into the hall, one finger still raised. He'd even forgotten to lock the bloody door!

I gave him another mouthful and walked over him, stamping on his chest. Then I made my way upstairs to go to bed and try to forget the whole business. At the top of the stairs I turned and looked down at him. He was still lying in the hall staring at the ceiling. First he farted. Then he burped. Then he burped again and muttered 'Hic-Haec-Hoc' in that stupid voice of his. Then he began to laugh. I knew he was seeing again the picture of the bowling ball striking the legs of Jones, the Managing Director. Hearing again the crack it had made against the ankle bone. Seeing the poor old bastard's face turn white before he keeled over.

And now there he was. Malcolm. Keeled over as well. Lying on his back. Drunk. With one finger still pointing up into the air. I went into the bedroom and slammed the door.

Example 3b

'Coming Home At Midnight' again, but this time with a different slant and emphasis on the way in which the writing is constructed. This time written in the third person, with two characters speaking in reported speech within the narrative. No sound effects. This last exercise is beginning to prepare the writer/student for the writing of dialogue. Notice how the speaker has now changed from the woman herself to a narrator.

NARRATOR: As the taxi pulled away Malcolm fell over. He raised an arm to Kim, but she just stood and stared at him. She was throbbing with rage. As he slowly began to try to find his feet, she began to walk off. He began to stumble after her, shouting 'Kim' in a thick, drunken, voice, but she kept walking slowly in front of him without looking back.

Although it was after midnight, the heat from the stifling July day was still in the pavement, and she stopped to kick off her shoes, which she then picked up in one hand. She walked on towards their house, reflecting on the events of the evening. It had been the annual summer dinner thrown by her firm. Fancy dress. She had gone as Queen Elizabeth the First and, as she walked, Kim still dragged her train behind her. Malcolm had gone dressed as Sir Francis Drake coming back from playing bowls and beating the Spanish Armada.
Suddenly overcome again with anger, Kim turned and shouted, 'You effing nutter! Throwing that stupid bowling ball at the Managing Director's legs. I'll be lucky to have a job tomorrow.' She ran back down the pavement and shook an enraged fist under his nose.

'My Lady has not the best of humours, I trow,' said Malcolm in a thick, slurred voice.

'You bastard', said Kim and pushed him in the middle of his chest. Malcolm staggered slowly and drunkenly back and sat down heavily in the middle of the pavement, from where he again waved a regal hand at her.

Kim shook her fist once more, then walked the other

hundred or so yards to their front door. She began to search her bag. 'That bloody key', she said.

Malcolm, having regained his feet, crept up behind with the exaggerated slow-motion of the drunk, then leaned over her shoulder attempting to fondle her breasts. Kim retaliated by hitting him across the side of his head with her bag. This time Malcolm didn't fall, but simply swayed on his feet like a boxer who has taken a tremendous punch – the half-bottle of vodka always carried by Kim in her bag providing weight to the delivery.

'The key!' she then shouted in his face. 'What have you done with the key, you bloody Sozzle-Pipe? Where is it?'

He raised one finger at her and rolled back his eyes solemnly. 'My Lady …' he began and then stopped. He tried again, 'My lady …'. At this point Kim yelled, 'You've lost it, haven't you?!' and pushed him towards the front door. He fell slowly back against it. The door opened under his weight and he stumbled backwards into the hall, one finger still raised.

With another curse Kim walked over him, stamping heavily on his chest. And then trudged upstairs determined to forget all about it. Malcolm lay in the hall staring at the ceiling. First he farted. Then he burped. Then he burped again and muttered 'Hic-Haec-Hoc'. Then a picture came to him of his bowling ball striking the legs of the Managing Director of Kim's firm. What a crack it had made against the old fat bastard's ankle bone. How white his face had gone before he keeled over. Malcolm began to laugh silently. Lying on his back. Drunk. With one finger still pointing up into the air. From this position he heard Kim enter the bedroom, the door slam, and the key turn.

Exercises (2)

Which of the two 'Coming Home At Midnight' accounts, when you read it, do you feel is the more immediate and paints the better pictures and gives the more accurate account of the two people involved? Do you hear/see either as you read them? Why do you think this is? Test this by recording and then listening.

As a way of further developing awareness about what different radio channels offer to their listeners, student writers could monitor various radio stations, then gear one of the set exercises towards that particular station. That is, 'Leaving Home' might be written for a Radio 4 audience; the second exercise, 'Lunch Break', for Radio 5; the third, 'Coming Home At Midnight', for Radio 1. Or write one of the three for a commercial radio station that specialises in Country and Western music; one for a station that specialises in music for 'Bikers' or 'Truckers'. Try one written by a member of a wine-tasting society or 'real ale' society. One for an amateur dramatic society. Try one for Radio 3.

4 The radio short story

> He holds him with his glittering eye –
> The Wedding-Guest stood still,
> And listened like a three years' child:
> The Mariner hath his will.
>
> S. T. Coleridge, *Rime of the Ancient Mariner*

> To a critic who once asked him why all his characters spoke alike Hemingway answered, 'Because I never listen to anybody.'
>
> Quoted by Leslie A. Fiedler in *Waiting for the End*

There was apparently once a competition to find the shortest short story in the world – the winner of which was said to be 'Pair of baby's booties for sale – never used.'

This is good mindvisible radio – we immediately see the pair of booties in isolation, perhaps with a 'for sale' sign sticking out of one, and understand the sadness behind the fact that they will never be filled by the small feet for which they were bought. But while this one-line story is satisfying, it satisfies only as one image, and the listener is left to construct all the other events; before, after and around this image. Whereas the true job of the radio story, and any other short story, is to give the whole incident of what led up to the booties being empty, and what will happen next.

The radio story, like the radio talk, has been around since the inception of broadcasting. Like taxes, it is always with us; and although on the surface it may appear a cheap and cheerful source of entertainment, unless the time is filled properly, that entertainment can drag like a lifetime's debt.

In 1924 two children's annuals were published: *Hullo Boys! The Wireless Uncles' Annual* and *Hullo Girls! The Wireless Aunties' Annual*. These works were written by the radio 'Aunts' and 'Uncles', leading members of the newly formed British Broadcasting Company (later Corporation), and were compilations of stories and talks.

In one of these pieces, 'A Wireless "Leg-Pull"', by Uncle Jim of Newcastle, we have what seems to be the first account of a radio 'spoof'. Written up as a story, the incident, though pitched for children, is exactly the right weight and style, and bears all the hallmarks of a good, entertaining radio story. It is intimate and confidential, yet contains movement, space and light, and, most importantly, is humorous.

'A Wireless "Leg-Pull"' by Uncle Jim Newcastle

I wonder whether you would like to hear about a big 'leg-pull' by wireless? You would? Right! Here is the story:

You know, of course, of the 'relays' of speeches taking place at public functions, dinners, and the like. These speeches are usually delivered by well-known persons, about whom everybody has read, but whom, perhaps, comparatively few have seen, and still fewer have heard. Such 'relays' are always popular, and provide a welcome variety in the broadcasting programmes.

The idea occurred to us of devising a 'spoof' dinner with speeches all home-made and delivered in our studio. First of all, it was necessary to lay the plan of the 'Dinner'. What should be the festive occasion, and where was the feast to be held? Everything must be invented. Therefore the town must be one that had no existence. What about 'Purchall'? Good enough. So the 'dinner' was to be relayed from 'Purchall'. And the occasion? Well, the start of a society for promoting the principles and practice of 'mutual improvement' would perhaps serve. Therefore, we got so far: 'the inaugural dinner of the Purchall Mutual Improvement Society'.

Then the principal speakers. There was, of course, a chairman – preferably a titled person – so 'Sir George Brundellyer' took the chair. The Mayor of the town must, obviously, be present; so must a guest of honour. An Indian dignitary would be a fitting person; so the 'Nawab of Pingh' came into existence. One more speaker would be sufficient, and he must be one to reply to the toast of the visitors, and perhaps a canny Scot – one, preferably, with a broad accent. 'Mr. Hector McWhish' was chosen.

But the principal speakers were not sufficient. Perhaps one of the most interesting features of the relay of a big dinner is the hum of conversation of the guests, interspersed with gusts of laughter, and the remarks of those diners sitting near the microphone who have no idea that their artless scraps of conversation are being broadcast to the country. Obviously, therefore, we must have a 'crowd', who must maintain a flow of bright and lively talk – just loud enough to be heard in the mass, but not loud enough for all their conversation to be audible. One or two must be fairly near the microphone to supply the 'unconscious' dialogue which is so entertaining a part of the genuine relay. But I have forgotten an important item. We must have an efficient toast-master to chant 'Mr. Chairman, Your Highness, Ladies, and Gentlemen, pray silence for' etc., before each speech.

So much for the preparation. Now for the performance. At nine o'clock precisely the announcer came to the microphone and informed listeners that we were now going to switch over to Purchall for the speeches at the dinner of the Purchall Mutual Improvement Society. Then the 'crowd' at the back of the studio started their buzz of conversation, punctuated with laughter. This continued for seven or eight seconds, after which the toast-master rapped on the 'dinner table' – actually on a small piece of wood – the buzz of talk ceased, and in his penetrating monotone requested silence for the chairman. This gentleman, in a high-pitched, affected voice, explained how much privileged they were to be present at the birth of the society and to have as a guest the Nawab of Pingh. When he said he did not propose to detain and possibly bore the diners any longer there was loud applause. His Worship the Mayor was so much impressed with the beauties and possibilities of mutual improvement, and became so eloquent on the superiority of discovering and pointing out other people's faults to remedying one's own, that he actually misplaced one or two aspirates.

After a song by a tenor, the guest of the evening was announced – His Highness the Nawab of Pingh. In measured accents he said he was so much impressed with the principles of mutual improvement that he intended to put them into practice among his two million subjects in the small state of Pingh, in India. Mr. McWhish followed, in accents of broad Doric. His original family name, he explained, was McWhishkey, but his grandfather, a distiller, lost the 'key' of the distillery, and thus reduced his name to McWhish. The speeches throughout were punctuated with applause and laughter.

The 'relay' was brought to a close by the Chairman proposing the toast of 'The Nawab', which was drunk with musical honours. It is safe to say that most 'listeners' were taken in, and in spite of the papers on the following morning 'giving the show away', a number of correspondents confessed that they had looked up directories and maps to find out the position of 'Purchall'.

From *Hullo Boys! The Wireless Uncles' Annual*

The above story is a tight, complete world where every word counts and where a whole parcel of the human experience was delivered under plain wrapping. This is what is to be aimed for. By 1946, the short story was so well established that the BBC was bringing out books in which selected short stories which had been broadcast were published, called *Late Night Specials*.

The standard radio short story slot is for fifteen minutes at approximately 2,300 words. Fifteen minutes is a good, satisfying length that gives time to develop a main plot and, if suitably handled, a sub-plot. With students in a classroom situation this length can be modified to suit differing circumstances and abilities.

Short stories, and radio short stories in particular, are an intimate form. The first task of the writer must be to try to gain the empathy of the listener. That is, the work being presented must try to draw in the listener to a full comprehension, identification and sympathy with what is being related.

In life, the way to attempt to gain empathy from anyone is to speak to them on as honest and friendly a basis as possible, as if they alone understand and hold the solution to what you are telling or describing. In radio short stories, the best way of achieving this same intimacy is to have the story related in the first person by an actor with an identifiable and pleasing accent; and with a style of delivery that bears some relation to the content. This approach has been found to work very successfully; listeners feeling that they are being addressed confidentially by someone who wishes to share a secret with just them.

Overall, the radio stories that seem to come across best are those that are written as dramatic monologues of a confidential nature.

Simplicity, too, is worth striving for. You have to hold a listener's attention for fifteen minutes while you relate an incident – or a series of inter-related incidents.

Although a specific case can be made for flashback, first efforts should be concentrated in simple story progression. Keep the events of your story temporally sequential; that is, tell the story in chronological order. 'A' should be followed by 'B' and then 'C'. The man must stop the bus and then climb on to it. It is confusing for a listener for the man to be on the bus, refer back to climbing on to it, then refer back again to something that happened at the bus stop as the bus was arriving. The images should slot in causally so that the listener can soak up atmosphere and plot and character without having to juggle with adjustments in time and space. The scenery is passing quickly, the mind needs to be kept relatively clear in order to be able to view and judge accurately what passes through it.

Keep the style and words simple. Do not invoke difficult concepts. Simple, mindvisible ideas are what are needed. It may be a short story in name, but the listener has no script and cannot 'turn back' a page if something is misheard or not understood first time round. Literary 'short stories' are meant to be read on the page; a radio 'short story' is meant to be read by an actor but 'listened to' by the audience. The listener must hear and see simultaneously. The actor/reader must serve your cause by turning the words in front of him or her into a living oral tale, and should, like Kipling's bull in the bullring, attempt to become but 'the vessel of an emotion'. The reader should become a person colloquially relating a story from memory rather than performing a set piece from a page of script.

Humour, as ever, is appreciated, and the story will be expected to fulfil its brief by the time it has run its course. If there is a gun mentioned hanging on the wall in the opening sentences, it will be expected that it will have been fired by the close of the story.

All classically constructed writing works in the same fashion: Opening, Development, Argument, Resolution, Ending (ODARE). That is, the basic well-made story should contain these elements in sequence. We should have a firm, interesting

OPENING	which draws in the listener by an intriguing and positive beginning that captures the attention and introduces the main character(s) who
DEVELOP	the story by elaborating the plot, and set up the
ARGUMENT	which will usually mean pitching the main characters and their points of view/beliefs against each other until the
RESOLUTION	occurs, at which point the Argument or conflict is resolved, for good or bad, and the story moves into its

ENDING	where all the threads are finally pulled together and the listener is presented with a complete and rounded work where all queries have been met and all questions answered.

This ODARE formula should be learnt and practised until it is second nature. Once it has been mastered, and providing the initial idea is sound, a basic, competent short story can be guaranteed. It may, initially, be formulaic writing, but the thing about a tried and tested formula is that it works.

So, utilising the ODARE formula, and then passing through a further four stages, we will build up a short story from basics. We will use the oldest, favourite and most tested plotline in the world, the boy/girl, love/lose, repent/redeem, reconcile/regain, re-affirm/rejoice, scenario. A meets B. A loses B. A wins back B.

Using the ODARE formulation we begin by setting up a basic framework. Then, after this, the story is expanded in four separate stages. Stage 1: the five-statement outline. Stage 2: the five statements expanded to sentences. Stage 3: the five sentences expanded to paragraphs. Stage 4: the addition of the sub-plot/second interest.

Stage 1: the five-statement outline

OPENING	A meets B and gradually it becomes love.
DEVELOPMENT	A asks B to commit to a permanent relationship.
ARGUMENT	B declines; A has an unacceptable habit.
RESOLUTION	A reforms to suit the wishes of B.
ENDING	A and B together again. Wedding bells.

Now expand the categories. The basic idea is still the relationship between A and B (Bill and Ann), but in this first expansion, each of the five steps in the ODARE sequence now becomes a sentence.

Stage 2: expanding the outline to sentences

OPENING	Ann and Bill bump into each other at the local wine bar and are immediately attracted.
DEVELOPMENT	They continue to meet at the bar until one night Bill, after a particularly enjoyable evening, suggests to Ann that they move into his flat together.

ARGUMENT — Ann tells Bill that she really likes him, but feels he drinks too much and she could not commit to anyone with that sort of problem. Bill storms off in a huff.

RESOLUTION — After six weeks of worry on the part of Ann, Bill turns up with a diary in which he accounts for every evening; none of which were spent drinking.

ENDING — Ann, impressed by this show of will-power, agrees to take a chance, and she and Bill begin their relationship.

The next step is to make each of the ODARE elements a paragraph.

Stage 3: expanding the sentences to paragraphs

OPENING — Ann, feeling depressed after a bad day at work, decides to call into a wine bar. Turning with a drink she collides with Bill, who apologises, buys her another drink, and asks if he can join her as his colleague, Roy, is just leaving. Ann and Bill find they have a common interest in Bogart films, and agree it would be nice to meet again.

DEVELOPMENT — Bill rings a few days later, and Ann agrees to meet him in the wine bar. The relationship begins to blossom. They continue to meet at the bar, going back to either her flat or his flat on different occasions. After one particularly enjoyable evening together, Bill suggests that they commit themselves and move into a flat together.

ARGUMENT — Ann tells Bill that she really likes him, but the fact is he always wants to meet in the wine bar, and she thinks he drinks too much. Whenever she suggests a film or concert there is always some reason why it has to be the wine bar. As well as liking Humphrey Bogart, Bill seems to be modelling his own character on that of the film star. Bill tells Ann that he drinks because he is bored and lonely, and would be happy to give it up if he had something more permanent. Ann implies that talk is cheap – but what is under discussion is her/their possible future(s). Bill suddenly gets up and leaves the wine bar.

RESOLUTION For six weeks Ann sees nothing of Bill – although she fancies she catches a glimpse of him jogging. She is upset – but feels it is not up to her to make the first move. Eventually she calls in the wine bar but Bill is not there. She talks to Roy, who tells her that Bill has become much quieter, not going out drinking any longer. One evening, passing the wine bar, Ann sees Bill sitting in the window. He shows her a diary he has been keeping detailing his movements for the last six weeks. He has not had a drink.

ENDING Ann, impressed by this show of will-power, and by Bill's obvious seriousness as regards their potential relationship, agrees to take a chance with Bill.

At this stage we should try to add a second interest to the story which does not interfere with the main storyline, but acts as a complement.

Stage 4: adding the sub-plot/second interest

OPENING Ann, in the first person, tells how, after a bad day at work, she calls into a wine bar. Turning from the bar she collides with Bill, who apologises, buys her another drink, and invites her to join him as his colleague, Roy, is just leaving. Roy was leaving but now he's seen Ann he thinks he'll stay. The three talk, find they have a common interest in Bogart films, and agree it would be nice to meet again.

DEVELOPMENT Bill rings early next morning and invites Ann to meet him again in the wine bar that evening. She agrees, not thinking about Roy, who walks in on them and seems put out to see them there together. Ann's meetings with Bill become regular and they are often joined by Roy, who acts as a catalyst when Bill has had a few drinks too many – and is also used as the butt of Bill's jokes. Although Ann and Bill do not see eye to eye on everything, the relationship blossoms. They continue to meet at the bar, going back to either her or his flat. After one particularly enjoyable evening together, Bill suggests they move in together.

ARGUMENT Ann tells Bill that she really likes him, but the fact is he always wants to meet in the wine bar, and she thinks he drinks too much. Whenever she suggests a film or concert it always ends in the wine bar. She feels that, as well as being a fan of Humphrey Bogart, Bill is taking him as a role model. Bill tells Ann he drinks because he is bored and lonely, and would be only too happy to give it up if he had something more permanent. Ann implies that talk is cheap, but what is being discussed is her/their possible future(s). Bill suddenly gets up and leaves the wine bar.

Roy, who has been watching from another table, comes over and offers to take Ann home.

RESOLUTION

Ann then relates how for six weeks she sees nothing of Bill – although she fancies she catches a glimpse of him out jogging. She is very upset – but feels it is not up to her to make the first move. Sometimes she calls in the wine bar but Bill is never there. Roy rings her and she arranges to meet him. He tells her that Bill has been much quieter around the office, and doesn't seem to bother going out drinking any more. Roy confesses he loves her – and says that, although Bill is his friend – Bill will never change. Ann says she likes Roy very much – but not as a lover. Ann stops going into the wine bar but continues to go home that way. One evening she sees Bill sitting in the window with Roy. She goes in and Bill produces a diary he has been keeping detailing his movements for the last six weeks. He has not had a drink.

ENDING

Roy goes to the counter to give Ann and Bill a chance to talk. Ann, impressed by Bill's show of will-power, and by his obvious seriousness as regards their potential relationship, agrees to take a chance. Bill, with a shout, tells Roy to order another two bottles of wine! When Roy arrives back with the three bottles Bill immediately opens one and starts drinking the way he did previously. Ann, with a sinking heart, feels Roy looking at her but refuses to catch his eye. She senses her life moving towards unhappiness and ruin.

The slight sub-plot, the declared love of Roy for Ann, does not add much in dramatic terms, but allows the story to breathe a little and, if skilfully handled, can keep the listener guessing as to whom Ann will eventually choose between the two men.

A lighter approach to the same might be something along the lines of 'How Bill Lost his Bottle', told in the third person:

OPENING — Ann meets Bill in a wine bar and they are immediately attracted to each other. Anne is interested in musicals; Bill describes himself as an insurance salesman by day – but the owner of one of the world's best collections of rare lager bottles and labels in his real life. As if to prove this, Jeff, a friend of Bill and fellow label collector, staggers up to the table and demands Bill sell him a bottle with a label 'Well Stoned' from a brewery on Easter Island.

DEVELOPMENT — Ann and Bill begin to see a great deal of each other, hit it off well together, and eventually Bill asks Ann to move into his flat with him.

ARGUMENT — Ann tells Bill that she likes him very much, but she doesn't feel that she can live with his collection of empty bottles and labels. And besides, that trip Bill promised to the latest West End musical. That special £50 weekend offer. How *could* Bill have spent the money on a dozen rare bottles of Tasmanian lager – just for the labels! No, she doesn't feel she can move in with Bill yet, not while Bill prefers his collection of lager labels to her well-being. Bill, hurt and baffled, goes off in a huff to the pub. He is quietly standing at the bar, adding to his collection of lager memorabilia, when Jeff staggers up alongside. Jeff has heard of the rare Tasmanian labels and would pay anything – perhaps a tenner a bottle.

RESOLUTION — For a moment Bill hesitates, weighing hobby against happiness ... then he realises that all the empty lager bottles in the world mean nothing against Ann, and he closes the deal with Jeff.

ENDING — As the train pulls out of the station for London and the West End show, Ann and Bill laugh and joke

Exercises (1)

The following exercises are to give the student writer practice in building up a basic idea into a complete, professionally structured story.

1 Choose one of the following scenarios as an initial meeting place for A and B – or pick a location of your own: health club; job centre; drug rehabilitation clinic; auction rooms; football match; police station; court; checkout till in supermarket. Then, using the ODARE plan and the expansion method of statement, sentence, paragraph and sub-plot, write a short story of 2,300 words or so; that is, a fifteen minute story in broadcast terms. Choose either the first or third person to relate the story.

2 From 'Contemporary issues' in the Appendix choose a scenario, and again, using the ODARE and four stages method, construct a short story of 2,300 words.

3 If the story is intended to be broadcast on a college radio station, use the above outlines to construct a 500–700 word story, which will give a good three–five minute short story.

together. Bill asks Ann if she would like something from the bar – she tells him – 'Anything, Dear, except lager.'

Read the following short stories twice before going on to the exercises on p. 77.

Here are two Radio 4 broadcast short stories to read/discuss/analyse as radio. 'Birdsong' and 'Mr Ossie's Rolled-Gold Fish and Chip Shop', are about childhood, adolescence, the confusions of 'growing up'.

'Birdsong' is very simple, told with a continuous, gradually developed plot and sub-plot. The story was developed from an initial idea of the actor James Ellis, who read the work. A sub-plot was added. It was produced by Michael Earley.

'Birdsong'

'Come on!' said my Ma, grabbing my foot and shaking it. 'It's your birthday and the birds are singing. Come and see what he's bought you. It's on the table next to your plate.'

'Birdsong' I said to myself, and once more saw it streak past the winning post in my dream. I felt both frightened and excited. I didn't often have dreams. Especially not about winning horses.

I went downstairs, looked for a pencil and paper, wrote down 'Birdsong', then went to the table. My Da's place was empty – gone hours ago to the shipyard for his Saturday overtime.

At my place there was an expensive-looking jeweller's box. I couldn't believe it. I had jokingly asked for a watch for my thirteenth birthday – 'Lucky for some, eh, Da?' I never expected it. Half the time the clock didn't work.

As I was winding it up my Ma came in from the back kitchen with egg, black pudding, fried bread. 'He came up on the fixed odds,' she said. 'On the football coupon. We're even going to get electricity in – get rid of these gas mantles for good.' She laid five shillings down beside the plate. 'Happy Birthday!' she said, and kissed the side of my head.

'The Pools'. The 'fixed odds' held no interest for me. I was a racing man. I fancied I knew every horse in training and used to try and have a small bet every day after school on one of the last races – threepence or sixpence each way. Saturday I'd catch the bus to town and hang round the bookie's all day. Today was Saturday. No one knew. No one could know. My Da would go wild at my age. It'd be a belt job. The leather across my legs. But not the buckle like some of my mates got. Da was basically all right.

I glanced sideways at the two half-crowns as I mopped up the egg with the bread. Five shillings, I thought, plus three I had already. Eight bob. Eight bob to go to the bookie's with – and 'Birdsong' a winner in my dream.

I didn't recognise the name and this sort of worried me. But there would be one or two I wasn't familiar with – had to be. I stood up from the table and stretched. I had a few things to do. Chopping firewood and the like. Besides, it would pass the morning ... And then ...

On the bus I sat on top up at the front. The unopened newspaper on my knee. I looked out the window. Grey street, grey sky, grey people. With steady rain coming in on the wind from the west.

I tensed, then quickly opened the paper at the racing pages. Seven meetings. Hundreds of horses, it seemed. I ran my eyes down. No 'Birdsong'. I went through again. No, nothing of that name. I couldn't believe it. The dream had been too real. Too vivid. Once more I searched the pages, slowly, carefully. Still nothing. I hunched over the columns of names, feeling confused.

The betting shop I used on a Saturday was near where the city proper began. Crowded but anonymous. Opposite was a pub. The other end of the block a pawnbroker's. A triangle, the sum of the sides of which would always give a minus.

The first race was in half an hour. The shop began to fill with men who steamed gently as they quietly came in out of the rain. Or shook the wet from their hair after sprinting across the road from the pub. There were low greetings, a couple of old, well tried jokes, a whispered exchange of last minute information from 'someone who knew the trainer' – but mainly they leaned against the walls, newspapers up, concentrating in silence on the names, numbers and odds before them as they prepared themselves for the first race.

The door opened and a woman wearing a headscarf came in. She had on a long coat and was carrying a shopping basket. The men pretended not to see her. Not to know her. As if they did not wish to compound what they saw as her shame. She did her business quietly at the counter then left without ever looking directly at anyone. Some nervous laughter broke out as the door closed behind her but most behaved as if it had never happened.

The loudspeaker, which had been crackling into life now and then with starting prices and 'on course' information, suddenly announced they were 'going down'. There was a last minute rush at the counter. Then they were 'Off'. There was no commentary. After a time the loudspeaker would simply announce the names of the first, second and third horses.

As the race began most of the men stood still – staring at the floor or at their newspapers, or at the large white sheets pinned to the walls with the horses in heavy black type. Others ran back across to the pub.

I stood near the door. A boy in a man's world who knew his place. Who could always claim to be 'sheltering from the rain' if the police entered.

I lost on the first race, got an each-way place in the second, lost on the third and decided to go for a walk to clear my head. I thought about my dream. About 'Birdsong'. It must be running Monday. That meant taking a day off school. More problems. As I strolled along a clock chimed from a church. I checked it against my new watch. I saw someone glance at me doing this, and pulled down the sleeve of my jumper. I wanted everyone to notice it while keeping it a secret.

In a small café I had a cup of tea and counted my money. Down to about six shillings. I finished my tea and stood up – time to begin seriously.

Towards the end of the afternoon I had two shillings and some coppers left. The last race was at five-thirty but I'd be wanted home for my tea by then. Five o'clock would be my last chance to get something back. I stared towards the entrance lost in thought; then the door opened and Jimmy walked in. I felt, simultaneously, embarrassment, anger, despair.

Jimmy was about sixty. He was small, thin, toothless, dirty, undernourished. He wore a pair of glasses with lenses like two opaque pebbles. Close-cropped iron grey hair, and a threadbare 'mac' that was so greasy it could have stood up by itself.

The first time I'd come in the shop he'd asked me to verify a horse's name he was trying to make out by holding the newspaper pressed against his nose. Flattered by being addressed on equal terms by a man, any man, I'd struck up a conversation. He'd asked me what I'd fancied for 'the next' and I'd told him. He'd put on a shilling each way and it had won. I became his 'luck'. He consulted me on every bet he had, and was driving me mad. I pretended not to notice him, but he found me by somehow sensing me as he edged round the walls.

He asked me how it was going. I told him. He asked me if I 'knew anything' and I said 'no'. He was shivering with cold but I didn't even bother to ask him how he was. He jingled money in his pocket. He'd been to the next shop along and made a killing. He had, he told me, won twenty-five bob. A 'fortune' was what he called it.

He said that he'd buy me some fish and chips, and tried to give me a packet of cigarettes. I could hardly bear to look at him. I stared at the clock. Quarter to five, and coming up for the last race. The shop was now nearly empty as most of the money was gone and the pubs were now semi-open again.

In an effort to escape I told Jimmy I wanted to check something on one of the big sheets of runners tacked to the walls. I stood staring blindly at the list of names for the five o'clock. Then I saw it. 'Birdsong.' My mouth suddenly went dry. I went back to my newspaper. There it was! But written underneath the main entries for the race. Below even the call-over prices – among the 'Also Engaged'.

In those days a trainer might enter a horse for a number of races at a meeting and run him in just one. These horses, being entered for more than one gallop, were necessarily 'Also Engaged' and listed, in much smaller print, under the main entries for any and every race for which they were put down.

I had not checked the 'Also Engageds'. I looked at 'Birdsong's' price, 20–1. I saw it was a two-year-old, never been out, which is why I didn't at first recognise the name.

I stood for a moment to steady myself then turned casually to the counter. Jimmy picked up the scent immediately and was treading on my heels.

'Shilling each way,' I said, and handed in the slip.

'What have you got?' he whispered. 'Jesus, I can tell you've got something!'

I shook my head, almost afraid to speak.

He gripped my arm in a vice-like trembling grip, and brought his face close to mine. His breath smelled of almonds. 'Give it to me, pal!' he pleaded. 'Jesus, son. Don't let a pal down!'

'Outside,' I whispered. 'Let's go out for a breath.'

Outside, in the rain, I told him. About the dream. The clarity of it. And the fact I'd never heard of the horse which surely must mean a supernatural sighting – a vision.

He almost had a seizure. He shook, trembled – but this time with excitement. 'My luck,' he said, 'I knew you were my luck! Count my money,' he added. 'Search the lining. Put the lot on. Every halfpenny. Every farthing.'

I dug into his pockets. I found twenty-six shillings. More than he'd probably had at any time in the last twenty years. He gripped me by the arm again and pushed his head towards me. 'Put it all on, son. Put it on. We're rich. Jesus, we'll lick the bastards yet!'

I was about to turn back into the shop with his money when something struck me, and I stopped dead.

'What is it?' Jimmy asked. 'What is it?'

I stared at him as I thought. I had a shilling each way. Jimmy would have thirteen shillings each way. Compared to him I'd win nothing. My dream, my effort, and he'd make the killing. I told him to wait and ran off with him shouting after me.

The man in the pawnshop was bringing out the shutters but I dragged him back into the shop. I showed him the new watch. 'A birthday present, brand new,' I explained.

'How much?' he asked.

'Five pounds,' I said. He laughed and offered two.

'Make it a bit more, mister,' I pleaded. 'Another quid if you can. It's well worth it.' He wouldn't budge, there was little if any time, so I took the two pound notes and ran back to the betting shop.

They were still not off. 'Win' or 'each way?' I thought. 'Go for the win?' Two pounds at 20–1. Forty-two pounds! Rich. More than rich! My head spun. But I hadn't the nerve and went for each way. My two pounds, plus Jimmy's twenty-six shillings – thirty-three shillings each way! I scribbled the slip and got up to the counter. Then they were 'Under Starter's Orders'. I took a breath and held it – I felt physically ill. Then they were 'Off'.

The few fellas left in there caught that something was going on. They moved over to ask Jimmy if I'd had some sort of tip-off.

Jimmy never cracked on about the dream – just that I'd had a hunch. Ay, well, those fellas weren't the sort that followed the hunches of thirteen-year-old schoolboys, but still they settled themselves against the walls to see the outcome. Sure, if the horse touched with that sort of money on it wouldn't there be a pint? – And if not, well, wasn't that what life was about?

Jimmy and I stared blindly into each other's faces. There was dead silence in the shop. The loudspeaker crackled, then fell silent, then crackled again. First, second, third were read out. 'Birdsong' wasn't mentioned.

I half-started towards the counter to ask for some sort of check. But even if there were an objection and one horse was disqualified the other two would just move up a place. The dream had failed.

Obsessed by my own bad luck, I had forgotten Jimmy. His twenty-six shillings. His 'fortune'. He was suddenly in my way. I waited for the abuse, the accusations. Instead he offered me a Woodbine. It was all old territory to Jimmy.

I brushed past him, muttering something about seeing him on Monday. I knew I would never go back there again. I still had a few coppers for the bus home. It was only when I reached the house I realised the watch was missing. And that Da would be there for tea.

At the table I sat with my sleeve drawn well down. Reaching for the bread and butter like a pirate trying to hide his hook. Nothing was said until near the end of the meal.

'Did you like the watch?' asked me Da suddenly.

'Sure it's great, Da. Ma told me about your pools win. I couldn't believe it ... I ... I ...' – I stopped exhausted with my lack of imagination in one direction, though I had all too much in another.

'Where is it?' he asked casually.

'At Johnno's,' I said, falling easily into the way of things.

'Go round after tea and get it back. You know how much that cost?'

Ma, who had been staring at me with bright eyes, said quickly,

'I don't want him out again today. He's wheezing enough as it is. In that rain all afternoon, he was.'

There was a pause while my Da thought. 'Tomorrow,' he finally said.

'He's playing football tomorrow for the under fifteens, is Johnno,' I said. 'An away friendly match. Twenty miles or so. An all-day job what with the coach and that. I'd have to go dead early – and even then I might miss him. He'll bring it to school on Monday.' In my voice I pitched for mercy and understanding.

Da thought again. 'Monday,' he finally said. 'Be wearing it when I get home from work.'

The belt was never mentioned, never looked at, but it was as if he'd already taken it off and laid it across the table.

I had forty-eight hours to find two pounds odd. God help me.

The old triangle – betting shop, pub, pawnshop – had put on their lights and opened their doors for me on my thirteenth birthday. They had held out the dream – 'Birdsong'. And like many others of my kind, before and since, I had accepted it, unquestioningly, and taken it up.

'Birdsong' is relatively simple. A direct first-person narrative intended to flow continuously and gradually build to its resolution and ending without any side tracking. The sub-plot of the watch was entered early and mentioned from time to time in the narrative to keep it firmly fixed in the mind of the listener.

'Mr Ossie's Rolled-Gold Fish and Chip Shop' is more complicated and technically complex, and uses flashback and multi-layering of character. It was produced by Pam Fraser Solomon.

'Mr Ossie's Rolled-Gold Fish and Chip Shop'

Rummaging through a drawer yesterday I came across a box containing a silver ten piastre piece dated 1916, and a one pound note issued by the Anglo-Palestine Bank. Immediately, a picture came to mind of a small, bald, fat man with bushy black eyebrows, large brown eyes, a putty-soft face, and a neck so thick all his shirts had to be worn open at the collar. Along with this picture came the smell of fish and chips, and an unpronounceable surname we shortened to 'Mr Ossie'.

Everton were playing an away cup-match and John Quigg, who had an uncle with plenty of money and a car, had offered to take me to the game. 'You'll need about seven-and-a-tanner,' Quigg told me. 'He always goes in the stands. How much have you got?'

Quigg, who breathed heavily through his mouth, had pale green eyes as close together as lights on an old tractor, a flat nose covered in freckles and shaped like a spade, loosely curled sandy hair, and a chin like Desperate Dan. He was about five foot tall and walked as if there was a very large weight in one of his pockets. He watched very closely after asking about the money.

'Five bob left from Christmas.' I took the two half-crowns out in my closed hand and shook them against each other. I carried the coins everywhere with me. 'Because you never know the minute,' as my mother always said. Quigg nodded and left it at that. The match was a fortnight away. Looking back, I have to admire his finesse.

I discussed the possibilities of finding the other half-crown with my mother and father, who stared at me blankly; and with my friends who were equally at a loss. I ran errands, visited relations as if they were all at death's door, went to early morning mass three days on the run, searched down shop-grids with a piece of soap stuck on the end of a brush pole – all to no avail.

Then I started thinking about Mr Ossie.

Mr Ossie had arrived on the road out of the blue and opened a stationers. This had failed immediately in a district where pencil and cheap lined writing paper were the norm, and those only used for bets and notes of absence to the school.

Mr Ossie then opened a chip shop – which immediately succeeded. It being silently understood that it was acceptable for someone of Mr Ossie's looks and background to serve us food and drink.

But the urge to spread literacy, or penmanship, would not be denied, and Mr Ossie had brought with him from his stationers a glass display case full of gold-capped fountain pens which he placed behind the counter of the chip shop. No customer had ever seen him touch the case or refer to it, and in time it passed into myth and beyond comment, but secretly it confirmed our opinions of our own superiority. It was something 'we' would never do.

'Thick as a canteen cup,' the father of one of my mates would say about Mr Ossie. 'Just about fit to run a chip shop. Could do with a good wash.'

I had made it my business to get to know Mr Ossie and had gradually wormed my way into his confidence. In time I could 'go behind the counter' and clean a bit, and stack the newspapers the chips were wrapped in, and even venture as far as the 'door into the back'. In the back there was said to be a 'Mrs Ossie' but I never saw her.

Mr Ossie and I became friends – though I tried to make it clear I would never be able to acknowledge him in public.

One afternoon, when the shop was closed between sessions and we were wiping down, Mr Ossie brought out a wooden box full of foreign coins and notes. It was then he gave me the silver ten piastre coin and the Palestine pound note. Nothing was said.

Part of my duties was to degrease the case that contained the fountain pens. I had never opened it, but when we were alone I had often seen Mr Ossie lift the lid and stare quietly at the contents – like the priest at benediction standing before the tabernacle. His broad back hiding the mysteries.

The week of the cup match came – I was still no nearer the other half-crown. If you took a good bundle of newspapers to Mr Ossie you got free fishcake and chips. I suggested to Mr Ossie I go round the doors knocking for these newspapers. This would save him money – which he would then hopefully give to me.

He didn't say anything. I took this to mean 'no'. Later I realised that Mr Ossie meant 'no' because he knew the local women hoarded their newspapers against the end of the week when the money ran out – when a bundle of papers could mean something to put on the table.

I was stuck. A chance to go to an away match. Have a ride in a car. Sit in the stands. All for half-a-crown.

I told John Quigg I couldn't make it. He asked if I had anything to sell. I said I had an album of stamps I'd swapped some time ago for a steering cart. He looked at me. 'Those pens of Mr Ossie's,' he said. 'That red marbly one with the gold top. I'd give half-a-dollar for that one. In fact I'd give a dollar. Five bob.' He stopped and waited. He said if we went to the match his uncle would probably stop at a pub on the way back. There'd be lemonade and crisps. We wouldn't get home until all hours. It would be the trip of a lifetime.

The next day, when I cleaned the display case, I tried lifting the lid. It gave without a sound. I eased it back and went home to think.

The following afternoon, after school, I went in again. Apart from the outset, when I needed to impress, I had never been in two consecutive days. Mr Ossie said nothing. I rubbed away at the side of the fat fryer. 'This grease,' I said. 'Any bleach Mr Ossie?' Nor had I ever asked for anything. Without a word, Mr Ossie opened the door into the back and disappeared.

The pens were in two rows of ten. I lifted the lid, took out the one Quigg wanted and adjusted the others to fill the gap. I closed the lid and went back to rubbing the fryer. Mr Ossie returned with the bleach. He didn't look in the direction of the case. I rubbed a bit longer, coughed, and made a show of trying to fasten a blazer that had no buttons. 'See you,' I said. And began to saunter towards the door. Somehow he was there before me. I stopped and looked at him. Eyes expressionless, he asked, 'You want fish? Chips? For your work?' I grinned a sickly grin. 'I'll have them tomorrow, thanks, Mr Ossie,' I said. 'I'll call in about teatime.'

He nodded briefly, then said, 'You want to buy it?' Then asked, 'How much you think it is worth?'

We were obviously talking about the pen. I saw the police coming to the house. A beating from my father. The trip to court. Then the beating in front of the whole school. Laid over a bench and six or eight with the cane. This was mandatory for anyone who appeared in court. No screams, or pleas from mothers, were ever accepted. Once, someone had got a doctor's note, but the derision from staff and pupils had been merciless. And if you wouldn't bend over willingly you were forced and held over. And there were very few who had ever had eight off this Headmaster quietly, or without vomiting.

I swayed slightly. Mr Ossie must have noticed. I felt he knew exactly what I was thinking – even before I was thinking it myself. Foreigners weren't supposed to be able to do that. The fat ones weren't supposed to be able to move quickly. What was going on? 'How much?' he asked again. 'How much it worth?'

'Five shillings,' I said desperately, feeling the two half-crowns in my pocket.

He stared at me.

'Five shillings,' I repeated. I took out the coins and showed him. He picked them off my palm.

'I sell to you,' he announced. 'I sell to you for five shillings.'

'Thank you,' I said in a whisper. I grinned a terrible grin and leaned forward in relief. I would escape physical punishment. That was all I could think of. I was embarrassed, ashamed, close to tears. But felt I'd got away with something. I had conned him somehow. I began to prepare the tale for my friends. I took a hesitant step forward. He didn't move.

'What you do with it?' he then enquired. 'Not to write with. No?'

I shook my head in agreement. I was ready to agree to anything at that stage. Just to get out and lick my wounds; work up my story. 'No, not to write with.'

'So, what you do?' he repeated in that same level voice. 'Why you want it?'

'To sell,' I said, looking at the floor. 'I was going to sell it.'

I knew by now that his honour was unimpeachable, but in my panic I reverted to the fable that this was the sort of thing his kind were supposed to appreciate. Buying, haggling, selling. 'Boo! Boo! Your mother's a Jew. Your father's a Proddy, your sister's one too!'

He nodded. 'How much? This good pen. You understand? Very good pen. How much you sell for?'

I thought, 'If I say too much he'll know I think it's worth more than five bob and that I've tried to fiddle him.' I stood calculating while attempting to look both ashamed and contrite.

'A shilling,' I finally said.

He nodded. I'd fulfilled all expectations. 'You sell for a shilling?' he repeated.

'A shilling,' I agreed in what I imagined was a firmer voice. We stared at each other. I looked him in the eye. His were still expressionless.

'I buy from you,' he announced.

I blinked, began to try to see my way through it all. Where was I? Let's think. The pen I had stolen from him he had then sold me for five shillings – he had my two half-crowns, I had the pen. But now he wanted to buy the pen back for one shilling – the price I'd told him I'd get for the pen on the street. Had I got it right? What was he up to?

From his pocket he took a shilling. He held it out and I hesitantly lifted it from his palm. He kept his hand outstretched and I put the pen into it. My mind juggled with the figures, then the mist dissolved. I had given him five shillings for the pen I had stolen from him. I had then told him the pen was worth a shilling to me if I sold it. From my five shillings he had given me back a shilling and regained ownership of the pen. He now had four shillings of mine and the pen. I had one shilling and total humiliation.

He gazed at my sad, bewildered face. For a moment something flickered behind his eyes, then he stood to one side and opened the door for me.

I slowly walked out onto the road.

I went down and had my tea. I had decided to bully my sister to tears but she wasn't in. My mother asked me about the football match money. Was I any nearer finding it? I muttered something, pushed away the plate, and then went to the top of the street to a shop doorway in which we always stood. I practised spitting while waiting for the rest of the lads. Quigg appeared. He gazed at me expectantly, then asked how much I was now short.

I blurted out the whole thing. I was hoping, I really believed, he might say something like, 'It doesn't matter, La, I'll talk to my uncle, he'll take you for nothing. He's a good skin.' Instead, once he'd heard about the pen, he said in a flat venomous voice, 'What's this about you looking up our Josie's knickers?'

I shook my head.

'Moggo told me. That you "knew" they were coloured green so you "must" have seen them. And that you said the elastic had gone in one leg and you could "SEE IN"!! You dirty bastard!'

Quigg punched me in the mouth with a rhinoceros fist, then triumphantly lurched away with his thirty degree list, and shapeless blue raincoat with the belt hanging down the back.

After about twenty yards he stopped and turned. 'I'll tell my Ma who'll tell your Da and you know what you'll get then!'

After that, whenever I had to go past Mr Ossie's, I always crossed to the other side of the road. I never went in the shop or spoke to Mr Ossie again.

I like the Palestine pound note, but of the two I prefer the coin. 'Ten Piastres', '1916', and the rest in Arabic enfolded within a beautiful filigree wreath running round the rim of the coin. But solid silver. And worth more than four shillings – no matter how you weigh it.

I wonder if Mr Ossie saw this at the time. He saw everything else.

Exercises (2)

1 Choose one of the two stories and break it down into the components of Opening, Development, Argument, Resolution, Ending. Then write out each of these individual sections as a paragraph. Then as a sentence. Then as a statement. Finally, say what you think the story is about in one word.

2 Then choose one of the stories and translate it from the first person to the third – at half its present length. Record, listen, analyse.

3 Write down an idea of your own. Choose something about which you know.

People it from your own group or background. Stick to a vocabulary with which you are familiar. Pick from your memory an incident that always makes you laugh, or cry, or fills you with rage. Then, working from the ODARE formula, write a short story using the four stages statement, sentences, paragraphs, second interest (sub-plot).

5 The radio play and the drama-documentary

For want of a nail the shoe was lost.
For want of the shoe the horse was lost.
For want of the horse the message was lost.
For want of the message the battle was lost.
For want of the battle the Kingdom was lost.
All for the want of a nail.

Anon.

History is written by the winners.

Radio plays have been around from the very beginning of broadcasting. Plays for voices alone even longer. Peter Lewis, in *Radio Drama*, refers to W. M. S. Russell's conference paper 'Sound Drama Before Marconi', which mentions Seneca's plays for voices.

Seneca (8 BC–AD 65) wrote plays purposely designed to be read by actors to a select audience. Closet drama. This seemed partly a political move, as Seneca had by this time upset Nero – not a difficult thing to do. As Michael Grant (1973) puts it: 'Nero was born of murderous parents ... And he too was murderous. But only when frightened, though unfortunately he got frightened easily.'

Seneca, by having his works more or less secretly performed, felt this might save him – but it never does.

Like any good play for radio, Seneca's works contain scenes that cannot be staged – the dismembered body of Hippolytus being pieced together, for example, in *Phaedra*.

CHORUS: You, sir, shall set in order these remains
Of your son's broken body, and restore
The mingled fragments to their place. Put here
His strong right hand ... and here the left,

Which used to hold the reins so skilfully ...
I recognise the shape of this left side ...

Trans. E. F. Watling

The BBC radio drama department was established in 1924 with R. E. Jeffrey as head and Howard Rose, a radio playwright, as his deputy.

According to Briggs (1941), the first play actually written for broadcasting was 'Danger' by Richard Hughes, produced in 1924. Set in a coal mine and containing a reference to the lights having just gone out, it grasped the nettle of what radio could offer by producing a setting in which there were no visual aids except those which could be conjured up by the mind.

The play was commissioned by Jeffrey, who had firm ideas as to what could not, and should not, happen in radio plays. He believed that no radio play should last longer than forty minutes, but that the best radio plays had an advantage over stage productions because of the grip which they could exert on the listener.

Between August 1924 and September 1925, 141 'plays' were broadcast (some would now be classed as features, 'One Hundred Years of Railways', for example).

Since then, radio plays have been written about every conceivable subject, set in every conceivable place and covering all times. Only now is the flow beginning to dry up, with greater and greater limits imposed on the length and availability of 'slots' for original work. The pressure is on to find something cheaper than employing numbers of actors and paying a playwright – because this means more money can be diverted to television.

Script layout

Before we approach the writing of plays it is essential to learn standard script layout. This enables a writer, quickly and professionally, to lay out his or her stall. This will save time and create the right impression of professionalism when a script lands on the desk of a reader/producer in a radio station.

Few people would turn up for a job interview looking as if they had crawled from under a bed; though many scripts arrive looking as if they have come from under a bus. Neatness and tidiness are as important in the presentation of work to a potential script buyer, as they would be to a potential employer looking at an interviewee.

People who receive and buy scripts are used to a certain type of layout and are never happier than when a script arrives in a format that can be easily judged for time, clarity and length of speeches. A good script editor can usually tell from the look of a script how good or bad it is – simply from riffling through it quickly.

An enormous number of unsolicited scripts arrive every year at all stations which produce written radio, all of which, theoretically, should be read and generate an impartial written report as regards potential.

In the past, this task fell to what were known as 'script readers', who read the script and, if they felt there was any good in it, passed it on to a producer. The producer, if he or she agreed with the reader's judgement about the script, would then look for a commission. This meant the work was passed on to a department editor, who could choose to take the script to a 'script meeting' where a final decision would be made by a panel of producers. Usually, one person alone could not buy or commission a script.

These days, producers, their personal assistants and sometimes a 'researcher' do the best they can. Whoever does the reading has much to do and little time in which to do it. A script which arrives in what is more or less standard format will make the reader's job easier and enable the play in question to be assessed both accurately and quickly.

All scripts should be considered on merit, but a work which arrives handwritten in green ink, sprinkled with Greek epigrams, illustrated in sepia half-tone and accompanied by the first movement of an atonal string quartet, may require the sort of time that is not available.

In short, in a handwritten work many words can be unclear. A misreading of these words may alter the sense of a speech, which may alter the thrust of a scene, which may alter the impact of the play – the nail and horseshoe effect.

Finally, make sure your script is radio script and not a film/television/theatre script that has been refused everywhere else, and is now to be tried on radio – where, it is well known, they will accept anything.

Scripts of this nature often arrive, with commands in the accompanying letter dictating which 'stars' will be required to fill the main roles – and instructions to send the commissioning fee by return of post.

Submissions like this are in themselves a comedy. To the trained eye, scripts that have been written for another medium, and then 'disguised' by the addition of sound effects and so on, are immediately identifiable as such – and are treated accordingly.

At this stage it may be helpful to look at a script especially written and contrived to give an idea of basic radio layout and radio drama script conventions. It is entitled 'Stolen Promises'. Explanatory notes will be found at the end of the script.

STOLEN PROMISES

A Play For Radio

by

Writer's Name

Writer's Name
Street
Town
Postcode

tel: 0000 000 0000

Broadcast Length: 30 mins

Cast in Order of Speaking

MAIN ROLES in capitals, subsidiary parts/possible doubles in lower case.

GEORGE RIKER	Midlands accent	35 yrs old
SUSAN KERR	Standard received	26
DONALD JOHNSTON	Scots	50s
Ann Donnelley	Standard received	50s
1st shopper	Female, south-east	40s
2nd shopper	Female, south-east	40s
Barman	Northern Irish	20s
Waiter	London	30s
Voice on tannoy		
Shopping crowds		

SCENE 1 LANDING OUTSIDE SUSAN KERR'S FLAT

FX: WE HEAR BANGING WITH HAMMER AND SOMEONE EXPELLING BREATH WITH EFFORT AFTER EACH BLOW. IN BACKGROUND WE HEAR MUSIC – CHRISTMAS LINKED, PERHAPS 'RUDOLPH THE RED NOSED REINDEER'. IT IS SLIGHTLY DISTORTED AS IT IS COMING FROM INSIDE THE FLAT OF SUSAN KERR.

1. RIKER: (SOFTLY) Trouble, Miss ...?

2. SUSAN: (STARTLED) Oh! ... I didn't hear ...

3. RIKER: Riker ... George Riker ... Flat upstairs. Just on my way to work ... (PAUSE) ... Trouble?

4. SUSAN: This screw. I bought a new lock ... try and beat the burglars. Being so near Christmas ... And the police and media talking about security ... The one that was on here was falling to pieces.

5. RIKER: Here, let's have that hammer ... You don't hammer them, you see, screws. Nails you hammer. But screws ... you screw ...

(RUDOLPH ENDS, INDISTINCT DJ'S VOICE FROM BACKGROUND RADIO) ... Got to make a hole, first ... Give it a start ... Now! ... (BEGINS TO FIX LOCK) You seen them about this?

6. SUSAN: Them ...?

7. RIKER: The brothers ... Ones that own the house. Must have got your rent book off them. On Benefit, are you? They like girls on Benefit ... (PAUSE) ... Now that plate ... That's the one ... They'll want a spare key, you see. For when they look round your room ... (PAUSE) ... See what you're hiding ... (PAUSE)

[PAGE 1]

1. SUSAN: I didn't think ... they had the right ... to look round people's rooms ...

2. RIKER: London ... isn't it? ... (PAUSE) ... As I said before, Riker ... George Riker ...

3. SUSAN: Oh, yes. Sorry. Susan Kerr. Pleased to meet you.

4. RIKER: Not from round here, then?

5. SUSAN: The North. No work, so I came down to take some temping. Starting in the new year ...

6. RIKER: Listen to that. On your radio. 'Jingle Bells' ... (PAUSE) ... Lonely business, Christmas away from your loved ones ... Boyfriend? ... (LONG PAUSE) ... Maybe a festive drink across the road then ... one evening?

PAUSE

FX: 'JINGLE BELLS' BROUGHT UP AND ISOLATED

7. SUSAN: Thanks ... But, well, I don't drink much really.

PAUSE

8. RIKER: (SOFTLY) Does something to your insides, doesn't it ... Susan?

9. SUSAN: What? ... What does?

10. RIKER: Why ... The thought of travelling on a one-horse open sleigh ...

[PAGE 2]

SCENE 2 UNDERGROUND STATION

TUBE TRAIN SCREAMS INTO STATION. DOORS OPEN. RUSH HOUR CROWD BOARDING. DOORS CLOSE. TUBE PULLS AWAY. WE GO INTO INTERIOR MONOLOGUE IN RIKER'S HEAD AS HE STRAP-HANGS. SOUND OF TUBE HELD UNDER IN BACKGROUND.

1. RIKER: (INTERIOR MONOLOGUE.) 'Oh, sorry ... No! ... Don't drink!' (LAUGHS) Not bloody much! ... We know the type, though, eh, George? ... Blonde hair ... tight sweaters ... We've seen them before. Had dealings with them ... (FADE UP TUBE, FADE BACK AGAIN) Seen their faces crumble ... Forced them to look at us as persons ... way they never would if they passed us in the street. (LAUGHS AS TUBE BEGINS TO DECELERATE) ... Why, George, one of them even killed herself over you! (WE ISOLATE SOUND OF GIRL SOBBING)

FX: TUBE SHRIEKS INTO STATION. DOORS OPEN.

CUT TO –

SCENE 3 DEPARTMENT STORE

FX: BUSY DEPARTMENT STORE. TILLS RINGING. PIPED CHRISTMAS MUSIC. WE HEAR KNOCK ON OFFICE DOOR. DOOR OPENING. THEN ALL STORE SOUNDS SUDDENLY CUT OFF AS DOOR CLOSES.

SCENE 4 OFFICE OF DONALDSON. STORE MANAGER.

2. DONALDSON: Ay, come in, George. Won't be a minute ... Just sorting out the last of the orders. Right, Ann, top up the menswear before 'C' day as we'll call it ... That's 'C' for Christmas, of course, George.

[PAGE 3]

3. RIKER:	Thanks.
1. ANN:	(TO HERSELF, MAKING NOTE) ... Menswear ...
2. DON'SON:	And if you come back about eleven, Ann, we'll look at some of the stuff for the sales ...
3. ANN:	Right. Coffee, now, Mr Donaldson?
4. DON'SON:	If you please. You'll join me George? ... Right! Coffee for two, Ann.
5. RIKER:	Lots of sugar, Ann. You know I've a sweet tooth, don't you?
	PAUSE
FX:	DOOR SLAMS.
6. DON'SON:	You've a way with the girls, George, and no mistake.
	PAUSE
7. RIKER:	Anything in particular, Mr Donaldson?
	Etc. ...

[PAGE 4]

These scenes attempt to show how a script is laid out, and to point up and analyse some of the conventions used within radio drama – 'Interior monologue', 'Rapid change of scene', 'Atmosphere-enhancing music', 'Sound effects' …

Suggestions for layout

Students and writers eventually adjust their pages to suit the amount of material they wish to fit on to them. That is, they may wish to have enough material on a page to fill a minute's broadcasting time, to enable a rough guess to be made as to how long a particular script is at any given stage. The following is only a very rough guide:

1 One-and-a-half lines of space to be used between all lines of dialogue.

2 Double spacing to be used between dialogue speeches, and between dialogue and sound effects.

3 Sound effects to be denoted on left-hand side of page as FX or SFX. Sound effects themselves to be in capitals.

4 All dialogue speeches to be numbered in sequence 1, 2, 3, and so on, beginning anew on every page in order to facilitate reference and correction. That is, if someone wished to speak to the writer over the telephone about certain aspects of the play, they could do so by referring to 'Page 5, Speech 6' or 'Page 12, Speech 1'. This cuts out much fumbling around in finding various speeches on different pages.

5 … (X) … identifies an interruption point; that is, in a speech, this signifies that the next speaker interrupts or breaks in at this point.

The text

With 'Stolen Promises' we have a title page with the writer's name, address and telephone number, and also the length of the play. This is important as it indicates to a script reader a producer to whom the play might go – that is, one who possibly specialises in half-hour 'thriller' plays.

Further points

CAST LIST

From this a producer would get some idea of how many actors would be needed; and what ages and accents might be required.

PAGE 1

Sets up the first scene. We learn that we are on the landing outside SUSAN KERR'S flat. That RIKER is another tenant in the house. From the FX the producer would know what sound effects would be required. The two main characters, RIKER and SUSAN, are introduced. We also learn that it is approaching Christmas from the music coming from inside the flat.

RIKER begins to pressure SUSAN. His tone becomes indefinably menacing … telling her that the brothers who own the house (P. 2, Sp. 7) '… like girls on Benefit'. He seems to know things … that 'the brothers' will

PAGE 2

also search SUSAN'S room while she is out. We also sense that RIKER is someone who can do things … fix locks … that, in a way, he is a controller of things and people.

We learn something about SUSAN – where she is from; what she does for a living. We sense she may be vulnerable. RIKER constantly pumps her for information – in a seemingly semi-friendly fashion. Where she was born – what she does for a living. Whether or not she had a 'boyfriend'. He speaks softly and there always seems to be a second meaning implicit in the remarks which he makes. A sort of sexual innuendo hangs over everything …

Then he asks her out for a drink – at which point 'Jingle Bells' is brought up and isolated in order to set the cheeriness of the Christmas music against the menace sub-textually posed by this seemingly casual invitation by RIKER.

And then an almost direct sexual reference – P. 2, Sp. 8, 'Does something to your insides, doesn't it … Susan' – and when, in panic, she questions him, P. 2, Sp. 9, he turns the question to an innocent answer: 'Why … The thought of travelling in a one-horse open sleigh …'

And we cut to:

PAGE 3 Scene 2. Radiophonically we immediately pick up on the 'travelling' and 'sleigh' and go to a tube station. RIKER's menace is suddenly intensified by this scene change to the Underground and the train shrieking into the station. We go into the radio convention of 'interior monologue' (P. 3, Sp. 1) whereby we learn what RIKER is thinking. It is about SUSAN. The images are particularly simple and mindvisible – 'blonde hair ... tight sweaters'. We are still in the dark as to who and what he is. Then we have a short flashback sequence when RIKER tells us a girl killed herself over him and we isolate and bring up the sound of a girl sobbing. This build-up about RIKER pulls us forward into the play. We begin to ask ourselves questions. Why did the girl kill herself? What is so special about RIKER that he could provoke such an extreme reaction?

Then the train begins to decelerate and as it shrieks into the station we cut to:–

Scene 3. Abruptly we change scene again. We are suddenly in a department store. There is a totally different ambience. Christmas and jollity. Shoppers, music ... Then we prepare to change the mood again. To do this we again change the atmosphere. We move to the office of MR DONALDSON (P. 3, Scene 4).

All the extraneous noise is cut out. We introduce another main character. The seemingly bluff, common-sense DONALDSON, manager of the store. DONALDSON is busy sorting out last-minute Christmas problems with his secretary, ANN. RIKER is forced to wait and listen to some of the day-to-day business of the store (P. 2–3, Sp. 2–4). This lets us know something about the store and also prepares the characters of

PAGE 4 DONALDSON and ANN. Then RIKER becomes involved again. He is asked by DONALDSON if he would like a coffee (P. 4, Sp. 4) and replies to the secretary (P. 4, Sp. 5) 'Lots of sugar, Ann. You know I've a sweet tooth, don't you?'

The secretary, ANN, exits, slamming the door to show her distaste of RIKER. The manager, DONALDSON, reinforces this opinion by telling RIKER, 'You've a way with the girls, George, and no mistake' (P. 87, Sp. 6).

And with RIKER's final speech on page 87, 'Anything in particular, Mr Donaldson?', we move out of the opening of the play and begin the development.

So here we have an example of a script laid out properly, which would allow a script reader/producer to see, at a very quick glance, exactly what is there in terms of length and ability. The length of speeches is always a good indication of the expertise of an author. Very long speeches, page after page, denote someone who has yet to learn the compression and shortcuts needed to present effective dramatic writing.

Plays, like chess, are both a science and an art, and both tactical and strategic skills are required. Immediate effects and gains must be sought constantly, but at the same time a long-term strategy for the shaping, cohering and bringing together of all the elements of the task must be worked towards; and always kept in view.

Notice in our example how the names were brought out early and repeated to fix them in the consciousness of the listener. How the play was full of life and spirit and moved around, taking the listener with it.

Riker is a store detective. A store detective who arrests only women. A year or so previously a girl occupying a room in the house where he lives had hung herself after Riker had arrested her for shoplifting. There was a question as to how much Riker was involved in driving her to her death, but nothing was ever proven. Susan Kerr is the dead girl's sister. She has decided to find out what happened in her own way.

Now to the writing of plays in general. You have chosen a subject or incident from the Appendix, at the end of the book, or an incident about which you yourself wish to write, and are ready to pull this into dramatic shape.

The three major elements in any standard dramatic work are the plot, the main characters and their development, and the dialogue. In a radio play, the characters involved will speak in dialogue in order both to tell us about themselves and to inform us of the events of the storyline in which they are involved as characters. That is, the characters, using dialogue, will unfold themselves and the plot.

If we take a play as a living human body, the characters would be the major organs and the dialogue the nervous system, but both of these, in order to function properly, have to be attached to a skeleton. And the skeleton of the body dramatic is the plot. For, as well as telling us the story, the plot will also give the play its dramatic shape and unify the whole. Without a plot, just like a human body without a skeleton, all you get is a puddle of entrails, tissue, muscle and organs spread over the floor.

As with the unfolding of the writing of the short story in chapter 4, the unfolding of a play's plot will present the listener with the same five elements necessary to maintain the classical structure of any play in any dramatic medium. That is, Opening, Development, Argument, Resolution, Ending. There will always be experimental works in which characters on Hampstead Heath stand up to their necks in giant jam-jars full of sand talking about Jean-Paul Sartre; but true drama demands a rigid structure.

From time to time accredited, and even 'famous', playwrights and screenwriters appear on radio, television and in the pages of the reviews and announce, 'No, I'm afraid I can't really handle plot'; or, 'Plot, well, I know this sounds frightfully ignorant but ... well ... that's not for me ... never could handle one.' Remarks of this nature usually seem to be made with no embarrassment or sense of failure. In certain cases, there seems an almost ingenuous delight in confessing to this basic inability. Nor do those to whom such confessions are made seem to exhibit any anxiety. Reviewers, heads of drama departments, critics, fanciers from the arts boards – all nod the head understandingly. In many cases, admissions of this nature seem only to act as an incentive to buying yet another shapeless mess from a particular writer.

This leads to one of two conclusions. That those who are buying material, in many cases from out of the public purse, do not know what they are doing. They cannot distinguish a good play from a bad play, nor do they have any knowledge of how a piece of drama should be constructed; or, they are deliberately cultivating unsound writing, and ridicule, for reasons known only to themselves. Imagine a leading, celebrated songwriter confessing to being unable to write a melody.

Plot

> An intrigue, an affair complicated, involved and embarrassed, the story of a play, comprising an artful involution of affairs, unravelled at last by some unexpected means.
>
> Johnson, *Dictionary*

We return to the ODARE scheme, plus the three basic types of dramatic plot:

- Simple spiral plot.
- Simple plot with complications.
- Plot plus sub-plot.

The simple spiral plot is the easiest type of play to write and one that falls naturally under the hands of the majority of writers. In a 'spiral plot' a new writer takes a story that has had a thousand outings and presents it in its simplest form. Take the wine bar story again:

OPENING	Ann and Bill bump into each other at the local wine bar and are immediately attracted.
DEVELOPMENT	They continue to meet at the bar until one night Bill, after a particularly enjoyable evening, suggests to Ann that they move into his flat together.
ARGUMENT	Ann tells Bill that she really likes him, but feels he drinks too much and she could not commit to anyone with that sort of problem.
RESOLUTION	Bill disappears for six weeks and then turns up with a diary in which he accounts for every evening; none of which were spent drinking.
ENDING	Ann, impressed by this show of will-power, agrees to take a chance, and she and Bill begin their relationship.

As a radio play:

How Bill Lost His Bottle

SCENE 1	WINE BAR
FX:	LAUGHTER, GLASSES, 'HOUSE/INDY' MUSIC IN BACKGROUND.

1. BILL: Whoops … sorry … Someone nudged my arm … Honestly … Here, let me get you another …

2. ANN: (LAUGHS) All right … White wine and soda please …

3. BILL: Look, where are you sitting? … I'll bring it over …

4. ANN: Here's fine … I'm alone as it happens …

5. BILL: Not for long! I'm Bill … Bill Bottle!

6. ANN: Oh, Ann … Ann Jones …

FADES DOWN/FADES UP TO

SCENE 2 ANN'S FLAT

FX: ALARM CLOCK RINGING. PART YAWN/PART GROAN AND THEN ALARM CLOCK SUDDENLY STOPS.

7. BILL: Ann! … Ann … Time for work!

8. ANN: (SLEEPILY) Already …

9. BILL: Come on! … (PAUSE) … Good night, eh? …

10. ANN: Was until you had that last bottle …

PAUSE

11. BILL: Well, Bottle by name, Bottle by nature … Ann … have you thought? … About what I said …? About us moving in together …?

12. ANN: Bill … You drink too much … too much for me to take on anyway …

13. BILL: I get bored, Ann … At least I did 'til I met you … Come on, how about it?

14. ANN: Throw me that bathrobe, will you …?

PAUSE

15. BILL: If that's what you want …

CUT TO

SCENE 3 ANN'S OFFICE

FX: (BUSY OFFICE SOUNDS. KEYBOARDS, PHONES, ETC. WE HEAR ANN MURMUR), 'Let's see how that finance account looks …'. THEN WE HEAR A PRINTER KICK IN. THEN WE HEAR, 'I suppose I could ring Bill ... see how he is ...'. THEN PHONE PAD BEING PUNCHED OVER PRINTER. AND PHONE RINGING OUT ... AND RINGING ... AND RINGING ... AND

CUT TO

SCENE 4 BUSY STREET. CARS, BUSES, etc.

1. BILL: (OFF-MIKE. SHOUTS) Ann! ... (COMING ON MIKE) ... Ann ... Ann, how are you, love?

2. ANN: Bill ... Oh, Bill ... What happened? ... Six weeks it's been ... And no word ... And look at you ... you must have lost at least a stone ... I hardly recognised you ... I mean, just look at you ...

3. BILL: While you look at this ...

4. ANN: Your diary ...?

5. BILL: An entry every day since we last spoke ... Here, have a look.

6. ANN: (READS) Monday – jogging ... Tues. – health club ... Thurs. – five-a-side football ... What's been happening ...?

7. BILL: You have Ann ... For the last six weeks ... No wine bar ... No booze ... No nothing. Sorting myself out for you ... Show you I could do it. Well ...?

PAUSE

CUT TO

SCENE 5 WINE BAR AS IN SCENE 1

FX: AS SCENE 1

8. BILL: So what'll it be ...

9. ANN: White wine and soda, please, for me ... Lemonade for you! ... Then home, James, for a cup of tea!

10. BILL: (FADING OUT) ... 'Cup of tea!' And to think I used to be Bill Bottle!

ENDS

This is spiral drama. You start at the top of the stairs and fall down.

Exercises (1)

To practise layout, and to begin to use the dramatic conventions of radio drama, write a short spiral plot play on the A meets B, boy meets girl, theme – using the wine bar play as a guide. But because a drama reader, with a pile of scripts on his or her desk like a chapatti mountain, would be looking for more than a simple spiral play, we must find something new in the A meets B scenario – either in setting or treatment. Below are two ideas for your short play.

A and B might meet under circumstances peculiar to our day and age. Perhaps at a gathering of a sinister 'fringe' religion that both may have attended out of curiosity. They begin a relationship. Then A is overtaken by the religion and its followers. In this case, A being reunited with B may mean a physical and psychological battle by B against the powers which hold A in thrall.

Alternatively, A meets B and all is set for marriage. Then A suffers an accident which incapacitates her either mentally, or physically, or both. The thrust of the drama would then revolve around B either accepting the changes – and the deeper bonding this will hopefully bring – or the gradual/outright rejection of A by B and the taste of betrayal, and the despair/resolution that follows.

Use one of these two ideas to write your short spiral play, or see the Appendix.

Plot plus sub-plot

Above we have seen two examples of how to circumnavigate the staleness which tends to creep into stories set in familiar surroundings, but what we have is still simple spiral drama.

What is needed to lift these plays is the addition of another ingredient to the mixture – another flavour altogether but one complementary to the main course – plot plus sub-plot. If, against the main story of the play, there is the constant thrust of another storyline that is intertwined with the main plot, though usually subordinate to it, then this is known as the 'sub-plot'. We find the same in music, where one melody can be sung in conjunction with another – both totally different but enhancing the overall effect of the piece.

To pursue our old theme of A meets B, A does meet B and gets on very well with B. A is a rep. who travels all over the country, and after a whirlwind courtship A and B marry.

It gradually unfolds that part of the reason why A travels is to visit his/her other family, who live a couple of hundred miles away. A is a bigamist. This gives the chance to run two storylines together either comically or tragically. The lives of the two families could be entirely separate or at times intertwine, the radio technique of cross-fade being perfect for this. For example, in the play A might be a man. In the first home he might be the dominant partner, in the second he might be firmly subordinate to the second wife, C. In the first home we could hear A order his wife to begin washing the dishes. We could hear the tap being turned on, then cut to home no. 2, where we hear a tap being switched off as A finishes cleaning the dishes on the instructions of C. This way, the character of A could perhaps be examined as a 'split personality'. C will provide the sub-plot.

A set-up such as two homes leaves room for many twists to be added. A might be a member of a race relations board whose job is to travel between cities with high ethnic populations. A's two spouses, B and C, could belong to different races. A could also be bisexual, one partner could be a man, the other a woman. Due to the strain both marriages could collapse – A's two partners could meet and then decide to marry each other. There seems no end to it – there never is.

It could be argued that the above is merely the result of a great deal of 'plot tinkering', that 'it couldn't really happen'. Which leads to the question of how far is it possible to go? How much can people be asked to believe? While it is true that no one ever went bankrupt underestimating public taste – are there dramatic imaginative limits even within the cloak of 'artistic licence'? The whole question is usually discussed within the framework of what is known as 'the suspension of disbelief'.

Mark Twain (1835–1910) observed about some character, possibly himself, that 'There were things that he stretched, but mainly he told the truth.' And some writers do present scripts whose compressed, complex, dramatic, tangled and unbelievable incidents pulse like a ball of maggots. Sometimes they state, truthfully, 'But it happened to me!' And so it might, for fact is stranger than fiction, especially in the world of letters.

But if you are presenting a fictional situation to a reader or listener, then that reader/listener must be drawn into crediting the situation. He or she must feel, through the skills of the writer, that however outlandish the sequence of events presented, there is no reason, given the handling of the play, that these events could not occur.

The most famous example is, undoubtedly, Orson Welles's radio broadcast to the citizens of New York when he announced, as a news flash, that New York was being invaded from Mars. Many of New York's inhabitants panicked, and scenes of chaos ensued. That was in 1938. Extra-terrestrials erupting on to the streets of New York today would probably mean as little as a volcano erupting in Central Park.

While some writers might possess Welles's sense of seizing the moment, few have access to seizing the New York public broadcasting system. To sell work, authors generally have to rely on realistic plays about realistic people – which can present a problem if those people are to be put in unnatural or unrealistic situations.

For, on one level, the rules of realism are always with us. Writers can argue along the lines of 'I'm writing fiction so, by definition, I can make Calcutta the capital of Japan or put the Sphinx inside the Coliseum.' And while this is true, it is unconvincing, because an audience is being asked to believe in a totally unreal situation within a totally realistic framework, and the two will not marry. In a world where Calcutta and Japan exist as physical entities as we know them, it is impossible for any normal listener to see them as anything other than what they already are. In this case the suspension of disbelief simply does not work.

The problem, however, has been resolved in a number of ways. First there is the setting up of a human society that is able to organise itself to rules of its own devising – with laws and customs outside of those which usually pertain. An example is *The Admirable Crichton* by J. M. Barrie (1860–1937).

In *The Admirable Crichton*, the Earl of Loam, his family and his butler, Crichton, are marooned on a desert island after being shipwrecked from their yacht.

Crichton, prior to being cast away, believes in a social order where everything has its place and every man has his – Crichton's being that of an upper servant within the Loam household. Crichton, initially, is portrayed as simultaneously observant and obsequious:

1. LADY MARY: Do go on speaking. Tell me, what did Mr Ernest mean by saying he was not young enough to know everything?

2. CRICHTON: I have no idea, my lady.

3. LADY MARY: But you laughed.

4. CRICHTON: My lady, he is the second son of a peer.

This is Crichton talking to Mary, Loam's eldest daughter. Mary's character is established in fast visual radio writing early in the play, in a speech she delivers when told she and her two sisters will be allowed only one maid between them on the yacht:

5. LADY MARY: But who is to put us to bed, and get us up, and how shall we ever know it is morning if there is no one to pull the blinds?

As in the Gorky extract about Chekhov, we hear nothing specific about Mary and her life – but such is the underwriting in this one bit of dialogue that everything about her becomes immediately apparent.

Once on the island, however, due to his natural abilities, Crichton takes charge, becomes almost a king, and is on course to reach an understanding with Mary, who has become a courageous, competent and a complementary partner for Crichton. The party is rescued, returns to England, and life goes on as before, Crichton falling acquiescently into his old role.

By placing his scene on a desert island, where all normal laws were suspended, Barrie could handle his material as he wished, with a complete 'suspension of disbelief' on the part of his audience. He could make the statements he wished concerning the privileges conferred by the accident of birth against the rewards of being born with normal abilities and common sense. Like the man who deliberately threw himself from his horse and feigned concussion for the rest of his life in an effort to be accepted by the country set.

Taking things a step further, though staying with the same author, we have *Peter Pan*. Here, fairies, pirates, crocodiles which have swallowed alarm clocks and human beings are all thrown together. Similar sorts of ingredient can be found in Lewis Carroll's *Alice in Wonderland*.

After this mixing of the human and non-human, the next step is to present complete non-humans in a non-human situation – the genre of science-fiction. Here, alien beings in the form of many-headed green monsters, crystals that walk, talk and float, or things that 'just are', are set in motion in worlds that defy all Newton's laws and most people's credulity. The only hindrance to a dramatist mining this field is lack of imagination.

One further category that deserves mention is the anthropomorphising, or the giving of human personality, to non-human creatures and objects.

The History and Adventures of an Atom, published in 1769 and written by Tobias Smollett (1721–81) is this type of narrative. In this satire an atom, ostensibly living in the body of a native of Japan, relates its experiences. The characters in the work are based on political personalities contemporary to that time.

In the same vein is *The Adventures of a Guinea*, a satirical narrative by Charles Johnstone (1719?–1800?), published in 1760–5. In this work, a guinea describes its several owners. It includes an account of Dashwood's 'Hellfire Club' at Medmenham Abbey.

A radio play utilising this approach, and using cockroaches, was 'Who Is Sylvia?' by Stephen Dunstone, directed by John Tydeman.

'Who Is Sylvia' tells the story of a family of cockroaches living in a specimen case in a laboratory. They are taken out one by one to be made the subject of hideous experiments. Henry and Angela are the cockroach mum and dad, and they have, initially, ten children, or nymphs. Sylvia, one of these nymphs, is the apple of her parents' eye – everything a good daughter could be.

The experiments are carried out by Sir Archibald Sopwith-Plackett and his assistant, Michael. Sir Archibald, too, has a daughter named Sylvia. Michael is in love with Sylvia, but is afraid his love is unrequited. Sir Archie's wife, Lady Mary, may have cancer.

The play plots the lives of the two groups – human and insect. The cockroaches try to understand a world where their children are systematically taken from them and, if returned at all, come back dying or mutilated; the humans live in their world with, for them, its own share of death, worry and ignorance of the ultimate meaning of things.

The most horrifying experiment of all is reserved for the young female cockroach, Sylvia.

Towards the end of the play Sir Archibald finds out his wife is not suffering from cancer. He also hears news that his daughter Sylvia, after kicking over the traces for a time at Cambridge, where she is a student, is again interested in Michael. He is a happy man.

Cambridge is the spiritual home of the experimenters – as, indeed, it is of the cockroaches. Angela, the cockroach mum, declares proudly, near the beginning of the play, how her ancestors came from the kitchens at Magdalene College.

In the experiment tank the cockroach father, Henry, is not so happy, as he tries to make sense of why his family have all been destroyed. All, that is, except Sylvia, who is before him implanted with cancer and grafted upside down on to another cockroach, Darren, who has been beheaded but still lives through her.

'Who Is Sylvia?' ends on a sad and disturbing note – but at least it ends in a fashion that can be understood – even though understated.

A final area in this category is to give totally inanimate objects human sensibilities. This short play was developed from a student exercise, and gives human life to two women's blouses:

Big Girls' Blouses

SCENE 1 BLOUSE RAIL IN A CHAIN STORE

FX: BUSY CHAINSTORE SHOPPING SOUNDS. THEN FADE DOWN AND OUT TO

1. BLOUSE A: Oh, hi! ... Welcome to the rail ... (PAUSE) ... You OK?

2. BLOUSE B: To be frank ... no, I'm not.

PAUSE

3. A: Why's that, then?

4. B: Well, this isn't really my sort of place ...

5. A: Oh ...

6. B: Well, I mean, I'm DESIGNER! But the firm went bankrupt. And I was sold off in a job lot! A JOB LOT! (BURSTS INTO TEARS)

7. A: There now ... At least you're a nice colour. Look at me ... Bright purple! A bright purple blouse!

1. B:	But a chainstore! In a provincial town. You can't imagine!
2. A:	Hang on, here's a couple of punters come in. Heading this way ... Blimey, look at the one in front. Size eighteen ... yellow shoes, and just itching for something in purple to go with them. My seams won't take it!
3. B:	And the other!
4. A:	Looks all right to me ...
5. B:	My dear, pure Volvo! Thinks a Corniche is some sort of pastie! And I know she's going to take me ... I know it! ... Oh! Unmanicured nails! Oh ...!
6. A:	(CALLING) Bye, now! ... (NORMAL) Right. Here comes Moby Dick ... Hope she treats me like my label says ... (MUTTERS TO HERSELF) ... Hold on to your buttons, girl ... You've been bought!
SCENE 2	RESTAURANT
FX:	BUSY RESTAURANT SOUNDS. FADE BACK, HOLD UNDER.
7. A:	Oh, hi! It's you again! You've done well. Being taken to places like this. Hang on ... mine's got to drop off another fork at that table over there ... (BRING UP RESTAURANT THEN FADE BACK AGAIN) ... Right, where were we ...?
8. B:	It's him. That bastard sitting opposite. Her husband. He takes her to posh restaurants like this so he can take the babysitter home later. Sweet sixteen, I don't think. Some of the things I've heard in that wardrobe ... I'd've turned pink if I wasn't this beautiful powder blue ...
9. A:	Still, you're looking well ... Nicely pressed ... just like new. Mine's hardly got time to give me a quick rinse ... What with the three kids and two jobs ... Her fella's long gone ... Left her to it ...
10. B:	Do you know? There hasn't been a dozen of champagne in that house since I arrived!

1. A: To be honest, I don't think I've got much longer. What with the grease spots ... and the steam and stuff ... It's playing havoc with my fibres ... And the owner lets them eat what they want ... So she stuffs her face with all this crap ... chocolate and cream and that ... I'm bursting apart ...

2. B: Of course, mine will find out about him and *Young Lady Crotchless*, and you know what that might mean, don't you? ... After the split and divorce? ... We are talking SEMI-DETACHED!! ...

3. A: Don't know what will happen to me when the balloon bursts ... Hang on, she's off for a fag and to rest her feet ... Bunions like cricket balls ... See you ...

SCENE 3 BACK OF A CHARITY SHOP

FX: DEAD SPACE

4. A: Look, love, I know you've just arrived but there's no need to shove. I'm giving you what space I can ... (PAUSE) ... Oh, it's you again ... (PAUSE) ... Didn't expect to see you here ...

5. B: (WHISPERS, FRIGHTENED) Where are we? ... It's so dark ...

6. A: Charity shop ... (PAUSE) ... Well, the back of a charity shop ... Didn't you know?

7. B: A CHARITY SHOP! I don't believe it! What's going on?! ... Is there NO GOD?

8. A: It could be worse ... Well, maybe ...

PAUSE

9. B: Of course, one has heard of such places ... But ... well ... I was given the impression there were rails of half-wearable clothes ... Even a decent label or two with whom one could ... (PAUSE) ... It's so musty here ... so cramped ...

10. A: I did say the *back* of a charity shop ... (PAUSE) ... What happened? ... You were looking great last time I saw you.

11. B: That *effing* bloody baby-sitter I was telling you about.

She offered to do some ironing for *Madame*, because then she could spend more time in the house with *Mr Randy*, being touched up from arse to breakfast time ... Of course, the little cow knew no more about ironing than ... well ... THE QUEEN MOTHER! ... A HUGE scorch mark down my front! I was picked up, thrown in a bag ... and that's the last I remember! ... The one consolation is *Madame* was going to send one of his old suits with me ... went through the pockets ... and found a note from Little Miss Big Knockers! ... So that's them on route to the lawyers, I'M PLEASED TO ANNOUNCE! ... (PAUSE) ... And you? ...

1. A: Oh, she went out clubbing with a couple of mates. Got drunk, picked someone up, brought him back. They got off their heads properly, and he made a grab at her ... just ripped me off her back ... One of my arms is only on by a few threads ... She couldn't be bothered sewing me up ... what with the grease and stuff from the restaurant ... So that was that as far as I was concerned ... (PAUSE) ... I'm not a pretty sight.

PAUSE

2. B: How DO these people exist?! ... (PAUSE) ... When do we get moved out front?

PAUSE

3. B: Why don't you answer?

4. A: It's the *back* of the shop ... Behind the curtain ...

5. B: And?

6. A: You've a big scorch mark ... My arm's hanging off ... No one's going to buy us, love ... I mean, would you ...?

PAUSE

7. B: So what happens?

PAUSE

8. B: So what happens?

9. A: Pulped ...

10. B: Pulped!

1. A: Boutique or bargain basement, it's all the same in the end, love.

2. B: Oh, God! (STARTS TO CRY) If only Luigi ... that's Luigi Spaghetti ... THE Luigi Spaghetti! ... My CREATOR! ... could see what's happening to me ...

3. A: Don't ... It's not that bad ... Not really ... We just become something else ... paper, I think ...

PAUSE

4. B: We're not burnt are we ...? Not incinerated! ... I couldn't stand that.

5. A: No ... I don't think so ... Paper ... or something ... But I think it's paper ... (PAUSE) ... Here, you might end up as a few pages in a best-seller about the rich and famous ... You'd like that ...

6. B: How can you! Bloody joke! At a time like this!

PAUSE

7. A Yeah ... Sorry ...

8. B: No, you're right ... (PAUSE. WHISPERS) ... Aren't you frightened?

9. A: No ... well, not a lot ...

10. B: I am ... (PAUSE) ... a bit ...

11. A: Don't be ... It's just life ... Hello, someone's coming down the shop ... Curtain's going back.

FX: (SOUND OF CURTAIN GOING BACK ON RAIL) ... Light at last! ... Great!

12. B: (WHISPERS) Don't leave me ...

13. A: 'Course not ... I wouldn't do that ... Well, this is it ... here we go ... Into the bundle ... Here, take my hand ... We'll stick together ... Come on ... Chin up ... Mustn't let them think we're Big Girls' Blouses.

END

Before passing on to construct a play ourselves, a word in general about beginnings, middles and endings.

Sitting down to write a basic radio play you are there to tell a story as simply and as economically as possible. Part of this economy should be directed to exposing the substance of the plot as quickly as possible.

You are asking a potential listener for a chunk of his or her time, and so you should, to some extent, show in return what is on offer. And if it seems interesting, if it seems that something worth waiting for is on the way, there is every chance a listener will stay with your dramatic development.

A theatre audience allows twenty minutes for the plot to be exposed, before becoming bored, but, in radio, the plot should be both immediate and intriguing – because if your play looks as if it is going nowhere then neither are you.

A radio play called 'The Finger of Suspicion' opens with the university rag-day parade passing Lewis's store in Liverpool. On the pediment of Lewis's is a statue by the sculptor Jacob Epstein. Inspector Crust, the main character, is standing watching the parade. Suddenly a helicopter appears and lowers a sling. Masked figures appear on the roof near the statue, hook up the sling and the statue is stolen. Later a finger is cut from the statue and sent with a ransom note. A plot like this presents a strong opening and would immediately interest a potential producer/listener in the rest of the play.

The middle sections of a play, the development, argument and denouement, are pretty much uncharted territory where the writer wanders without maps, guided only by instinct and talent. It is where a writer's gifts for dramatic tactics and strategy become apparent – where the overall shaping of a play takes place. It is a minefield for those whose gifts are discursive rather than structural. As Tartakower observed, pointing at the as yet undisturbed chess board, 'The mistakes are there, all waiting to be made.' And that is where the mistakes really begin – after the opening.

Everyone has a different way of handling material once they are into the central sections of a play. And it is in these sections that many writers leave the marks and techniques by which they are known.

Some writers, after their development, may have a very slow build-up to a crashing resolution and a one-sentence ending. Others may have an early resolution, say a battle, which is prolonged and prolonged again as we switch from one corner of the battlefield to the other, perhaps learning about various protagonists, the play drawing out to a long tapering flicker as the dead are numbered and the cost finally realised. Middle sections are usually very personal things, and to many people the real touchstone of a writer's ability.

But whatever happens in the opening and middle sections of a play, all things must come to an end. And as the ending of a play is the last immediate memory a listener will carry of your work – make it memorable.

Listening to radio is very much a solitary vice. People tend to listen while alone or while engaged in some other task – decorating, cleaning, driving. It is therefore of the utmost importance that the ending of any radio play is absolutely clear – just as the beginning must be absolutely gripping.

If a listener gives you their time and concentration, it is only fair that the play is rounded off in such a way that he or she feels they have had value for money. One way to give this value is to try to produce a 'closed' ending.

In plays which are 'closed' the plot is stated, developed and, after the central argument and resolution, is ended to the full satisfaction and understanding of the listener. The rules of propriety, dramatic and human, could be said to be satisfied. The gun which was hung on the wall in scene 1 has been taken down and fired; there are no unanswered questions.

Then there is the 'open' play. This type of play again states the plot, develops it, moves through argument to resolution but, instead of a crisp, rounded ending, an 'open play' might well end on lines of dialogue such as the following:

CHARACTER X: But what of the Duke's assassin? What happened to him?

CHARACTER Y: That, my friend, is another story!

FX: RURITANIAN MUSIC. SHOUTS. CANNON SHOTS. BELLS. BUGLE CALLS. CLOSING CREDITS ... ETC. ...

Another story it might be. But if this missing information about the Duke's assassin leaves even one strand of the work unresolved in the listener's mind, then the play could be thought to have failed in both construction and believability.

Radio, to repeat a point, is not the theatre or cinema, where the person in the next seat can be consulted (often at some peril) as to what a particular writer might have had in mind in ending a play or film in this or that ambiguous fashion. In radio drama the listener deserves, and should have, absolute clarity of purpose in the main body of the play and a firm, self-explanatory ending.

And now, using the ODARE format, and the thoughts on openings, middles and endings, we could perhaps try to construct our own play, first as a simple spiral plot – and then adding a sub-plot. A contemporary play, with an element of comedy, hopefully believable, though requiring at the same time a bit of 'suspension of disbelief'.

We write a radio play

To you, O mighty sages of the pit
Henry Fielding (1707–54)

Bed, Bored and Banjaxed

(It is usual, in submitting a proposal, to identify the characters in capitals.)

OPENING JOHN GREEN meets MARY WHITE. They come together through bumping into each other in the refectory of an FE college. They hit it off immediately. JOHN is a local boy, MARY from out of town. They agree to meet after lectures.

DEVELOPMENT JOHN is now going to MARY's flat almost every evening. MARY is never invited to JOHN's home. When she raises the issue, he always side-steps. Is he ashamed of her? Is he already married? She consults a friend, JOAN, who tells her she must have it out with JOHN or, at least, see the student COUNSELLOR at the college.

MARY thinks this a good idea because she knows JOHN is on familiar terms with the COUNSELLOR – in that John has a common interest with the COUNSELLOR (perhaps a football team they both support).

MARY approaches JOHN who refuses to discuss his home life with her or to go to see the COUNSELLOR with her. She decides to approach THE COUNSELLOR herself. THE COUNSELLOR calls a meeting.

ARGUMENT At the meeting, JOHN, under pressure, admits the reason he never invites MARY home is that his

MOTHER is a bed-bound invalid who uses JOHN as a slave and would never countenance the appearance of another female in her, or her son's, life.

The COUNSELLOR'S advice is that if JOHN and MARY are to have any life together, they must confront JOHN'S MOTHER. He asks if there is anyone whose help JOHN might be able to invoke. JOHN answers that the family DOCTOR has always appeared sympathetic towards his predicament. The COUNSELLOR advises JOHN to consult the DOCTOR.

JOHN goes to the DOCTOR, who says that for a long time he has suspected that JOHN'S MOTHER may not be as bed-bound as she appears. The DOCTOR offers to come to the house and talk to the MOTHER on JOHN'S behalf.

RESOLUTION

The principals gather in JOHN'S MOTHER'S bedroom. There are explanations, pleas, threats, excuses. JOHN'S MOTHER will not budge. She states that JOHN belongs to her, and is there to look after her – a poor bedridden invalid. The DOCTOR asks if she is sure she can't walk. After all, the X-rays she had taken years ago showed nothing really wrong with her back. JOHN'S MOTHER goes into hysterics at the implication that she might not be as ill as she has always maintained.

JOHN'S MOTHER then insults MARY, blaming her for all the trouble that has recently descended on the household. MARY leaves in tears.

ENDING

From this point the play could close in a number of ways. JOHN could irrevocably fall out with his MOTHER and go off after MARY, leaving the DOCTOR to tend to his MOTHER. Or, JOHN'S MOTHER, towards the end of the scene, could have a stroke and JOHN could really be left with a bed-ridden invalid on his hands. Or, there could be a final scene in a railway station where MARY, having seen the depth and intimacy of the relationship between JOHN and his MOTHER, decides she is going away while JOHN makes up his mind. She could leave JOHN a telephone number with an instruction not to call her until he has finally decided. There could be a pause then we could hear a telephone ringing out. MARY answers and JOHN tells her his decision one way or the other. The play could end on this note.

The above is a short, simple, spiral drama of the A meets B, A loses B, school. It needs to be strengthened and made more interesting. In some ways, it is more like a short story than a play. So what could be done to breathe more vibrancy and life into it?

Return to the opening again and look at the most important character after John and Mary – John's mother. Because of her dramatic importance, she should appear earlier in the play, and this appearance should be used to give some hint as to what the play, on one level, is going to be about. That way the listeners will have some idea *why* and *for what* they are giving up their time. We will insert a new scene near the beginning of the play where John is about to leave for college. In this new version, the play will open in John's kitchen.

We hear background radio and time pips. We hear John mutter ... 'time to go', then a tap running and then switched off. Then the radio is switched off. John is humming softly. We hear a banging on the ceiling. A muffled shouting. John groans, and goes to the bottom of the stairs. He shouts up to ask his mother what she wants. Mrs Green first berates John for leaving her alone – then tells John to remember to call en route to the college to see Doctor Brown to collect her 'tablets'. John says he will go that evening as he doesn't want to be late on the first day of the new term. 'No. NOW!' his mother shouts, 'And bring them back to me at dinner time!'

We hear the front door slam as John sets off to college. We then cut to the bedroom, where we might hear his mother muttering to herself:

SCENE 3 MRS GREEN'S BEDROOM

FX: MRS GREEN IS IN BED. WE HEAR BED MOVE AS SHE CONSTANTLY ADJUSTS POSITION

1. MRS GREEN: (UNDER. TO HERSELF) I don't believe it. His own mother. That college. Fend for myself day after day. I thought after the first term he might get tired with all that studying ... You'd better be careful, Betty, my girl ... otherwise he could be off for good ... Who knows who he's meeting at that place ... Now where's that last novel he got me from the Medical Romance

> Library? ... (GROANS) ... On the chair by the door ... (CREAKING AS IF MRS GREEN IS BEGINNING TO GET OUT OF BED). Just let me move this tray ... (THEN SILENCE. PAUSE) ... Ay, there'll be plenty after him at that college. Only too ready to bump into him by accident. Same as Theatre Sister Frobisher knocked into Doctor Chinley while he was carrying that liver transplant ... (GROANS) ... Gorr ... shouldn't have had those prawns last night ...

And then we could cut immediately to the college canteen/refectory where John has just bought his tea and where he and Mary will shortly collide while carrying their trays. And begin their relationship.

The small scene at the beginning serves a number of purposes. It sets up the master/servant relationship between John and his mother, essential information for the listener to have. It also casts doubt as to whether Mrs Green is actually bedridden. It prepares the way for another of the major characters, Doctor Brown, and the mention of food and drink at the end provides an immediate link to the next scene, set in the college refectory.

After meeting Mary in the refectory, John could then go to Doctor Brown. Brown, the family's GP, would ask casually how things were with John at college. John would reply that his mother was totally against John trying to get any qualifications – and John would then ask point blank just how ill his mother actually is. Brown, sensing there is a particular reason for John's asking this, would reply that Mrs Green's X-rays had never shown any reason why she could not leave her bed – it was simply her word that she was incapable of movement. Brown tells John that if he can be of further 'assistance' John need only let him know.

We then cut to Mary and her friend, Joan. Joan is listening to Mary talking about John. Joan is studying A-level sociology/psychology, and prefers to reserve judgement of John until she has a chance to examine him at close quarters. (The role of Joan, although subsidiary, is one of importance. She will be the dramatic convention whereby we will learn what Mary is really thinking at any given time. Mary, during the course of the play, will discuss John, John's mother, Doctor Brown and any other characters with Joan, which will give the listeners further insight into those characters and into the characters of Mary and Joan.)

So, at the moment, we have a half-hour play shaping up with four main characters – John, Mary, John's mother and the Doctor – and an important subsidiary character, Joan. The college counsellor may or may not be a subsidiary character – depending on what part he/she would take in the main action.

The next phase could be John and Mary in Mary's flat, and Mary wondering when John is going to invite her back to meet his mother, an issue John, using a variety of less and less believable excuses, continually evades. The evening could end on a sour note with Mary asking John to go as she has some 'course work' to prepare.

Next day, Mary could tell Joan that John didn't seem to want to discuss his 'home life' ... And the pressure would be on until John finally revealed what his secret was – that he was an unpaid, unwilling, but more or less undemanding, servant to his mother. Mary then begins the 'her or me' scenario.

The play could progress with John's mother coming under more and more pressure from John to give him a life of his own – but with her always seeking not to do this by pleading the fact that she is bedridden and would have no one to look after her should John leave.

She categorically refuses to meet Mary, and John turns once more to Doctor Brown. Mary, John and Brown finally devise a scheme to find out if John's mother can, or cannot, walk.

John could simply bring Mary to the house, Mary deliberately enraging John's mother so much that she lurches out of bed to get at Mary. Alternatively, Doctor Brown could arrive unexpectedly with John to make an 'assessment examination' of John's mother, as there is a new treatment for her condition. He could ask various questions about her mental and physical state, compare it with something on his clipboard, and tell her he wishes her to go to hospital for further 'tests' as he feels with the 'new' treatment she may shortly be able to walk again. John's mother would ask to see this 'new' treatment which the doctor has written on his notepad. The doctor would refuse, pleading confidentiality.

Brown could then suggest they make her a cup of tea and he and John could quit the room, leaving the clipboard on a chair near the bedroom door. Outside the door John, Brown and Mary could wait and listen for a few moments, then fling open the door to find John's mother standing next to the chair trying to decipher Brown's notes from the clipboard. After this a firm, unequivocal ending would round off the play.

As added strands the college counsellor could perhaps be a very attractive female who has her eye on John. A priest could also be involved, who perhaps comes to give John's mother communion every week – and is firmly on her side. He might walk in as she is standing near the chair reading the notes and immediately proclaim a miracle.

The above, hopefully, is a simple plot with simple sub-plot, and with interesting and diverse characters. It has movement between house, college, surgery, pubs, coffee bars, buses, etc. ... perhaps one scene at a fairground, perhaps one at the seaside. All these things hopefully use radio to its best advantage.

Exercises (2)

This exercise is to help the student writer complete a full-length work (twenty to thirty minutes). Using the above notes and suggestions, and following the outline given, write the radio play 'Bed, Bored and Banjaxed'. As it is radio, you can go anywhere and have any effects you want. Bear this in mind, as 'open air' scenes will provide a good contrast to the stuffiness of the bedroom, surgery and college settings.

In 'Bed, Bored and Banjaxed' we saw the mother utilise in her first speech the convention of 'interior monologue' to save vital development time.

This way we learned a great deal about her very quickly without having to suffer a lengthy exchange of dialogue. This is one method of speeding a play along in radio – necessary when the listener's interest has constantly to be plucked forward. As well as 'interior monologue', there are two other methods in radio to gain that extra economy which leads to extra clarity: 'flashback' and 'narration'.

Flashback

Flashback is a convention used to reinterpret current dramatic action by reference to earlier events. It can explain or show why a character acts or thinks/talks in a certain manner in the present, by allowing us into a segment or segments of his or her past life. The segment may or may not contain characters involved at the present time with the main protagonist.

Flashback can also be used to relate the whole of a person's past life from the earliest time of dramatic interest to the audience/ listener up to the point that is the dramatic climax of that character's life.

Take a play which might open with a private detective on a stake-out outside somebody's flat. We might hear the announcer read the credits for a play, 'Stake-out', then go to:

SCENE 1

FX:	CAR SLOWING THEN STOPPING. ENGINE SWITCHED OFF.
1. AGENT:	(NARRATING) On the surface it was the easiest job I'd had for a long time. 'Park opposite her flat,' Control told me. 'She'll leave about five. Follow her, then report back here to me – I'll be waiting. Just one more thing ...'. He stopped short, stood, stretched, then walked towards the cupboard on the wall ...

SCENE 2 CONTROL'S OFFICE

FX:	DISTANT TRAFFIC. AMBULANCE SIREN.
2. CONTROLLER:	Whiskey ...?

And at this we have gone into flashback to learn what that other thing was.

A good example of flashback in an actual broadcast play was that in 'Typhoid Mary' by Shirley Gee, which was directed by David Spenser and based on a true story.

The Typhoid Mary of the title is Mary Mallon (Molly Malone), who emigrates from Ireland to America at the turn of the nineteenth century. In America she finds employment as a cook, the worst possible choice of career – as, unknown to herself, she is a carrier of typhoid. In going about her job, she leaves a trail of death and devastation behind her.

She is finally tracked down by Dr Soper, who has her isolated on a small island where she can do no more harm. At the end of the play Mary, on the island, is helping Soper as his assistant.

When the play opens, Mary is presented to us as already being in captivity on the island – already caught by Soper and isolated as a carrier. In her first speech she establishes her state of captivity, and then takes us into flashback to the Dublin of her childhood where we begin to learn about her life. Through flashback we follow her whole career from Dublin to a New York tenement, where she meets the first of the many that she will eventually infect. And then on to various other domestic positions and an ever-lengthening trail of bodies.

'Typhoid Mary' is a relatively straightforward use of flashback. Mary, speaking from her isolation ward on the island, leads us sequentially through the events that have brought her there.

There are times when flashback can get out of control and the play can fail because of it. This occurs if we intend to move in and out of totally different sets of time bands within the main plot. An example is a project that was submitted as a possible idea for a programme, but which progressed no further than the proposal stage because of difficulties foreseen in the flashback sequences against the levels of flashback which the average listener can assimilate.

The proposal was for a play in which character A is involved working on a piece of restoration in an old church in England. Character A spots an antique artefact and asks the meaning of it. A is told that the artefact relates to a French count, character B, who lived a hundred years previously and whose story is well worth hearing. At that stage it was intended that the play would go into flashback to a scene in a death chamber in a French chateau a hundred years earlier where character C is dying.

Character C, in order to reveal why character B's story is well worth hearing, would then go into another flashback to dramatise events that occurred fifty years earlier in an Italian catacomb; events that were themselves dependent on an arranged marriage in Spain at an even earlier time.

In the first three scenes of this play, we would have had three time bands in three different countries, and a promise of more to come. The concentration required would be that needed to take a driving test in Trafalgar Square with a piece of red-hot grit in one eye.

Radio plays, to truly engage, must be immediately clear and fall easily into place as regards both chronology and plot. To be used to its best effect, 'flashback' needs a fine sense of overall structure and timing – perhaps even more so than narration.

Narration

Purists have argued, and will continue to argue, over the use of narration in drama. Their argument is that a play containing narration is not a play at all as it does not fulfil dramatic criteria as they understand it; that is, plays should contain dialogue, which equals drama, rather than narration, which equals prose.

Those opposing this view simply point to the Greek chorus, a form of narration, as a precedent. The roundabout begins to turn; the descent into the maelstrom begins.

Perhaps the answer lies in the amount of narration used. If, every three minutes or so, a huge chunk of prose is inserted into the dialogue, then the identity of what is being broadcast may well be called into question. But certain types of radio play require detailed exposition, and in these cases there seems no reason, in the interests of economy, why some form of help cannot be offered to both dramatist and audience.

Narration also offers the chance to construct a play, as it were, in the first person; to give the narrator's view of the events by making the narrator part of the cast rather than an outside commentator. This would be done ostensibly in the character/narrator's head, to him/herself, but in reality it would be used to serve the audience's interest as a source of explanation and interpretation utilising the convention of 'interior monologue'.

But perhaps narration is most powerfully used to set atmosphere and open up character.

In Nathanael West's classic novella *Miss Lonelyhearts*, the Miss Lonelyhearts of the title is a male 'agony aunt' on a large New York daily paper. Initially, Miss Lonelyhearts accepts the job because he hopes it will lead to promotion to the social column – but gradually he begins to realise that the letters he receives, begging for advice, are not a joke to those who send them.

Through religious mania, drink, sex and his increasing inability to cope with the horrors contained within the letters, Miss Lonelyhearts gradually disintegrates. He dies, shot by a cripple he has befriended, but whose wife he has seduced.

The work was written in the speakeasy era, channelling the spirit of that era into a conduit that led eventually to Oliver Stone's *Natural Born Killers* and the final song of the film, Leonard Cohen's 'The Future', with its line 'I've seen the future, brother, and it's murder.'

Here is the quietly cynical narrator describing the aftermath of one of Miss Lonelyhearts's visits to Delahanty's speakeasy. Note how the narration uses long sentences for reflection and description; short sentences for information:

SCENE 10	OUTSIDE DELAHANTY'S
FX:	FOOTSTEPS CRUNCHING IN FRESH SNOW.
1. NARRATOR:	Miss Lonelyhearts had long stopped listening to his friends in Delahanty's. Telling their stories until they were too drunk to talk. Aware of their childishness, yet not knowing how else to revenge themselves. At college, maybe for a year afterwards, they had believed in literature, beauty, and personal expression – and when they lost this they lost everything. Money and fame meant nothing to them. They were not worldly men ...
FX:	FADE UP FOOTSTEPS IN SNOW. FADE BACK.
	... For a while at the start of the evening he had felt warm and sure. The whiskey had tasted good, and through the light-blue tobacco smoke the mahogany bar had shone like wet gold. The glasses and bottles, when touched by the bartender, had rung like bells ... He forgot the bomb in his heart and thought back to his childhood when once, waiting for his father to come home from church, he had gone to the piano
FX:	and played a little Mozart dance ... (MOZART DANCE UNDER) ...To his amazement his younger sister, who had never danced before, began gravely to step to the music ... He stood at the bar, remembering, and swaying slightly to the long forgotten measures. A picture of children dancing came to his mind. First one, then another, until there was not a child on earth who was not dancing. Lost in this vision he stepped back and accidentally collided with a man carrying a glass of beer. After listening carefully to his apology, the man had punched him in the mouth ...

In all, narration in radio can be a perceptive way of taking a dramatic short cut. It has also been understood to be a very valuable method of providing information to children in schools programmes, as it provides a strong linear narrative line within a play.

The BBC Schools Service, which reached its zenith in the 1970s, commissioned material which had to be presented in a certain dramatic fashion. Robert Lamb, who wrote over two hundred plays, stories, and features for schools and who called on narration time after time within his work, states:

> The idea was to make the subject live and immediate – to wake up the kids' imagination – make it picture book rather than text book. Darwin – Medieval Guilds – Captain Cook – it didn't matter – the academic subject had to be lifted off the page and into the imagination – which fixes facts in the minds of children. The use of drama, backed up by narrative fact or observation, is a tremendous fixer. And it's fail-safe because the more vividly anything is presented the more certain they are to remember. And they remember much more through drama – the whole thing – dates as well. Making the facts visual, through the writing, did everything. There was a separate Schools Repertory Company, too, in the BBC at that time – actors who were sympathetic to children and whose job it was to bring that bit extra to the writing – if the actor doesn't see it nor does the audience. They were there to bring the material to life – and were chosen for their gift of visualising scripts.

BBC Schools was developed from an ideal to bring knowledge to children everywhere.

Mary Somerville, in 1924, was sitting in a country schoolmistress's parlour with the mistress and three pupils. She heard Walford Davies speaking on music and noticed the impact this had on the children. From then on she devoted herself to developing schools broadcasting.

She did this in conjunction with people such as J. C. Stobert, of whom it was claimed, 'he didn't know one end of a child from another'; until, in 1927, an estimated 3,000 schools in England and Wales were listening. At the beginning of the war in 1939, the number of participating schools was 9,953.

As Mary Somerville noticed, BBC Schools programmes were especially valuable as regards music and dance. Many small rural schools had no music specialist, and the Schools music programmes were, in many cases, the only instruction available to the children.

But to return to school plays with the use of narration, here is the opening of Robert Lamb's 'A Time For Giving', produced by Geoff Marshall-Taylor, in which narration sets the scene in a way that serves both the plot and the listening children:

FX: (WOLVES)

1. NARRATOR: Not so long ago, when wolves still howled on winter nights in Wales, there lived a small farmer named Owain, whose small house looked almost like one of the many boulders and rocks scattered on the harsh hillside. He had a few sheep, a couple of goats, and some scrawny chickens that lived on their wits. It was a hard life, and people in the nearest village knew him as 'Poor Owain Up There' ...

The play describes three farmers, Owain, Marlais and David. Owain and Marlais are poor, David is rich and mean. Owain and Marlais, alone on Christmas Eve, decide, independently, to take the other a small bag of grain as a gift. Due to a storm on the mountain, they pass without seeing each other, and each arrives at the other's house to find it empty. Marlais thinks Owain has been lost in the storm; Owain thinks the same about Marlais.

Owain goes to David to ask his help to find Marlais – David agrees if Owain will work Christmas Day for nothing. Owain agrees and David gives Owain two labourers to help him search. Then Marlais turns up at David's, looking for Owain, and the same bargain is struck.

The search proves fruitless and the next day both men, tired out after a night on the mountain, turn up at David's house to find they have been fooled.

Instead of causing trouble, David is amazed to find that both men declare it is the best Christmas Day they have had – as they have found happiness in learning about the effort each of them was prepared to put in to help the other. And that they will always keep and treasure the small bags of grain to remind them of what has passed.

David, like Scrooge, is forced to examine his life. The play ends:

NARRATOR: David rushed into the house. He knew that Owain and Marlais would not break their bargain and would work until nightfall on Christmas Day. But later in that week he took some of his own workers – and good ones at that – to help put Owain's farm, and

Marlais' farm, in good order. The first time he'd ever given anything freely. And found himself happy. It's surprising how giving brings happiness, in the most unexpected ways.

So narration, in a certain sense, saves time, but there is another way of taking a short cut, which, though not exactly narration, saves a lot of time, dramatic energy and dialogue. This is to have an announcer/narrator at the beginning of a play, say something along the following lines:

1. ANNOUNCER: Midnight at the laboratory of Doctor Frankenstein, maker of monsters. Geneva, 1818.

FX: WOLF HOWLS. MAN SCREAMS. MANIACAL LAUGHTER.

The announcer not only introduces us to the play, but lets us know exactly where we are and what we are in for in terms of background and content – pre-emptive subliminal plot planting.

Exercises (3)

- Construct a narrated opening of a play in which a character describes him/herself and background. Try using short sentences for hard information and longer sentences for reflection and description.
- Construct a short opening by the announcer (with sound effects) to set up the background and probable content of a play. A further example in the Frankenstein mode might be:

FX: (HOWLING, SHRIEKING BLIZZARD.)

1. ANNOUNCER: Below the summit, Mount Everest, 1933.

FX: FADE BACK BLIZZARD. BRING UP SPIRIT STOVE HISSING INSIDE TENT. ...

But plot, though perhaps the most important aspect of a radio play, will not sell a play by itself. The skeleton still needs its nervous system and major organs. The major organs in our body dramatic are the characters.

Characters and their development

Dramatic characters, generally, can be said to be set in motion and explored by the expedient of either putting an ordinary person in extraordinary circumstances or putting an extraordinary person in ordinary circumstances.

To return to *The Admirable Crichton*. When the play opens, Crichton is butler in an aristocratic household and firmly believes in the superiority of his masters. The circumstances, for Crichton, are quite ordinary. Then the family is shipwrecked and the circumstances become extraordinary.

At this point the 'ordinary' character of Crichton begins to develop to meet those extraordinary circumstances – which gives the play its classical aspect of character development.

So a definition of character development might be that, in any dramatic work, the main character(s) must, at the play's close, have developed from the manner in which they were portrayed at the outset. They can be worse or better, but the play will have travelled nowhere if they have not changed. In *The Admirable Crichton*, Lady Mary, who begins as a haughty, proud, languorous aristocrat, develops to become the adaptable and courageous hunter of the group, and wife-to-be of Crichton.

A play, therefore, should resolve some crisis in the lives of its main characters – or precipitate one.

So, how to accomplish this character delineation and development in radio, in sound alone? A picture that gives all the detail that in other, visual, dramatic media the camera or eye would provide.

First, it is essential in a radio play that the listener can cope mentally with the number of characters involved. In radio, the audience has to hold all the characters on a mental stage, and too many characters arriving too quickly are apt to prove too much. A main character must usually make a substantial contribution to the dialogue before the listener feels he or she has a complete picture of that character, and this cannot be done if a main character is being constantly crowded out by other voices.

In a half-hour play, there would be, perhaps, four main characters – as in 'Bed, Bored and Banjaxed', the play we devised earlier. In a work of this length four characters would give a writer time to develop all fully; and the listener equal time to build up a composite mental and physical picture of each. To facilitate this assimilation, it is important that the characters are introduced at discrete intervals to give the listener time for individual assimilation. Going back to our play, you will remember that the doctor was not introduced until John, John's mother and Mary were all up and running.

A second point is that, as it is impossible to see any radio character before they speak, it is very helpful to have immediate identification by sex, accent or age. Take any standard character. There is the immediate broad differentiation of man or woman, upper/middle/working class, plus that of region, plus that of age.

By skilfully mixing possible permutations, a radio dramatist can offer a sort of 'character shorthand' that may allow a listener to identify that character by the first few sounds he or she utters – A sex/class/regional/age mix (SCRAM).

Using SCRAM will help people a play with characters who are at least vocally different from each other, depending on the backgrounds given to them.

To return to 'Bed, Bored and Banjaxed', John could be a young, working-class London male; his mother, a working-class female. Mary might be a middle-class girl from Bristol. The doctor could be Northern. The college counsellor could be standard received and the priest from Scotland.

And if, instead of being relegated simply to British accents, we have total freedom in casting, although still setting the play in London, we could get something like – John and his mother, still London; Mary, Canadian; the doctor, African; the counsellor, German; and the priest, Irish.

This is veering towards choking the cat with cream. Attempting to facilitate the listener's task to the point of no return by offering a play in which accents range from the Old Transvaal to Old Trafford, and with an age range stretching from the pipings of infantility to senility. Sometimes adding heavy 'nuances' to inform the listener all is not quite 'right' with the character in question. The window-cleaner (or anybody else) who whistles Scriabin, the Eliza Doolittles who have bought the way they speak and, courtesy of the writer, cannot help but let it show once in a while; the dog that actually does bark in the night. Everything presented in day-glo and slow-mo.

If the writer is lucky, a play like this will be rejected out of hand. Imagine, later, having to look back on something of this nature if it were bought and broadcast.

Exercises (4)

If you were casting 'Bed, Bored and Banjaxed' what SCRAM mix would you use? What would you see as the most effective way of intimating friction between John's mother and Mary, and the doctor and clergyman on casting alone? For example, if John's mother and Mary were both working class do you think this would cause more friction than if Mary was middle class?

The grotesque

Chekhov said something to the effect that when a man is born he is faced with three roads. If he takes the road to the left he is eaten up by wolves. If he takes the road to the right he eats up the wolves. And if he takes the middle road he eats up himself.

Grotesques can eat up a writer until they take over his or her play, having eaten up all the other characters en route. Grotesques are usually enthralling larger-than-life creatures. They can save much dramatic time by not being bound by the rules which govern ordinary characters. They are not responsible and, therefore, while they are in dramatic motion, the writer is not responsible – a rare freedom.

But if grotesques are over-used in a play or, what is worse, cast as main characters, they tend to dissipate dramatic tension and weaken the whole structure to the point where 'suspension of disbelief' begins to be called into question.

In a play already mentioned, 'The Finger of Suspicion', the stolen Epstein statue is traced by Inspector Crust to a deserted American airbase outside Liverpool where a helicopter was seen landing. Crust thinks the statue may have been dropped off there.

At the airfield he and Julia, another main character, find Billy living in one of the deserted hangars. Billy was 'put into the community' from a home for the mentally ill, then taken up by some travellers who looked after him for a time, and now haunts the airfield waiting for 'them' to arrive from outer space to save mankind. Billy is an expert on the Book of Revelation of St John.

1. INSP. CRUST: Billy, these others ... where are they coming from?

2. BILLY: The sky ... Up there ... One came yesterday ... In his chariot ... and wonderful clothes who cried mightily ... (IN LOUD EVANGELICAL TONES) 'Babylon is

fallen, and become the habitation of every foul spirit and hateful bird!'

1. JULIA: (UNDER, TO CRUST) Someone in a helicopter, wearing a flying suit?

2. CRUST: This chariot. Billy, was there anything slung under it?

3. JULIA: And these clothes, Billy ... What were they like?

4. BILLY: (STILL PROCLAIMING) 'And I saw a woman arrayed in purple and scarlet, decked with gold and pearls, and a cup full of blasphemy and abomination and the filthiness of fornication ...', (BEGINS TO SHOUT AS HE TURNS AWAY AND GRADUALLY FADES) ... And on her forehead, 'O Mystery! O Babylon the Great! O Mother of Harlots and Abominations!'

5. JULIA: And exit back to his hangar.

Billy is value for money but is only used twice in this 1975 play – a little of any grotesque goes a long way.

Exercises (5)

Invent a radio drama scene between an explorer/mountain walker who comes across someone who has chosen to live in a cave to escape from the pressures of the modern world, and who has a particular obsession. This obsession can be anything from the meaning of the pyramids to the history of the sea serpent.

The stereotype

Another danger for new writers is the use of stereotypes in minor, or even major, roles. The policeman who always says 'Hello, what's all this, then?' The barman with the eternal 'Time, gentlemen, please.' The clergyman with the unctuous and mumbled 'God will provide.'

This sort of writing lends a dispiriting air to any production, and gives the impression of a writer who keeps these sorts of character on a shelf above his or her head, and then, when necessary, brings one down, dusts it off and sets it into motion. And once they are in motion they sound, especially in radio, exactly what they are – cardboard, two-dimensional cut-outs.

The answer is to give every character the individuality that befits all individuals. Why not the pub manager who releases his Doberman dogs at closing time to accelerate the departure of his customers? The policeman who charges his suspects in rhyming couplets? The clergyman who fires a starting pistol from the pulpit to gain the undivided attention of his flock and put them in mind of the crack of doom? The English poet/clergyman Skelton (*c.* 1460–1529) held up his naked illegitimate child from the pulpit to prove that it was, after all, the same as those children his parishioners had conceived in wedlock.

Exercises (6)

Write a couple of pages of dialogue between the people suggested below and one other person whom they might meet in the course of their usual duties. Attempt to present them in a more interesting fashion that that in which they are usually offered to an audience:

- A person distributing a milk round.
- A person working behind a bar.
- A person on a school crossing.
- A person driving a bus.
- A door-to-door salesperson.
- Any other person you feel to be doing a job that, in the eyes of the majority of people, seems completely stereotyped.

These brief notes have hopefully examined, in a basic fashion, character and its development. For some writers, however, the problems posed by the creation of dramatic characters are far more deep seated. Writers often face a 'block' as to how to set any character in motion at all – or even how to find a character in the first place. That is, some writers can find a plot but not the characters to fill it.

There seem to be two immediate ways of approaching the problem that might be of help. The first is to take a character directly from life. Someone whose background and psychology are already known, and who can be altered to meet the twists and turns of the plot, but who will always provide a bedrock of known ability and response as far as the writer is concerned. This can annoy friends and acquaintances, who partially or fully recognise themselves, but it does provide one answer.

The second way is to attempt to devise an absolutely original character. Here, writers may begin by constructing, outside the play, a fictional biography for the character they are going to build inside the play. The writer will compile a detailed history of the proposed character's life up to the point that he/she is set in motion within the play. This will include parents, childhood, education, health, adolescence, and so on – until the writer feels there is now a complete character about which to write.

This method, for some writers, provides the springboard from which to set a character in motion and keep it moving. And by reference back to the character's manufactured 'life', writers are often then able to predict how the character will behave within the twists and turns of the plot.

A very good example of this latter method was in the setting up of the first great British radio serial character, 'Dick Barton – Special Agent'.

From Geoffrey Webb's *The Inside Story of Dick Barton* (1950), we learn that what was required was a 'cliff-hanger' serial with a strong central character possessed of an abundance of 'knightly' qualities and 'infinite resourcefulness'. He might have a couple of 'satellites' but he was to be the main focus of attention. His world would be our world, but his existence a fantasy. Just like life. By August 1946 a brief on the character was worked out, but there was still no name.

After disregarding such alternatives as Michael Drake and Bill Barton, 'Dick Barton' was settled upon. 'A single syllable Christian name usually balances with a double syllable surname commencing with an explosive consonant to drive it home.' They now had the character – now to build a background.

To have given Dick a London background would have fixed him for all time as 'a metropolitan type', so a more universal gestation was formulated. He was born in High Wycombe. His father was from Sheffield, his mother from Ealing. His father began as an errand-boy in a flourmill, but eventually became its senior partner. Dick, as a child, was the possessor of an interest in the sort of home-made toys that fit together. Neighbours thought him a 'clever dogged little chap' and advised Mum and Dad to give him an engineering training.

So Dick, a Sagittarian, captained the school football team for two years, then took his 'well formed person … oval face … long Grecian nose … chestnut hair … jovial, active and intrepid disposition' off to Glasgow University (1930–33) and then to the drawing office of a firm in Liverpool.

He did not take to this, and seeing a job in a Liverpool paper offering 'an interesting life in Peru' sailed for South America. Then to Persia, and then to a construction post that gave him travel all over the world.

In 1939 he joined the army as a Sapper, was commissioned in the Royal Engineers, and was later evacuated from Dunkirk. He gained the MC and then joined No. 20 Commando. He was demobilised a captain.

After the rigours of his life so far, he naturally turned to the BBC. Six trial episodes about his life were written and recorded in Birmingham and sent to London for a final verdict. A signature tune was found, 'The Devil's Gallop' by Charles Williams. Two assistants, 'Snowy' and 'Jock', were enrolled to Dick's cause. And 'Dick Barton – Special Agent' was broadcast as a light programme for the first time at 6.45 p.m. on Monday, 7 October 1946. The programme initially went out five evenings a week. It was blamed for everything from the juvenile crime rate to 'pandering to the bourgeoisie'.

The *Daily Worker*, quoted in Webb, began by stating that the programme was 'that bad it was beyond criticism' and ended by simply calling him 'A Fascist lackey … or is he just a fine boneheaded young Englishman who does not know the meaning of fear?'

The right wing, in letters to *The Times*, blamed the BBC for taking children's minds away from 'prep'. This was answered by an announcement that there would be an omnibus edition on Saturday mornings so everyone who wished to do 'prep' in the evening had a clear run at it.

Dick was discussed in Parliament, was the subject of one of George Bernard Shaw's postcards, and 'everyone who has not heard of him is viewed with mingled suspicion and pity'.

His followers were drawn from a spectrum embracing a sixty-year-old professor of anthropology from Wales and a six-year-old girl who wrote, 'On hearing your lovely voice I immediately sweated.'

Whether they sweated, or simply perspired, an average of seven million adults and eight million children listened every night. A star was born.

Before he became a true icon, and beyond ordinary desires and appetites, he was romantically linked to a girl – Miss Jean Hunter, 'a Dundee lass', five-foot six, hazel eyes and auburn hair who took 'size nine in stockings'. And who never allowed herself more than two drinks.

Dick dealt with spies, death rays, bombs, booby traps, quicksands, floorless lifts, a shower bath of acid worked on the whim of a white rat, apes trained as knife fighters, man-eating orchids, ghosts, synthetic icebergs, Nazis, volcanoes, more man-eating orchids, sharks, storms and sunken treasure ships – which took the listeners to the end of the first series.

Eventually the fan mail rose from 600 letters per week to 2,000. By the time the programme went off the air for the summer of 1949 there had been 444 broadcasts. By this time Dick, understandably, had given up women, drink and cigarettes.

Boys everywhere took to heart his philosophy to fight crime and save lives; and he became a moral force. The 'Thirteen Commandments' were drawn up:

- Barton is intelligent as well as hard hitting.
- Barton only uses force when peaceful means have failed.
- Barton never commits a criminal offence.
- Barton may deceive, but never lies.
- Barton's violence is restricted to clean socks on the jaw.
- Barton's enemies have more latitude, but may not indulge in sadism.
- Barton and colleagues do not willingly involve members of the public.
- Barton has now given up drink altogether.
- Barton adventures are such that sex plays no part.
- Barton does not become involved in plots with political themes.
- Barton's adventures should avoid horrific effects (prowling gorillas, vampires).
- Barton's adventures must contain no character who swears.
- Barton and colleagues may not use 'cut-throat razors'.

Dick passed on eventually, like all good things, but this is a noteworthy example of how to build a character from scratch.

America had led the way in this sort of thing in the 1930s though not with the dedication that had been shown in bringing Barton to life. Louise Tanner (1968) refers to the show 'I Love a Mystery', featuring three characters called Jack Packard, Doc and Reggie, the 'Britisher'.

The travels of these three embroiled them with vampires, snakes and the headwaters of the Amazon. One episode was set in an old castle where murder after murder occurred to the strains of Brahms's 'Lullaby', being played on a huge pipe organ by a pair of ghostly hands. Perhaps those of Brahms himself, who played the piano in a brothel while a child – a setting not too removed from these serial fantasies.

To conclude, a good character and its development allow the audience to become involved with, or even identify with, the blossoming, or destruction, or sometimes both, of another human spirit. By courtesy of the writer we gain a glimpse into another human 'psyche'.

The construction of this character might be contrived by the writer; it might be based on a person known to the writer. It may, in the case of a historical figure, be drawn from contemporary letters and accounts. But it is the dramatist's target to isolate that character and make it completely different from all the others within the work – and then to shape the plot so that the crisis in the character's life is exposed. And then to share with the listener feelings that the character experiences during this crisis.

The way those feelings, on radio, will be brought before the listener is through dialogue.

Dialogue

> If you would be pungent, be brief, for it
> is with words as with sunbeams, the more
> they are condensed the deeper they burn.
>
> Saxe

People, all too many, say, 'I heard an awful radio play the other day' – and that's usually the end of it. But if the same work were on television the response might be, 'As for last night's play, well, the plot and characterisation weren't that hot but the settings … The direction … And didn't she look marvellous with her hair dyed that sort of tawny colour? ... Do you think he does those sorts of things to his wife in real life?', and so on.

And what has failed on radio because of its 'dialogue' is more than half-way towards a success in the visual media.

This shows the importance of competent dialogue in radio and how, without it, the whole edifice of a play will collapse. In building terms, plot and character may be the foundation and bricks – but dialogue is the cement. What does radio dialogue do?

Radio dialogue helps to isolate, delineate and develop character. It informs the audience of the plot, and indicates through 'signposting' (hints) in which direction that plot will be going. It describes physically the people of the play, and the surroundings within which they move and have their dramatic life.

Dialogue, in fact, provides everything needed to understand, visualise and vitalise the play. It does so in a fashion that is highly artificial and contrived, but which can appear, through the skills of the writer, to be completely natural.

Plays are not life – they simply represent life; good dialogue being the catalyst that successfully effects this representation. One of the first tasks of dialogue is to edit the slice of life under consideration in an effort to make it palatable and of an acceptable strength to the listener.

Take the last time you sat around talking with two or three friends in a pub or café – perhaps for an hour or so. Later, you decide that in your next play you will set the first scene in that same pub/café, and you will use the conversation had by you and your friends as the basis of this proposed scene.

So you repeat the sixty minutes' conversation on the page. This, while accurate and realistic, would immediately alienate every listener on the planet who happened to be listening at that time.

No matter how interesting a writer might think an hour of his or her casual conversation in a pub with friends might be to an audience, that audience would have different ideas, and would really only want to learn five things from the opening sequence:

- That the scene was set in a pub.
- Where and when in time that pub was.
- Who the characters were in the scene.
- Why these characters were in the pub.

- Where the play was moving on to from the pub.

And after this information, given as concisely as possible, we should move on to the next scene.

But while this information is being loaded into the dialogue, something else should also be happening – the dialogue given to the main characters in the play should be beginning to differentiate between them. And because of the amount of information that needs to be packed into the dialogue, it is necessary that emotion is also loaded into what is given to the actors to say. Apathy, anger, mirth, malice, ambivalence – these are things that, in film or television, can be given in a one-camera close-up or by gestures on the stage; but the only gestures in radio are 'silent' gestures – an 'angry' silence ... 'embarrassed' silence ... 'affirmative' or 'negative' silence. Or by loading these same emotions into the words themselves. This places a further burden on the actors, who perhaps might be driven into 'hamming it' in order to produce the effect required by the dialogue.

The writer should aim to give the actors the right tools – not to put those tools in a basket so heavy it cannot be lifted.

Here is a dialogue extract from the *Under Milk Wood* BBC Radio script, a work which has always drifted between a play and a feature, and is, in essence, neither; but in which the writing combines information, identification and emotion – and some very fine mind-visible pictures – painted by dialogue alone.

Dylan Thomas (1914–53) From *Under Milk Wood*

1. SECOND VOICE: Come closer now ... (THE SOUND OF BREATHING ALL ROUND) ... Only you can hear the houses sleeping in the streets in the slow deep salt and silent black, bandaged night.

2. FIRST VOICE: Only you can see, in the blinded bedrooms, the combs and petticoats over the chairs, the jugs and basins, the glasses of teeth, Thou Shalt Not on the wall, and the yellowing dickybird – watching pictures of the dead.

3. SECOND VOICE: Only you can hear and see, behind the eyes of the sleepers, the movements and countries and mazes and colours and dismays and rainbows and tunes and wishes and flight and fall and despairs and big seas of their dreams.

From where you are, you can hear their dreams. Captain Cat, the retired blind sea-captain, asleep in his bunk in the seashelled, ship-in-bottled, shipshape best cabin of Schooner House dreams of ...

Another role for dialogue in radio is to supply a form of 'character shorthand'; a type of aural identification which saves both time and exposition.

For example, if it is established early in the play that a certain character has the habit of using an expression such as 'No way!' or 'Right on!', then, in a crowded club/pub/party scene, this expression being heard above the general hubbub points dramatically to the presence of that character without further identification being necessary – the character need not even have to speak 'on mike'. Alternatives to the 'set phrase' can be the habit of humming a bar or so of a tune, a cough, a bronchial wheeze. Any conventions such as the above, once established, convey instant identification.

The words 'My dear Watson' always, and always will, carry with them the clue to one of the most famous creations in writing, Sherlock Holmes. Likewise P. G. Wodehouse's Bertie Wooster will always and forever be identified with 'Right-ho, Jeeves'.

Such catchphrases establish character immediately, but dialogue, correctly wielded, can give a far wider range of impressions to the listener – even in the course of a single speech. It can give at a stroke, in fact, an immediate grasp of the political, social, moral and financial standing of one of the play's protagonists. Here is an example written for the occasion. Contrived, overwritten and overdone, but which may quickly make the point of just how much one speech can say about a character.

First, let us look at the scene as it might appear in the theatre or on television:

SCENE 1 LIBRARY IN MAJOR HARRIS-TWEED'S COUNTRY SEAT

THE MAJOR, BURNT BLACK BY THE INDIAN SUN, APPEARS WEARING A BIG GAME HUNTER'S HAT ON HIS HEAD, AND CARRYING AN ELEPHANT RIFLE. SOAMES, HIS ARCHETYPAL SHAFTESBURY AVENUE BUTLER, CREEPS DEFERENTIALLY BEHIND HIM ACROSS THE SET.

THE MAJOR PICKS UP AN EMPTY DECANTER

FROM A TABLE, HOLDS IT UP TO THE LIGHT, SHAKES HIS HEAD WITH RAGE, GRINDS HIS TEETH, THEN THROWS THE DECANTER INTO THE FIRE-PLACE.

THE MAJOR'S DAUGHTER, GEORGIANA, ENTERS AND GIVES THE MAJOR A FILIAL PECK ON THE CHEEK. GEORGIANA IS ACCOMPANIED BY GREASE. GREASE IS WEARING A BRIGHT ORANGE CAFTAN, A PAIR OF DOC MARTEN'S BOOTS, AND AN IRON CROSS AROUND HIS NECK. THROUGH HIS NOSE IS A SAFETY PIN, HIS HAIR IS DYED PURPLE AND GREEN, AND RUNS IN A SHAVED STRIP DOWN THE CENTRE OF HIS HEAD.

THE MAJOR GAZES PARALYSED FOR A SECOND OR TWO, THEN BEGINS TO BREAK OPEN HIS GUN WITH SHAKING HANDS.

Now for radio:

SCENE 1 LIBRARY IN MAJOR HARRIS-TWEED'S COUNTRY SEAT

1. ANNOUNCER: Major Harris-Tweed has returned from India.

FX: CRASH OF HEAVY DOOR BEING THROWN OPEN.

2. MAJOR: (OVER SHOULDER) Where else would I hope to find a drink but the library! ... (ON MIKE) Soames, Fetch that decanter! (CRASH AS SUIT OF ARMOUR FALLS) What's that suit of armour doing here? ... Lady Georgiana's rehearsals? ... Protest play? Against 'Hunting'! Hell's Bloody Bells! ... Three months visiting the Rajah and I come back to find my house full of poets chasing m'daughter. The covert's full of poachers chasing m'birds. And the claret with more cork in it than a lifejacket! Where is Georgiana, come to that? ... Behind me! ... Ah, there you are, m'-dear ... How was 'The Season' this year? ... That young FitzTightly lurking behind you in the doorway? No? ... Then? ... My God, Soames ... He's wearing a dress ... And a parakeet on his head ... It's his HAIR! Soames ... break out the elephant gun – and give the undertaker a ring!

Simple, straightforward and totally overboard – with the Major presented as a caricature. But a caricature who hopefully reveals all in one speech.

Exercises (7)

Write the above scene again as radio, from the point of view of the butler, Soames. Then write it as radio with three characters: the Major, Soames and Georgiana.

The Major's dialogue is of a type, and needs study.

Another type that needs even more study is dialogue between children. Actors are said to dislike appearing with children because of the innate ability of children to steal the show by simply standing there. But there are other reasons why, in radio, scenes between young children are best avoided.

In radio, young children in long scenes can tend to sound mawkish, going on precious, because in radio drama the characters must constantly speak – which is just what young children do not do in life.

In life, children below a certain age tend to confine themselves to grunts, rushes, runs and pushes – and to long silences where, though two youngsters may be standing side by side, each will behave as if the other is not present. When forced to speak, as they must in radio drama, the effect is un-natural because what is required of them is un-natural. One young child with adults, yes. Two children or more together, no.

A further complication can be a radio play that contains a large part for a small child. Children have very limited spans of concentration, and limited strength to sustain the take after take in front of a microphone that radio sometimes demands. An answer here is to use young women. Young actresses can be indistinguishable from children in voice, have the necessary energy and concentration, and do not require the careful husbanding that children require.

Another aspect of radio dialogue is that 'out of sight' is very much out of mind. On radio, if there are three people in a scene and the main thrust of the dialogue is between two of them, the third person is somehow effaced from the memory of the listener. It will startle everybody should he/she suddenly be given a speech near the end of the scene. On film or the stage a third character will always be a factor by his or her visual physical presence. In radio, a third character must be thrown a line from time to time at relatively fixed intervals throughout the scene.

Length of speeches, too, on radio, merits careful consideration. They must be neither too long nor too short. Ideally they should be of a length that divulges fact and establishes identity, without being allowed to reach the proportions that induce hysteria and precipitate sleep.

In a play, long speeches from one person, then another, then another, begin to make the work lose shape. The listener begins to feel that it is not a play to which he or she is listening, but some sort of three-handed polemic.

Very short speeches can also fail on radio, but for a different reason. Consider the following:

Four people, W, X, Y and Z, are questioning a fifth character, Q.

X: Then where were you

Y: On the night

W: In question?

Y: And how?

W: And why?

X: And where?

Y: And why?

Z: And with – WHOM!

And so on. In the visual dramatic media, seeing the faces of the interrogators would allow the mind to track the speech aurally as you watch the action visually, and therefore come to a complete and composite understanding of the scene. But, because of the speed of the dialogue and its shortness, just hearing the questions on the radio would not be enough, and the mind would not have time to put a face to each interrogatory remark. Aural tracking rather than visual–aural is probably all a listener could manage. The voices would be disembodied.

So, while this is the sort of technique that many radio writers might use to project the confusion of a prisoner under interrogation, to write this sort of thing as dialogue in a straight play is to ask for trouble.

Many script editors and readers have the ability to gauge the worth of a script by simply riffling through the pages when it arrives and glancing at the length of the speeches and the way they lie on the page. This is because dialogue has a shape, just like music. The notes in a musical score have a pattern, and there is always a flow in the note patterns in well-written pieces. The sound pattern of dialogue also resembles that of music in how it builds up and can attract and hold a listener's interest. Thinking of voices as instruments, a pattern such as

1. HE: – – – – ?
2. SHE: –
3. HE: – – –
4. SHE – – – – – – – – – – – – – –
5. HE: – – – – – – – – – –
6. SHE: –
7. HE: – –

is probably more interesting than

1. HE: – – – –
2. SHE: – – – –
3. HE: – – – –
4. SHE: – – – –
5. HE: – – – –

in which every speech is exactly the same length. Good dialogue has a discernible pattern, where one speech rolls into another, and yet at the same time is in tension against the next speech.

Finally, dialogue must prepare the listener for the denouement of the play. To give us all the answers. The name of the murderer. The identity of the man who unbolted the lion's cage. Why Smith changed his name and took to Scrabble.

The dialogue must contain the clues that prepare us for the surprise that isn't such a surprise when we go back over the play in our heads. The clues, however, will have been spaced out by the dialogue and maybe partially obscured, to prevent the cat being let out of the bag too early. At the same time the listener must be allowed, during the course of the play, to see the cat moving around in the bag and know that it is not a red herring.

So, with the nervous system of the dialogue now surrounding the major organ of character, and both attached to the bones of plot, your play has hopefully been formulated, if not written.

Exercises (8)

Write an essay (1,500 words) about the importance of dialogue in radio drama.

At this point we will leave straight original plays to discuss other forms of dramatic writing.

There are people who, for one reason or another, do not wish to write original drama – who prefer to write dramatic documentaries, or dramatisations or adaptations. Each of these forms has aspects that differ from a standard play.

The drama-documentary is the turning of real events into a blend of fact and fiction. The 'fact' element is that which is historically recorded or ascertainable through accounts and records, whether true or false; the fiction is the dialogue given to the characters as they work out these facts dramatically.

Almost all recorded history can be turned into drama-documentary material, but there are difficulties with this form of writing. One problem is making some of the characters involved sound plausible. How did Genghis Khan speak? We have no record of him except through hearsay; although his much-reported line that he would use the women of his enemies 'as night-shirts' gives an indication of his general philosophy. Similarly, the blind Hussite general, Ziska, who, on his deathbed, commanded his followers to make a drum out of his skin that God's enemies might be destroyed to its beating.

But is a modern international figure any more accessible? With someone like, say, Gandhi, we have letters, film footage and records of his speeches; but what of his 'small talk' when he was with his intimates?

With many figures of international history we have little or no record of their casual conversation and its tone. Once a person reaches world status, they usually become very careful as to what they say and how they say it.

A drama-documentary that purports to show the true face of a man or woman behind the public persona needs not only the written recollections of friends and enemies, but long thought from the writer as to what such a person would be like in unguarded moments. What drove a particular person? What really moved and motivated the actions that brought the fame or the infamy?

Any writer, in order to fix a character, must not only look at as much biographical material as possible, but also thoroughly probe and analyse character. Often it is not the major events in the life of a figure which provide the key to his or her personality, but rather what is inherent in Ernst Renan's (1823–92) observation that 'The truth lies in the nuances'. For often the true nature of a character is found in what are almost asides. Hitler remarked to an associate: 'It will be my duty to carry on this war regardless of losses ... Cities will become heaps of ruins; noble monuments will disappear forever. This time our sacred soil will not be spared. But I am not afraid of this.' Joachim C. Fest points out in *The Face of the Third Reich* that in these few sentences lies the epitaph of almost fifty million people.

To close, we come to a more hybrid type of work – the 'faction'. The 'faction' could be defined as a dramatisation which deals with the people and events of enduring, and usually contemporary and contentious, interest. It is usually applied to programmes where all the evidence to provide a clear-cut view is not available and the makers of the programme inject their own, necessarily subjective, view – no matter how heavily that view is said to be 'unbiased'.

'Factions' are, and have to be, written in a more immediate fashion than dramatic features, which is probably why they cause so much trouble. They comprise recent, often very raw, events, which can affect both the living and, usually, the recently dead. They concern emotive, bitter issues. That they cause trouble can only be understood through the nature of drama itself.

Drama can be a very powerful weapon, a fact known to all governments, everywhere. Novels are usually read singly and at one remove from their action. Drama can touch many people simultaneously and in an intimate fashion – especially in the theatre or cinema, where a sort of group consciousness can begin to take effect.

Therefore a good dramatist, much more so than a novelist, can cause trouble and embarrassment. A very good dramatist can cause lots of trouble and embarrassment. A good, very funny dramatist can cause most trouble of all.

Fielding, in 1737, had this power of ridicule. Walpole's corrupt administration was his target, and after Fielding's short afterpiece play, *The Historical Register for the Year 1736* was performed the Licensing Act was read and passed within a month, and British theatre was put into the hands of the censors for over two hundred years; yielding nothing to anybody except the collection of acting manuscripts the Examiner of Plays gathered unwittingly during that period. Fielding, at that stage, more or less gave up writing plays – just about the time he should have really begun to exercise his dramatic gifts.

So, while subjects such as strikes, shootings, bombings and unexplained deaths in and out of custody need to be brought before people in a readily digestible form, they are sensitive issues, and there remains the question of passing a verdict before all the evidence is in. Except of course, it is usually ensured that all the evidence is never in.

A writer may ask, because of the amount of conflicting accounts, is any dramatist justified in putting forward a view that may sway people but later may be found to be unreliable? That is a question that can only be answered by the writer – but it needs consideration, and careful consideration, before pen is set to paper.

Exercises (9)

Take any great or notorious figure or event and try to think of a different way of handling it than by the usual biographical method.

An example might be the Great Fire of London. Find out how it began. Then write a short drama-documentary on what it was like being a shopkeeper/householder who would lose everything unless the fire could be controlled.

An account from the horse's point of view of the suffragette, Emily Davidson, who threw herself under your hooves and prevented you from winning the Derby.

An account, by a survivor, of the last minutes on board the *Titanic*. Then another account, by someone left on board after the last boat had gone.

Good places to look for material are anthologies of accounts under one heading, such as 'Great Escapes', 'Great Sea Disasters', 'Great Discoverers and Discoveries', 'Tales of Hauntings and Haunted Houses', 'Great Discoveries in Medicine'.

A proposal for a medical series included the life of Ignaz Semmelweis. The following gives an idea as to how a submission should be made – the amount and density of the material needed for a producer to make an initial appraisal of the viability of a project.

'A doctor is a gentlemen ... a gentleman's hands are clean'

Professor Meigs, Philadelphia, *c.*1843, in answer to the accusation by Oliver Wendell Holmes, essayist, poet and physician, that women often died in childbed ... 'poisoned by their medical attendants'.

Proposal for 45 minute drama-documentary on the life of Ignaz Philip Semmelweis (Budapest, 1818–Vienna, 1865)

Ignaz Semmelweis began by studying law in Vienna, but eventually switched to medicine, specialising in obstetrics. He made a friend of Kolletschka, a colleague; but fell foul of Professor Klein, department head.

The obstetrics clinic had two sections, one run by students, the other by midwives. The mortality rate in the student section was triple that of the midwives. The causes given for deaths in student care were various: 'miasma', 'male examinations', 'wounded modesty'.

Semmelweis began dissecting the bodies of women who died in childbirth. He found no reason for the deaths. Klein was forced into an inquiry. This found that women were dying 'from injuries to genital organs', because of rough student examinations.

Semmelweis refused to agree, and ceaselessly dissected, trying to find the truth. Straight from these dissections Semmelweis, hands coated in cadaveric matter, would return to the wards and plunge those hands into those waiting to give birth.

Semmelweis, overstretched, took a holiday. When he returned he found his friend Kolletschka had died from a cut on the hand received from a scalpel during the dissection of a woman who had died.

Semmelweis called for the autopsy. Kolletschka's symptoms were those of all the women who had died in childbed fever. The truth struck home. The scalpel Kolletschka had been using was carrying cadaveric matter from the corpse of the woman. This material had entered his hand, then his bloodstream, then killed him. The same cadaveric matter that Semmelweis and his students carried on their hands to women in labour – whom they then examined internally. Pregnant women everywhere were being killed by their doctors. And the difference in the death rates between the student wards and those superintended by midwives was that the midwives did not dissect. Semmelweis realised his own non-stop dissections had caused hundreds of deaths. This affected his mental stability.

Semmelweis made it a rule that all who carried out examinations must wash with chlorine-water. The death rates fell immediately, but no one was interested. His efforts brought abuse and ridicule. He became the 'Hungarian crank!', 'a fanatic'. Doctors refused to accept that it was they who were killing their patients. Semmelweis resigned. His successor promptly restored the status quo. The deaths began again, and everyone was happy – except the women.

Semmelweis began to rage against the ignorance of the medical profession. He was dismissed for 'lack of moderation'. His personality began to disintegrate and he was committed to an asylum. Shortly before this happened, delivering yet another sick woman, Semmelweis cut his finger. As with Kolletschka, the wound became infected and the poison spread.

In 1865, Ignaz Semmelweis, who conquered septicaemia and whose message saved thousands of women, died while a patient in an asylum for the insane.

ENDS

The proposal for the Semmelweis drama-documentary necessitated consulting written and archive material and relying on documentation left by others.

A more exciting project is the putting together of a drama-documentary where there are still people remaining from the event around which the documentary is built.

BBC Radio 4 ran a series called 'Who Sings the Hero?' – devoted to acts of heroism that had more or less passed un-noticed. One episode of the series was 'Diana Jarman and the Sinking of the *City of Cairo*', produced by Martin Jenkins.

In 1942 the Ellerman Lines Steamship *City of Cairo* was torpedoed off the coast of south-west Africa. Open lifeboats were lowered and the majority of the crew and passengers escaped. These boats were eventually separated and all made different journeys. One sailed as far as South America; some were picked up by other ships.

Lifeboat No. 1 ended up carrying fifty-four people; Indian nationals who were part of the crew, and European crew and passengers.

Through a number of unlucky circumstances, No. 1 lifeboat eventually spent thirty-seven days at sea. The survivors fell from fifty-four to three amid scenes of great hardship, courage and humour; selfishness and cowardice. The three survivors were Diana Jarman, a young English widow whose husband had been killed fighting the Japanese; Angus MacDonald, a Scots quartermaster; and Jack Edmead, an English steward.

These three, *in extremis*, were picked up by the German blockade runner *Rhakotis*. Diana Jarman, who had contracted a throat infection while in the lifeboat, died on the operating table of the *Rhakotis*. The *Rhakotis* itself was then sunk by a British cruiser, and MacDonald and Edmead found themselves in lifeboats once again. Eventually both were repatriated.

MacDonald wrote an account of the time in No. 1 boat, detailing Diana Jarman's heroism and imperturbable good humour and support throughout the whole of their ordeal – her unsung heroism. A proposal was written and submitted.

The programme was commissioned and sources had to be sought. The primary source was Angus MacDonald's narrative, and various books and articles. Finally it came to light that the ship's doctor might still be alive. He was traced and interviewed. Although not in No. 1 boat, he, too, suffered privation and exposure in his particular boat. He had known all three survivors well – especially Diana Jarman, whom he had treated for a throat infection – the re-occurrence of which probably led to her death.

The doctor was asked what he thought now of the events of fifty years before. When he thought again of himself in the open boat, no more than a tiny dot in the middle of a trackless ocean. The sun beating down, and no idea of where they were, or what was to happen to them.

'Water', he replied. 'That's what I thought at the time. That's what I still think about. How much there was, when would we be given more, was anyone getting more than me, how could I get some extra … even why should the sick have more? … Always water … That's all I thought about then … and all I think about now when I look back …'.

Here is the beginning of MacDonald's account. Then the

opening pages of the script, to indicate how it was turned into drama. In order to attempt to present a balanced view, and to give the story movement and breathing, some early scenes were set in the U-boat that sunk the ship. The U-boat commander, Captain Merten, was responsible for one of the most famous and oft-quoted lines of the war. After the *City of Cairo* sank, Merten brought his U-boat up in the middle of the lifeboats. He questioned the survivors, then prepared to dive with the memorable line, 'Goodnight, sorry for sinking you!'

From the written account left by Angus MacDonald, Quartermaster, *City of Cairo*

I was a quartermaster and had charge of No. 4 lifeboat. After seeing everything in order there and the boat lowered, I went over to the starboard side of the ship to where my mate, quartermaster Bob Ironside, was having difficulty lowering his boat. I climbed inside the boat to clear a rope fouling the lowering gear, and was standing in the boat pushing it clear of the ship's side as it was being lowered, when a second torpedo exploded right underneath and blew the boat to bits. I remember a great flash, and then felt myself flying through space, then going down and down. When I came to I was floating in the water, and could see all sorts of wreckage around me in the dark. I could not get the light on my life-jacket to work, so I swam towards the largest bit of wreckage I could see in the darkness. This turned out to be No. 1 lifeboat and it was nearly submerged, it having been damaged by the second explosion. There were a few people clinging to the gunwale, which was down to water-level, and other people were sitting inside the flooded boat.

I climbed on board, and had a good look round to see if the boat was badly damaged. Some of the gear had floated away, and what was left was in a tangled mess. There were a few lascars, several women and children, and two European male passengers in the boat, and I explained to them that if some of them would go overboard and hang on to the gunwale or the wreckage near us for a few minutes we could bail out the boat and make it seaworthy. The women who were there acted immediately. They climbed outboard and, supported by the life-jackets everyone was wearing, held on to an empty tank that was floating nearby. I felt very proud of these women and children. One woman (whose name, if

I remember rightly, was Lady Tibbs) had three children, and the four of them were the first to swim to the tank. One young woman was left in the boat with two babies in her arms.

We men then started to bail out the water. It was a long and arduous task, as just when we had the gunwale a few inches clear, the light swell running would roll in and swamp the boat again. Eventually we managed to bail out the boat, and then we started to pick up survivors who were floating on rafts or just swimming. As we worked we could see the *City of Cairo* still afloat, but well down in the water, until we heard someone say, 'There she goes.' We watched her go down, stern first, her bow away up in the air, and then she went down and disappeared. There was no show of emotion, and we were all quiet. I expect the others, like myself, were wondering what would happen to us.

We picked up more survivors as the night wore on, and by the first light of dawn the boat was full. There were still people on the rafts we could see with the daylight, and in the distance were other lifeboats. We rowed about, picking up more people, among them Mr. Sydney Britt, the chief officer, and quartermaster Bob Ironside, who was in No. 3 boat with me when the second torpedo struck. Bob's back had been injured, and one of his hands had been cut rather badly. We picked up others, then rowed to the other boats to see what decision had been made about our future. Mr. Britt had, naturally, taken over command of our boat, and now he had a conference with Captain Rogerson, who was in another boat. They decided we would make for the nearest land, the island of St. Helena, lying five hundred miles due north. We transferred people from boat to boat so that families could be together. Mr. Britt suggested that, as our boat was in a bad way, with many leaks and a damaged rudder, and at least half its water-supply lost, all the children should shift to a dry boat and a few adults take their places in our boat.

When everything was settled we set sail and started on our long voyage. Our boat was now overcrowded with fifty-four persons on board – twenty-three Europeans, including three women, and thirty-one lascars. There was not enough room for everyone to sit down, so we had to take turns having a rest. The two worst injured had to lie down flat, so we made a place in the bows for Miss Taggart, a ship's stewardess, and cleared a space aft for my mate, quartermaster Bob Ironside. We did not know exactly what was wrong with Bob's back. We had a doctor in the boat, Dr. Tasker, but he was in a dazed condition and not able to attend to the injured, so we bandaged them up as best we could with the first-aid materials on hand. The youngest person among us, Mrs. Diana Jarman, one of the ship's passengers, and only about twenty years of age, was a great help with the first-aid. She could never do enough, either in attending to the sick and injured, boat work, or even actually handling the craft. She showed up some of the men in the boat, who seemed to lose heart from the beginning.

Once we were properly under way Mr. Britt spoke to us all.

He explained all the difficulties that lay ahead, and asked everyone to pull their weight in everything to do with managing the boat, such as rowing during calm periods and keeping a look-out. He also explained that as we had lost nearly half our drinking-water we must start right away on short rations. We could get two tablespoonfuls a day per person, one in the morning, one in the evening. He told us there were no passengers in a lifeboat, and everyone would have to take turns bailing as the boat was leaking very badly.

Before noon on that first day we saw our first sharks. They were enormous, and as they glided backward and forward under the boat it seemed they would hit and capsize us. They just skimmed the boat each time they passed, and they were never to leave us all the time we were in the boat.

The first night was quiet and the weather was fine, but we didn't get much rest. A good proportion of us had to remain standing for long periods, and now and then someone would fall over in their sleep. I was in the fore-part of the boat attending to the sails and the running gear, helped by Robert Watts from Reading, whom we called 'Tiny' because he was a big man. He didn't know much about seamanship, as he was an aeronautical engineer, but he said to me that first day, 'If you want anything done at any time just explain the job to me and I'll do it.' ...

This beginning was translated into a drama-documentary script:

Diana Jarman's Story

SCENE 1 MONTAGE

SOUNDS OF BATTLE. SHOUTS IN JAPANESE/ENGLISH AS WE WITNESS THE FALL OF SINGAPORE IN FEBRUARY, 1942, AT WHICH JOHN JARMAN, HUSBAND OF DIANA JARMAN, WAS KILLED IN ACTION. FADE DOWN BATTLE, FADE IN INDIAN MUSIC.

SHOUTS IN HINDI. MILITARY BAND ON QUAYSIDE, UNDER STEAMSHIP'S SIREN AS THE *CITY OF CAIRO*, CARRYING DIANA JARMAN HOME TO JOIN ONE OF THE WOMEN'S SERVICES, LEAVES BOMBAY, AT THE BEGINNING OF OCTOBER 1942, FOR SOUTH AFRICA/SOUTH AMERICA/UK. FURTHER SHOUTS, SIRENS, MILITARY BAND FADES BACK AND WE BRING IN WASH OF SEA ... WE FAINTLY HEAR EIGHT BELLS STRUCK ...

SCENE 2 WHEELHOUSE, *CITY OF CAIRO*

FX: TICKING OF SHIP'S CHRONOMETER.

1. ROGERSON: Morning, Sydney ...

2. BRITT: Morning, Sir ...

3. ROGERSON: See anything ...?

4. BRITT: Flat ... Calm ... Not a periscope in sight, Captain.

5. ROGERSON: Mmm ... Should be safe enough, now. Well clear of Bombay ... Capetown round the corner ... Passengers seem about early ...

6. BRITT: Difficult sleeping in this heat ... And nerves ... No one's going to feel safe until we're in the middle of the South Atlantic heading for South America ... out of reach of those bloody U-boats.

7. ROGERSON: That pair at No. 2 hatch ... Blonde ... and the middle-aged chap?

8. BRITT: Blonde's young Mrs Jarman ... Husband killed at the fall of Singapore ... only married fifteen months. Going home now to join one of the women's services ... Chap's Ronald Tasker ... Ex-Navy ... doctor ... something with Burma Oil ... He's taken a bit of a beating by all accounts ...

9. ROGERSON: Whole cross-section of the Empire in one small steamer ... Doctors ... judiciary ... missionaries ... Army ... Navy ... Air Force ... Anyway, I'll get below ... Usual instructions ... call me anything at all suspicious ...

10. BRITT: Captain ...

1. ROGERSON: (OFF MIKE) Yes ...?

2. BRITT: That rumour ... There's a pack of U-boats around Cape Town ...?

3. ROGERSON: Big loss of tonnage not long back ... But quietened lately ... perhaps they've all run out of fuel ...

4. BRITT: Or tenacity ...

5. ROGERSON: (LAUGHS SHORTLY) Little chance of that, Sydney ... Little chance of that ...!

EDGE INTO –

SCENE 3 GERMAN SUBMARINE. U-68.

FX: ESTABLISH INTERIOR OF SUBMARINE. 'PING' OF ASDIC

6. CAPT. MERTEN: Send this. Message to base (BEGINS TO TALK AS IF DICTATING TO MORSE OPERATOR) ... From Corvettenkapitan Karl Friedrich Merten, U-68. Am short of diesel and under constant threat from South African Airforce. Intend to return to base. Will proceed West, past Cape Town, into South Atlantic ... then head for home. I will, of course, at all times, attempt to seek out and destroy enemy ... (CONVERSATIONAL VOICE) ... Usual acknowledgements and signing off codes ...

7. RADIO OPERATOR: Commander ...!

FX: BRING UP PING OF ASDIC. FADE BACK. INTRODUCTORY CREDITS.

SCENE 4 ALONGSIDE: CAPE TOWN

8. MACDONALD: (NARRATION) Cape Town in wartime was very much like Cape Town at any other time. Brilliant colours, clear skies, Table Mountain. A bit more subdued than peace-time, maybe, but not too much so – no one was going to bomb South Africa ...

I'd been quartermaster some time now on the Ellerman 'City' boats ... Quiet and happy ships, generally, sort of vessels that suited my temperament. A lot depended on the Chief Officer, the Mate, of course, and this one, Sydney Britt, I always considered to be a real gentleman ... right to the end ... (PAUSE) ...

> We were due to sail that afternoon ... although we weren't supposed to know that, of course, and, as usual, everything was a bit of a mess ... I was on gangway duty with my mate Bob Ironside ... killing time ... waiting for night ... the next dawn ... and our chance to slip away ...

This is how it was decided that this particular drama-documentary would be set up. Instead of beginning with the escape from the ship in MacDonald's account, it was decided to lay the background to the story.

First play a montage to set the martial Japanese/Indian/British atmosphere; introduce the ship, the character of the captain and the mate. Give Diana Jarman and Tasker (both of whom would be in No. 1 lifeboat) an early mention. Bring in the submarine to begin the hunter/torpedoing sequence, and then enter MacDonald in his role as narrator/cast member, a role he would occupy to carry us through the rest of the programme.

The other way would have been to begin with MacDonald's account after the ship had been torpedoed. This would have meant much more in the way of narration as regards character, and ship movement, prior to the sinking. And it would also have posed real problems as to the setting up of the U-boat commander Merten's character, and the subsequent scenes in the submarine.

We needed to move out of the *City of Cairo* as much as possible early on – to the submarine and back. Because once the survivors were in No. 1 lifeboat, we would be in the 'one set' convention of the lifeboat until the rescue – which is always difficult to sustain with credibility and without loss of pace on radio.

Exercises (10)

Look through back copies of newspapers/magazines for headlines such as 'Dramatic Rescue', or 'Fireman/Policeman/Rail Worker/Passer-By ... Heroic Rescue Attempt', and so on. Choose an account of this nature and build it up into a 'faction'. Perhaps you will be able to gain more details or consult the people involved if you contact the paper. Or, just using the bare bones of the article, invent a background to the rescue and an aftermath – write this up as a prose account and then turn it into a radio 'faction'.

6 The radio adaptation and dramatisation

His adaptation will be the result of counsel, scheme and industry.
Paley

'Adaptation' is the process of modifying something to suit new conditions. In the context of this book, 'adaptation' will be understood to mean the modification of stage plays and film scripts into radio drama. 'Dramatisation' will cover the modification of novels and stories (short and long) into radio drama.

The dramatic adaptation has been around a long time in the BBC. Writing in 1924, Caractacus Lewis, the BBC's first programme organiser, discusses the drama that had been broadcast during the previous twelve months. This consisted of Shakespeare and short modern plays of that era – none of which, apparently, came over as entirely successful. Lewis felt this was because they had initially been written for another medium. He eventually felt all would turn out well.

Later, Captain Peter Eckersley (1892–1963), first chief engineer of the BBC, recalled what was probably the first drama broadcast ever made of adapted material.

At the beginning of his career, Eckersley was part of an experimental team working from Writtle, in Essex, in the early 1920s. His early impromptu broadcasts did much to popularise the new medium, his 'funny, unpredictable, irreverent half-hours' showing what might be possible, given 'the right spirit':

> We chose the balcony scene from *Cyrano*: it is played on the stage, in semi-darkness, with virtually stationary players and so it seemed very suitable for broadcasting ... 'Uggey' Travers, a young actress, and her brother came to help ... We sat round a kitchen table in the middle of a wooden hut ... and said our passionate lines into the mouthpieces of our separate microphones.

Peter Black, in *The Biggest Aspidistra in the World*, gives the first broadcast adaptation as a seventy-five minute version of *Westward Ho!* in 1925.

An interesting venture undertaken in America was the Lux Radio Theatre series of Hollywood film adaptations which ran for twenty years from 1935. Howard Fink notes that: 'As Cecil B. DeMille ran it, *Lux Radio Theatre* often became an oral version of the kind of expensive extravaganza for which his films have become famous ... inventing new radio codes and techniques ... of communicating action that had been visually conceived in its original form.'

Val Gielgud, head of BBC drama from 1929 to 1948, published a handbook on radio drama in which he discusses the adaptation of stage plays. In it, he mentions the type of writer who believes that any work under consideration for adaptation is best served by utilising three crucial steps. These are: (1) scratching out the original stage directions; (2) making a number of cuts to meet the broadcasting time available; and (3) adding the names of the characters to almost every speech in the hope that this will make the action intelligible.

He felt that to submit an adaptation of this kind was the next thing to trying to obtain money by false pretences.

So, how to obtain money by honest pretences? Three things seem necessary for a good, successful adaptation:

1 Sufficient editorial technique. That is, a strong enough editorial flair to enable the adapter to separate the rust from the coin – to know what to save in the way of plot, dialogue and characters, and what to discard – plus a thorough understanding of how a piece of radio drama is structured and an ability to translate aurally all necessary visual images.

2 Love of the work. This usually means having an empathy with the play or novel in question. The most successful adaptations are of works in which the adapter believes both morally and as pieces of literary art.

3 The ability to be true to a particular author's voice and message. To be able to catch the nuances of a particular authorial voice, and truly deliver the message of a text. To be able to invoke what ultimately makes Jane Austen, Austen; Charles Dickens, Dickens.

To give a musical example. The pianist Vladimir de Pachmann

was once described as belonging to no school, having no followers and making up his own rules as he went along.

Tales about him are legion. He and his wife would take seats at the back of the hall and then, when another pianist was playing, Pachmann would creep down the aisle and on to the stage, where he would kneel and kiss the tailcoat of the performer. Then he would rise and address the audience about himself and his abilities.

In his old age he dressed in a monk's habit (*à la* Liszt), and kept a herd of cows which he milked every morning to keep his fingers supple.

The great musical love of his life was Frederick Chopin. He specialised in the works of Chopin, and many at the time considered him to be the greatest Chopinist alive. He generally dressed in clothes he claimed had 'once belonged to Chopin'. Chopin's dressing gown, Chopin's gloves. He claimed always to wear one of Chopin's old coats when playing. And his technical ability when young, and his love of Chopin's works, possibly conferred upon him the right to do so. But as for exposing Chopin the man through the music, and passing on Chopin's message ...?

Pachmann would add his own octave passages, and modify generally where he thought the work could be improved. He tried to make the pieces Pachmann/Chopin instead of Chopin. He interfered with the tone of the original voice without the adequate creative equipment to do so; failed in the third category above, and therefore marred the whole enterprise.

Adapting stage plays

Today, onstage, the fashion generally is for two acts – with tight, spare, dialogue and economy of presentation – a natural blueprint for good radio drama. And a fair number of modern plays will readily translate across to radio. But, unless the adapter has personal relations with the dramatist in question, the question of copyright occurs. At its simplest, until an author has been dead for seventy years, permission has to be sought from his or her estate to adapt or alter his or her works. If the author is still living, permission has to be sought from source. The author, or the author's agent, will have to be approached.

To save all the bother of correspondence and contracts, many adapters tend to look further back for their material, or simply have an interest in drama outside of their own time. Plays from an earlier period usually require much from the adapter.

Prior to the advent of film, radio and television, a play was a full evening out at the theatre and not, as now, simply part of an evening. As usual, the work expanded to fill the time available. Plays from earlier periods can suffer much from overwriting, perhaps too many characters, and will almost certainly be too long.

They can present an even more serious problem. In a work of three or five extended acts, the plot may not be exposed until well on into the play. This, in a play that is not well known and familiar through hearsay and study, can be instant death for an adapter, as the listener may decide not to wait to find out what the work is actually about. A play like this, as well as being cleaned up generally, may require as a matter of necessity to have its plot moved to the beginning of the work.

Three Hours After Marriage is an early eighteenth-century satiric farce by Gay, Pope and Arbuthnot. It is important as being the only dramatic work in which Pope is definitely known to have had a hand. The main plot is a hundred guinea wager between the characters Plotwell and Underplot as to who shall be first to cuckold the old Doctor Fossile with his new young bride, Mrs Townley. In the play, this wager is not revealed until the third act.

It seemed to make sense to add a completely new scene at the beginning of the play to let the listeners know the idea around which the work was to be built:

Three Hours After Marriage

SCENE 1 TAVERN. LONDON. 1730.

FX: WHORES, THIEVES, BLADES, ETC., AT TABLES, DRINKING AND LAUGHING.

1. UNDERPLOT: (OFF MIKE) ... Plotwell! Richard Plotwell, thou rogue!

2. PLOTWELL: Ah! Friend Underplot! I must have missed you last night!

3. UNDERPLOT: You might have missed me, but I got my pistol off! ... (LOUD LAUGHTER) ... And Mrs Townley?

4. PLOTWELL: Susanna?! ... To be married quietly, I hear, tomorrow morning at seven ... (WHISTLES. MURMURS OF AMAZEMENT) ... to the famous Doctor Fossile.

1.	1ST VOICE:	The famous 'old' Doctor Fossile!
	FX:	LOUD LAUGHTER
2.	UNDERPLOT:	He'll be no match for her appetites ...
3.	2ND VOICE:	No, but one for her debts!
4.	3RD VOICE:	And need all his alchemical processes to settle that volatile spirit!
	FX:	LAUGHTER
5.	UNDERPLOT:	Then let's help him! ... Hundred guineas say I'm first to her ... Who'll go against me? ... You, Plotwell ...?
6.	PLOTWELL:	Surely!
7.	UNDERPLOT:	Then your hand, friend. – And send round the bottle, Landlord!
	FX:	LAUGHTER, SHOUTS, FLOURISH OF EIGHTEENTH-CENTURY MUSIC. CREDITS.

So the listener knows from the outset that the plot of the play is the hundred guinea bet between Plotwell and Underplot as to who will be first to cuckold Doctor Fossile.

A general point, to which particular attention should be paid in adapting any stage play, concerns the 'breathing' of a particular play. Plays that are too claustrophobic, plays with only 'one set', often do not breathe properly – because there is no physical movement. This could seem boring and stultifying to the radio listener through the unchanging mental scenery. A person sitting alone in a room listening to a play does not want that play to be set in a similar room for the whole of its course.

Judicious invention of scenes is an answer here. Move the work around. Take advantage of what radio has to offer in locations in space and time. The conservatory, garden, pub, bowling alley, cricket match. A walk along the seafront. A change of acoustic and air in radio can work wonders – like a change of air in life.

Sometimes, too, stage plays have very long 'two character' scenes set in one place. Again, possibly very boring. A convention worth considering here is perhaps to insert a shorter scene with minor characters within the longer scene, in a different part of the house or outside, and then to return to the original scene armed with information gleaned from this shorter scene. This, as well as allowing the listener to track the doings of the minor characters, allows the adapter to edit the main plot by allowing the two secondary characters to advance the story both structurally and in terms of general dramatic economy. Something along the lines of these scenes from the middle of a play.

SCENE KITCHEN

FX: LOUD MUSIC IN BACKGROUND

1. A: So it was C did the murder?

2. B: Probably ... and the first thing we need to prove it, he was at the taxidermist's convention ... Turn that radio down, will you? ... (FADING) and I'll tell you what I think happened ...

CUT TO

SCENE STUDIO

FX: SOMEONE IMPROVISING BADLY ON PIANO

3. C: So there's no way they prove anything unless someone saw me there ... which they didn't ...

4. D: How did you pay for travel ... cash?

5. C: Credit card ... (PAUSE) ... Oh, SHIT!

CUT BACK TO

SCENE KITCHEN

FX: RADIO NOW ONLY JUST AUDIBLE IN BACKGROUND

6. A. There must be some way ... some way of checking his movements ...

7. B: Like ...?

8. A: Like maybe he drew out money ... signed a bill ... fixed himself at a time and place ... Pass me that phone ...

In the above manufactured extract, characters A and B are discussing a problem in one room, where a radio is playing loudly. A wants to know something but asks B to turn down the music.

We then cut to another room, where C and D are exchanging

dialogue about this same event. We cut in to hear C idly banging away on a piano (thereby establishing a musical scene-change link) and then C and D have their dialogue.

Cutting back to A and B, we learn the outcome of both discussions centring around the credit card. So we have had a piece of deduction from two different points of view (the pursuers and the guilty), plus a welcome change of acoustic.

Finally, stage plays often tend to drag out their endings like Mahler symphonies. Five or ten minutes either way in a stage play seems to make little difference – indeed, many stage dramatists prolong their endings as if some terrible fate has been threatened should they ever lift pen from paper. In all radio plays, whether adaptations or not, endings should be short, sharp, self explanatory.

Dramatising the novel

All the troubles that have been detailed above can occur in the novel (although the one-set situation is rare). The major problem with the novel is that all too often novels are discursive rather than dramatic. This simply means that, technically, many novels are not structured to the ODARE format. Also, they often contain much more description than would be viable in a play.

So, how to bring a novel like this into dramatic format that complies roughly with ODARE and has all the right internal dynamics and tensions?

Rachmaninov observed that all works of music turn around a certain point in the score and so, it might be argued, do all other works of art.

Look at any good painting; your eye will be drawn to a point in it, its 'centre' – although this 'centre' can be anywhere on the canvas. From there the eye will take in the rest of the painting gradually until the mind has a composite and structured picture of the scene that the artist wished to portray. Bruegel's 'Hunters in the Snow', for example; a work that has seen more prints than Scotland Yard, and where the eye is naturally and immediately drawn to the crow and then outward into the rest of the picture.

So with novels. They have a section, the climax, which is the natural centre of the work, and around which all the rest is structured. One way to bring the novel into dramatic format is to read the novel until its events are fully familiar. Then extract this climax which will form the equivalent of the ODARE 'Resolution'. Then extract the other events which correspond to the 'Opening', 'Development', 'Argument' and 'Ending'. This will give you the initial shape of your adaptation.

At this stage, when you have isolated the five ODARE elements, it might be necessary to drop some characters. It might also be necessary to invent a character if the main protagonist of the novel is given to internal reflection in a big way – he or she may need someone to whom they can unburden themselves.

In a proposed adaptation of one of Kipling's novels, *The Naulahka*, the hero often talked things out with his horse. Another solution might be for the hero to 'brood aloud' – although dramatically even the horse might be preferable to this.

A better alternative is probably using a narrator – especially where a novel is concerned in which the narrator's voice is essentially part of the fabric of the work. Dickens's unique narrative voice, for instance. Or Jane Austen; or Fielding.

One final point to be taken into account is the actual physical demands of a novel's format. The author, to make the point he or she wished to put forward, may have constructed the novel in a certain manner – and this must be observed in the presentation of the work, as this is the reflection of the 'authorial voice'.

An example would be Nathanael West's classic American novel, *Miss Lonelyhearts*, which we discussed in chapter 5. Most longer prose works have discernible forebears. *Miss Lonelyhearts* seemed to have none. Research indicates it was possibly based on a series of German woodcuts made in the 1920s – the story of the moral fall of an artist.

This wordless series of woodcuts jumps from event to event. Nathanael West, in the writing of *Miss Lonelyhearts*, jumped from scene to scene in short chapters – and so the dramatisation had to be constructed in the same way.

So a novel must not only be examined for content but also for physical construction. Do all the chapters last for one page only; and can this be reflected in the dramatisation – or is it one unbroken mass like James Joyce's *Finnegan's Wake*?

Exercises (1)

A Christmas Carol is a universally familiar book. Read it again or, from memory, deconstruct it into ODARE. Find the Opening, Development, Argument, Resolution and Ending. Devote a paragraph to each of these. Then go to the exercise at the end of this chapter.

Short story dramatisation

Then said I, 'Lord, how long?'

Isaiah 6: 11

The first thing at which to look in any short story being considered for dramatisation is how much of the work is description and how much is dialogue and emotion. Short stories that are full of description make even shorter plays – unless a lot of original work is done.

So, although the plot or central idea of any short story must be sound, before you think of going any further look carefully at how much of the story will turn easily into good dialogue. Think of the one-line short story from chapter 4 again – 'Pair of baby's booties for sale – never used.' All that is here is the basic idea. Characters, dialogue, various scenes, would have to be invented. Such invention is a major undertaking (almost an original work), and not something to be taken lightly or without some guarantee that the whole thing will eventually be taken seriously when it arrives at the office of your producer.

Which leads to the selling of dramatisations/adaptations. What sort of market is there?

Dramatisations are popular. People who like a book or film believe they will equally like the same work as a radio play. Producers like them too because they cost less to commission than original work. Before beginning a dramatisation, especially of a fairly well-known and popular work, it is always wise to check with the intended buyer to ascertain if there is any interest in your idea. A company such as the BBC will check if the work in question has previously been handled as a dramatic adaptation. There can be few sadder moments than a writer having a manuscript returned not because of quality – but because the work was dramatised five years previously, or is at that moment being adapted by someone else who had the same idea slightly earlier.

The dramatisation

At Radio 4 a chance arose, for the first time, to dramatise the whole canon of the Conan Doyle 'Sherlock Holmes' stories in 45-minute episodes.

A certain unifying house style was agreed by Richard Imison, the deputy head of drama, and Enyd Williams, the executive producer for the series; and it was also decided that a short 'teaser' would be built into the beginning of each of the episodes to highlight a spring of the main action and draw in the listener.

One of the lesser-known Holmes stories is *The Adventure of the "Gloria Scott"*. Although full of good things, this story posed pronounced structural problems. Here is the opening of the story in prose:

A. Conan Doyle ***The Adventure of the 'Gloria Scott'***

'I have some papers here,' said my friend Sherlock Holmes, as we sat one winter's night on either side of the fire, 'which I really think Watson, it would be worth your time to glance over. These are documents in the extraordinary case of the "Gloria Scott", and this is the message which struck Justice of the Peace Trevor dead with horror when he read it.'

He had picked from a drawer a little tarnished cylinder, and undoing the tape, he handed me a short note scrawled upon a half sheet of slate grey paper.

'The supply of game for London is going steadily up,' it ran. 'Head-keeper Hudson, we believe, has been told to receive all orders for fly-paper, and for the preservation of your hen pheasant's life.'

As I glanced up from reading this enigmatical message I saw Holmes chuckling at the expression upon my face.

'You look a little bewildered,' said he.

'I cannot see how such a message as this could inspire horror. It seems to me to be rather grotesque than otherwise.'

'Very likely. Yet the fact remains that the reader, who was a fine, robust old man, was knocked clean down by it, as if it had been the butt end of a pistol.'

'You arouse my curiosity,' said I. 'But why did you say just now that there were very particular reasons why I should study this case?'

'Because it was the first in which I was ever engaged.'

I had often endeavoured to elicit from my companion what had first turned his mind in the direction of criminal research, but had never caught him before in a communicative humour. Now he sat forward in his armchair, and spread out the documents on his knees. Then he lit his pipe and sat for some time turning them over.

'You never heard me talk of Victor Trevor?' he asked. 'He was the only friend I made during the two years I was at college. I was never a very sociable fellow, Watson, always rather fond of moping in my rooms, and working out my own little methods of thought, so that I never mixed much with the men of my year. Bar fencing and boxing I had few athletic tastes, and my line of study was quite distinct from that of the other fellows, so that we had no points of contact at all. Trevor was the only man I knew, and that only through the accident of his bull-terrier freezing onto my ankle one morning as I went down to chapel.

'It was a prosaic way of forming a friendship, but it was effective. I was laid by the heels for ten days, and Trevor used to come in to enquire after me. At first it was only a minute's chat, but soon his visits lengthened, and before the end of the term we were close friends. He was a hearty, full-blooded fellow, full of spirit and energy, the very opposite to me in most respects; but we found we had some subjects in common, and it was a bond of union when I learned he was as friendless as I. Finally, he invited me down to his father's place at Donnithorpe, in Norfolk, and I accepted his hospitality for a month of the long vacation.

'Old Trevor was evidently a man of some wealth and consideration, a J.P. and a landed proprietor. Donnithorpe is a little hamlet just to the north of Langmere, in the country of the Broads. The house was an old-fashioned, wide-spread, oak-beamed, brick building, with a fine lime-lined avenue leading up to it. There was excellent wild-duck shooting in the fens, remarkably good fishing, a small but select library, taken over, as I understood, from a former occupant, and a tolerable cook, so that it would be a fastidious man who could not put in a pleasant month there.

'Trevor senior was a widower, and my friend was his only son. There had been a daughter, I heard, but she had died of diphtheria while on a visit to Birmingham. The father interested me extremely.

He was a man of little culture, but with a considerable amount of rude strength both physically and mentally. He knew hardly any books, but he had travelled far, had seen much of the world, and had remembered all that he had learned. In person he was a thick-set, burly man, with a shock of grizzled hair, a brown, weather-beaten face, and blue eyes which were keen to the verge of fierceness. Yet he had a reputation for kindness and charity on the country-side, and was noted for the leniency of his sentences from the bench.

'One evening, shortly after my arrival, we were sitting over a glass of port after dinner, when young Trevor began to talk about those habits of observation and inference which I had already formed into a system, although I had not yet appreciated the part which they were to play in my life. The old man evidently thought that his son was exaggerating in his description of one or two trivial feats which I had performed.

'"Come now, Mr. Holmes," said he, laughing good-humouredly, "I'm an excellent subject, if you can deduce anything from me."

'"I fear there is not very much," I answered. "I might suggest that you have gone about in fear of some personal attack within the last twelve months."

'The laugh faded from his lips and he looked at me in great surprise. "Well, that's true enough," he said. "You know, Victor," turning to his son, "when we broke up that poaching gang they swore to knife us; and Sir Edward Hoby has actually been attacked ... I've always been on my guard since then, though I have no idea how you know it."

'"You have a very handsome stick," I answered. "By the inscription, I observed that you had not had it more than a year. But you have taken some pains to bore the head of it and pour melted lead into the hole, so as to make it a formidable weapon. I argued that you would not take such precautions unless you had some danger to fear."

'"Anything else?" he asked smiling.

'"You have boxed a good deal in your life."

'"Right again. How did you know it? Is my nose knocked a little out of the straight?"

'"No," said I. "It is your ears. They have the peculiar flattening and thickening which marks the boxing man."

"Anything else?"

'"You have done a great deal of digging, by your callosities."

'"Made all my money at the gold fields."

'"You have been in New Zealand."

'"Right again."

'"You have visited Japan."

'"Quite true."

'"And you have been most intimately associated with someone whose initials were J. A., and whom you afterwards were eager to entirely forget."

'Mr. Trevor stood slowly up, fixed his large blue eyes on me with a strange, wild stare, and then pitched forward on his face among the nutshells which strewed the cloth, in a dead faint.

'You can imagine, Watson, how shocked both his son and I were. His attack did not last long, however, for when we undid his collar and sprinkled the water from one of the finger-glasses over his face, he gave a gasp or two and sat up.

'"Ah boys!" said he, forcing a smile. "I hope I haven't frightened you. Strong as I look, there is a weak place in my heart, and it does not take much to knock me over. I don't know how you managed this, Mr. Holmes, but it seems to me that all the detectives of fact and fancy would be children in your hands. That's your line of life, sir, and you may take the word of a man who has seen something of the world."

'And that recommendation, with the exaggerated estimate of my ability with which he prefaced it, was, if you will believe me, Watson, the very first thing which ever made me feel that a profession might be made out of what had up to that time been the merest hobby. At the moment, however, I was too much concerned at the sudden illness of my host to think of anything else.

'"I hope that I have said nothing to pain you," said I.

'"Well, you certainly touched upon a rather tender point. Might I ask how you know and how much you know?" He spoke now in a half-jesting fashion, but a look of terror still lurked at the back of his eyes.

'"It is simplicity itself," said I. "When you bared your arm to draw that fish into the boat, I saw that 'J. A.' had been tattooed in the bend of the elbow. The letters were still legible, but it was perfectly clear from their blurred appearance, and from the staining of the skin round them, that efforts had been made to obliterate them. It was obvious, then, that those initials had once been very familiar to you, and that you had afterwards wished to forget them."

'"What an eye you have!" he cried, with a sigh of relief. "It is just as you say. But we won't talk of it. Of all ghosts the ghosts of our old loves are the worst. Come into the billiard-room and have a quiet cigar."

'From that day, amid all his cordiality, there was always a touch of suspicion in Mr. Trevor's manner towards me. Even his son remarked it. "You've given the governor such a turn," said he, "that he'll never be sure again of what you know and what you don't know." He did not mean to show it, I am sure, but it was so strongly in his mind that it peeped out at every action. At last I became so convinced that I was causing him uneasiness that I drew my visit to a close. On the very day, however, before I left, an incident occurred which proved in the sequel to be of importance.

'We were sitting out upon the lawn, on garden chairs, the three of us, basking in the sun and admiring the view across the Broads, when the maid came out to say that there was a man at the door who wanted to see Mr. Trevor.

'"What is his name?" asked my host.

'"He would not give any."

'"What does he want, then?"

'"He says that you know him, and he only wants a moment's conversation."

'"Show him round here."

'An instant afterwards there appeared a little weazened fellow, with a cringing manner and a shambling style of walking. He wore an open jacket, with a splotch of tar on the sleeve, a red and black check shirt, dungaree trousers, and heavy boots badly worn. His face was thin and brown and crafty, with a perpetual smile upon it, which showed an irregular line of yellow teeth, and his crinkled hands were half closed in a way that is distinctive of sailors. As he came slouching across the lawn I heard Mr. Trevor make a sort of hiccoughing noise in his throat, and, jumping out of his chair, he ran into the house. He was back in a moment, and I smelt a strong reek of brandy as he passed me.

'"Well, my man," said he, "what can I do for you?"

'The sailor stood looking at him with puckered eyes, and with the same loose-lipped smile upon his face.

'"You don't know me?" he asked.

'"Why, dear me, it is surely Hudson!" said Mr. Trevor, in a tone of surprise.

'"Hudson it is, sir," said the seaman. "Why, it's thirty year and more since I saw you last. Here you are in your house, and me still picking my salt meat out of the harness cask."

'"Tut, you will find that I have not forgotten old times," cried Mr. Trevor, and, walking towards the sailor, he said something in a low voice.

'"Go into the kitchen," he continued out loud, "and you will get food and drink. I have no doubt that I shall find you a situation."

'"Thank you, sir," said the seaman, touching his forelock. "I'm just off a two-yearer in an eight-knot tramp, short handed at that, and I wants a rest. I thought I'd get it either with Mr. Beddoes or with you."

'"Ah!" cried Mr Trevor, "You know where Mr. Beddoes is?"

'"Bless you, sir, I know where all my old friends are," said the fellow, with a sinister smile, and slouched off after the maid into the kitchen. Mr. Trevor mumbled something to us about having been shipmates with the man when he was going back to the diggings, and then, leaving us on the lawn, he went indoors. An hour later, when we entered the house, we found him stretched dead-drunk upon the dining room sofa. The whole incident left a most ugly impression on my mind, and I was not sorry next day to leave Donnithorpe behind me, for I felt that my presence must be a source of embarrassment to my friend …'.

The rest of the story in synopsis:

After this opening and development Holmes returns to London. A couple of months later he receives a telegram from Victor imploring him to return. He does so and is met by Victor, looking thin and careworn.

On the drive from the station, Victor tells Holmes that Mr Trevor is dying. That the devil has come into their lives in the shape of the seaman, Hudson, who has gradually taken over the house. That he, Victor, and Hudson had finally had a blazing row. Old Trevor, to Victor's amazement, had come down on the side of Hudson and asked Victor to apologise to Hudson. Victor had refused and his father became even more distressed. And, after this, became more and more distressed and ill.

Then Hudson suddenly announced he was leaving and did so.

Old Trevor gradually began to recover, and then the final blow fell – a letter arrived from Fordingbridge in Hampshire where Old Trevor's friend, Beddoes, lived. Old Trevor read the letter and had a stroke. At this point Victor sent for Holmes.

Holmes asks what was in the letter. It was absurd and trivial, he is told by Victor.

They reach the house to find that Old Trevor has died. His last message was that 'the papers are at the back of the Japanese cabinet'.

Holmes asks to see the letter received from Beddoes – it is the piece of paper that Holmes showed Watson. Holmes breaks the code of the letter, which then reads that Hudson has told all.

At that point Victor takes the papers from the Japanese cabinet and in them the full secret is revealed. They are an account of the voyage of the *Gloria Scott* barque. We learn that Old Trevor began life as James Armitage (the J. A. tattoo on his arm). He worked in a bank and stole some money. He was caught and sentenced to be transported to Australia. During the voyage on the *Gloria Scott* he meets Jack Prendergast, 'a man of good family and great ability, but of incurably vicious habits'. One of Prendergast's great abilities was to defraud leading merchants of huge sums of money. Prendergast and Trevor struck up a friendship and Trevor learnt there was a plot to seize the ship – organised by Prendergast's partner, who was sailing on the ship as chaplain.

The mutineers took the ship in a pitched battle – killing most of the marines and officers. Prendergast wished to kill all those who were still alive, and had not declared for him and his cause.

Trevor could not agree to this cold-blooded murder, and so he and a few others of like mind were put in a small boat and set adrift.

They pulled away from the ship. A short distance away they saw the ship explode. They rowed back and found one young seaman left alive – Hudson. Hudson told them that on board the *Gloria Scott* the mate had managed to shake off his bonds and flee to the hold. He had broached a powder barrel and held a match over it – daring the mutineers to approach him. Someone fired at him – the musket ball sparked the powder – that was that.

The next day, those in the boat were picked up, passed themselves off as shipwrecked mariners; and Trevor landed at Sydney and made his fortune in the diggings.

He then returned to England with another of the convicts, Beddoes, and both became country gentlemen.

Twenty years later Hudson turned up again, as he did in the extract, and intruded himself on the Trevors, ruining their lives. Hudson then went off to blackmail Beddoes as well, at which point Beddoes sent the telegram, the reading of which caused the death of Old Trevor.

We return to Holmes's study, where Holmes rounds off the

loose ends by telling Watson that neither Beddoes nor Hudson was ever heard of again. The police thought that Hudson killed Beddoes, then fled – Holmes believes just the opposite – that Beddoes, feeling himself already betrayed by Hudson, killed Hudson, and fled the country with all the money on which he could lay his hands.

Dramatising this story posed certain problems, although it also gave great scope in terms of being able to take advantage of radio's gifts to go anywhere in time and space without incurring production costs. These opening pages included scenes on board ship; the mention of various countries; plus Cambridge, Norfolk and Holmes's chambers.

But they are only 'mentioned' and the major problem was that the whole thing is set in Holmes's rooms, and that all movement in the tale is in flashback and related by Holmes. Neither Holmes nor Watson, in this story, actually moves outside Holmes's study.

More serious was the fact that in this adventure Watson has nothing to do but listen to Holmes – Watson plays no active part at all. The story is also very short and would need to be expanded to fill the forty-five minutes required for each individual episode of the series. A method and way had to be found through all this, along with a 'teaser' that would hopefully draw in and hold the audience.

The critical scenes in the story occur on the barque *Gloria Scott*, when the convicts who are being transported stage their mutiny, so it seemed fitting that the 'teaser' should take place on the ship.

The bogus chaplain, the Rev. Wilson, is a prime mover in the mutiny, and so it seemed to make sense to give him prominence; and ambiguous dialogue that immediately cast doubt on who and what he was, and prepared the listener for the surprise that was no surprise.

From the end of this first scene on the ship, the ship's bell could be edged into the bells of Cambridge to signal Holmes's student days and lead into the information that it was Holmes's first case, undertaken while still a student.

From there we would move to Holmes's rooms and the dramatisation proper would begin.

This still left the problem of what to do with Watson – what sort of part could he play in something that was essentially a monologue? An idea presented itself in the cylinder containing the coded message. What if Holmes set Watson the problem of decoding the message in the cylinder? Then the narrative could break off at discrete intervals to cut back to Holmes's chambers, at which points Watson could make yet another ineffectual stab at decoding the message and thereby achieve an active, 'dramatic' part in the play.

Here is the information in the opening pages turned into dramatic format:

The Adventure of the 'Gloria Scott'

TEASER: POOP DECK OF CONVICT TRANSPORT SHIP *GLORIA SCOTT* AT SEA. EN ROUTE TO AUSTRALIA.

FX: WIND IN RIGGING. MODERATE SEA.

1. CAPTAIN: Morning Reverend. You're about early.

2. REV. WILSON: This terrible heat, Captain. And then one of the convicts expressed a wish to see me. Poor souls. To be crammed below. Between those fetid decks in this weather.

3. CAPTAIN: Ay, well ... the conditions are no concern of ours. And who knows ... maybe providence will come to their aid ... (LAUGHS) ... Rain down food and liquor ... even part the sea to make an easy passage! What d'you say to that Reverend?

4. WILSON: Why, simply that the ways of 'providence' are often like the Peace of God. 'Passing all understanding' ...

5. CAPTAIN: (UNEASY AT SOMETHING HE HEARS IN WILSON'S VOICE) Well ... eight o'clock ... near as dammit ... You'll excuse me, Reverend ...

6. WILSON: Of course, Captain ... the calls of duty ... I fully understand those ...

FX: SHIP'S BELL BEGINS TO STRIKE EIGHT BELLS. WHICH CROSS-FADE TO MUSIC AND CREDITS AND BELLS RINGING IN CAMBRIDGE, WITH DOG BARKING HELD UNDER. THEN CLOCK CHIMING HOURS FROM TOWER WHICH LEADS INTO CLOCK SOFTLY CHIMING IN HOLMES'S STUDY WHICH SWELLS THEN FADES BACK TO

SCENE 1 HOLMES'S STUDY

FX: TICKING CLOCK. FIRE.

1. WATSON:	Brrr ... another winter on us ... How much more depressing each one feels ... the older one becomes ...
2. HOLMES:	Watson ... Draw up to the fire I beg you. For here in these papers is something I warrant will snap you out of your gloom, as it concerns the stuff of youth ... My youth!
3. WATSON:	Really, Holmes?
4. HOLMES:	My time at Cambridge. More particularly, the freezing of a dog on to my ankle while I was a student there.
5. WATSON:	Good heavens ...
6. HOLMES:	Which event, however, led me to the undertaking of my first case ...
7. WATSON:	Ah ... At last ...
8. HOLMES:	Indeed ... You know you have often questioned me as to what turned my mind in the direction of criminal research? Well, the answer lies in these papers ... and in the contents of this little tarnished cylinder tied with tape.
9. WATSON:	Ah ...
10. HOLMES:	So while you untie this same cylinder, and read the message inside ... I shall enlarge upon the background details ... Here ...
11. WATSON:	(LEANING TO TAKE CYLINDER) Yes ... right, Holmes (MUTTERS) Some years, I think ... since these knots ...
12. HOLMES:	(SPEAKING ACROSS WATSON) The dog, of course, served no more purpose than to bring me into contact with its master, Victor Trevor. Who, though something of a lone wolf like myself, determined to become my friend. And it was Victor who ...
13. WATSON:	(TRIUMPHANT) Ah, that's got it ...!
14. HOLMES:	(LIGHTLY MOCKING) Oh, excellent, my dear fellow ... And the contents of the note within?
15. WATSON:	(READS SLOWLY) 'The supply of game for London is going steadily up. Head-keeper Hudson, we believe, has been told to receive all orders for fly-paper, and for the preservation of your hen pheasant's life' ... But what on earth does it mean, Holmes?

1. HOLMES:	Why Watson, I am looking for you to elucidate that.
2. WATSON:	Me?
3. HOLMES:	Indeed. This time you will play detective, and attempt to crack the code before I reach the point of my tale where I must reveal it to you … So, back to Cambridge, where after cementing our friendship, Victor Trevor issued an invitation for me to stay for a month or so in the long vacation at his father's place in Donnithorpe, Norfolk … you know Norfolk, Watson …?
4. WATSON:	(DISTRACTED AS HE CONSIDERS NOTE) Why, no, not really, Holmes …
5. HOLMES:	No. Nor did I … At the time …
	GO TO

SCENE 2	ROAD TO DONNITHORPE
FX:	RATTLE OF PONY TRAP.
6. VICTOR:	So, Holmes. What do you think of our countryside ?
7. HOLMES:	All steeple, field and fen, it seems, Victor.
8. VICTOR:	Which means, however, excellent duck shooting …
9. HOLMES:	Ah …!
10. VICTOR:	… and fishing …
11. HOLMES:	I see …
12. VICTOR:	And when I add my father has a small but select library … and a tolerably good cook …
13. HOLMES:	Then I am your man! … The two of you live alone?
14. VICTOR:	My father is a widower … my sister dead. My father … well … a man of resolution … shipped to Australia early in life … Made his way in the gold-fields … Returned to England … Is now the local Justice of the Peace where he puts up a fierce front … But in reality … well … his leniency from the bench is well remarked … Holmes, look, the house! … (CRACKS WHIP) … Hoa!
	FADES

And with the information packed into these opening scenes there should be a fair indication of the characters involved and where the plot may be going.

A writer should practise adapting/dramatising various types of work, especially plays or stories of other periods. Adapting plays teaches not only the structure of drama, but also how playwrights of earlier periods ordered and handled their material. The best way to know your own field is by going out to graze in it regularly.

In dramatisation there are what might be termed the 'Greatest Hits', ranging from *Pygmalion* to *Peter Pan*. These are works of abiding interest for adapters, that are seen to demand a tried-and-tested technique, and are usually allotted to those writers with a proven track record in adaptation plus, in many cases, credits for original work.

A writer coming new to dramatisation should perhaps look for something from a well-known author, but not one of that author's better-known works. Whatever it is that is chosen should contain action and interest and strong characters, and within it should be material that will use the full breadth of radio.

To sum up. In adaptations, especially of relatively unfamiliar works, it is probably as well to get the idea of the play, or germ of the plot, out into the open as soon as possible to help and attract the listener. Even if there is a pause at this stage while the natural development of the play occurs, the listener will know where things are going and be able to decide whether or not to stick with the play. Listeners will feel they are at least tracking the plot until it flows naturally and fully from the text.

In the case of one-set plays, or novels where the protagonist lies in bed for three hundred pages staring at a crack in the ceiling while searching for a flaw in the universe, set changes must be found to let the work 'breathe'. This can be achieved by change of acoustic, by use of a narrator, or maybe even by a flashback technique. Narration can tend to run on, and the less the better should be the rule here.

So as not to pose the double problem of working for the first time in an unfamiliar genre with an unfamiliar piece of prose or drama, your first dramatisations could be works with a wide currency – perhaps fairy stories. Try adapting the following for radio: 'Cinderella', 'Little Red Riding Hood', 'Hansel and Gretel'.

Attempt to give these fables an updated treatment in order to appeal to a modern-day audience.

In a modern-day treatment of Cinderella, the father of Cinderella could be a music promoter who has recently taken on to his books 'Prince' Valiant, the hottest thing in rock. The father has been given two tickets to attend a masked fancy-dress party to be given by Prince, at an exclusive night-club. Prince is known to be looking for a new partner.

Cinderella's (Cindy's) sisters commandeer the tickets and go off to the party, leaving Cindy alone to bewail her luck and wash the dishes.

A Fairy Vacuum Cleaner Salesperson arrives at the house, gives Cindy her card, and states that Cindy will be able to attend the party. The Fairy Salesperson makes up a dress and mask for Cindy from stapled-together vacuum cleaner bags.

Cindy, clad in her fancy-dress, flies to the party on a vacuum cleaner supplied by the Fairy Salesperson. This unfortunately has batteries which will run down at midnight, by which time Cindy must be home.

At the party the Prince and Cindy dance until midnight strikes. Cindy rushes off, leaving one of her training shoes behind. Prince picks it up, and seeing that it is not a 'brand' name, realises that Cindy needs help in more ways than one.

The next day, carrying the trainer, Prince turns up at the house of Cindy's father to discuss the aftermath of the party, and subsequent tour dates for himself and his band.

The two sisters see the shoe and ask its meaning.

Prince tells them that it belongs to a young girl he met the previous evening, but who left the club at midnight before he could discover much about her. She was wearing a vacuum-cleaner bag costume and mask so he would not recognise her, even were she standing in front of him. But dancing with her he felt things he had never felt before ... Strange yearnings ...

The sisters clamour to try the shoe, but it is too small to fit either.

Prince rests the shoe on a chair. Then, before returning to trash his hotel suite, he asks for a drink of water to help him take his morning uppers. One of the sisters shouts for Cindy to bring it from the kitchen.

Cindy comes in barefoot. When asked about this she says she

has lost one of her trainers – her only footwear. She sees it on the chair, and announces that she hasn't lost it after all. She has just found it.

At this point Prince announces that he has found his masked partner of the previous evening. He presents Cindy with his autobiography, a blank prescription pad and a list of tax shelters. And tells her he intends to take her away with him on a magic carpet. Cindy suggests a magic vacuum cleaner instead and, producing the card the Fairy Vacuum Cleaner Salesperson left, tells Prince she will order one up immediately. On this note the dramatisation would end.

Exercises (2)

1 Turn the above storyline of Cinderella into a radio dramatisation. Use the following ODARE criteria:

Opening	Cinderella (Cindy), father, sisters. Father, the agent of top rock singer Prince, has two tickets for Prince's masked fancy-dress party. Sisters claim tickets. Cindy to be left behind.
Development	Cindy alone and sad. Fairy Vacuum Salesperson arrives. Cindy can go to party on magic vacuum cleaner, but must be back at midnight when vacuum batteries will run down.
Argument	Prince meets Cinders at party. They dance and he declares his love for her. Will she accept it? Midnight strikes. Cindy runs off without Prince knowing who she is. Cindy leaves behind training shoe.
Resolution	Prince, heartbroken, arrives at Cindy's house to see her father about Prince's next tour. Prince carries the trainer. Explains it will fit his lost love. Sisters fight to try on trainer. Prince prepares to leave but requires glass of water to wash down his 'medication'. Cindy brings in water and sees trainer. Says it belongs to her. Prince overjoyed.
Ending	Prince and Cindy prepare to ring Fairy Vacuum Cleaner Salesperson to arrange transport.

Aim for a broadcasting time of about five minutes.

2 Give 'Little Red Riding Hood' a suitably modern setting. With 'Hansel and Gretel' use a narrator and perhaps set the story in its own time.

3 Choose a favourite short story of your own and attempt a simplified radio dramatisation.

The above exercise dealt with the dramatisation of prose into radio. Now we will look at the adaptation of a stage play for radio.

Here is the opening of a simplified stage version of *A Christmas Carol*, entitled 'Scrooge'. Read it as a stage piece and then go to the exercise on p. 176.

'Scrooge', A Play for the Stage

SCENE 1 OUTSIDE SCROOGE'S HOUSE

SCROOGE'S FRONT DOOR TOWARDS FRONT OF THE STAGE. FITTED WITH ORNATE KNOCKER. ABOVE KNOCKER A HOLE IN DOOR BIG ENOUGH TO TAKE THE HEAD OF JACOB MARLEY'S GHOST. NUMBER OF CHILDREN DIVIDED INTO TWO GROUPS ACROSS FRONT OF THE STAGE. THESE GROUPS, ACTING AS A CHORUS, PROVIDE A COMMENTARY ON THE ACTION OF THE PLAY. FOR A SCHOOL PERFORMANCE, THE GROUPS COULD BE OF MIXED AGE SO THE OLDER CHILDREN COULD HELP THE YOUNGER AS REGARDS VOLUME AND PACE. THE GROUPS COULD BE DRESSED AS CAROL SINGERS AND HOLD MUSIC SHEETS CONTAINING THE VERSES. THIS AGAIN MIGHT HELP THE YOUNGER MEMBERS OF THE CAST RECALL THEIR LINES. THE END MEMBER OF EACH GROUP COULD HOLD A LANTERN. THE GROUPS COULD SPEAK AS AN ENSEMBLE, OR BE SPLIT AS SUGGESTED IN THE TEXT

1. CHOR: Scrooge is cruel!
Scrooge is mean!
The meanest man
We've ever seen!
Hard as flint!
Sharp as bone!

But watch it, Scrooge
YOU'RE ALL ALONE!!

STROBE LIGHT GIVING THE IMPRESSION OF SNOW. STAGE GRADUALLY FILLS UP WITH RAGGED CHILDREN. FLOWER/MATCH/PIE SELLERS, ETC. WANDER ROUND AIMLESSLY BEGGING/IMPLORING WITH OUTSTRETCHED HANDS.

1. SINGER/ TINY TIM: Cold and hunger are our playmates,
And to suffer is our task.
Give a little, just a little.
Little's all we ask . . .

SCROOGE ENTERS, BEGGAR CHILDREN CONVERGE ON HIM. SING TO THE TUNE OF 'ORANGES AND LEMONS'

2. CHILDREN: Please buy our posies,
Our bouquet and nosegays,
Lilies, primroses,
So fine, yet so cheap.

AS THE FLOWER SELLERS REPEAT THIS QUIETLY, THE PIE SELLERS SING OVER THEM

3. PIE/MEAT SELLERS: Please buy our meat, Sir,
So tasty to eat, Sir,
So juicy and sweet, Sir,
So fine, yet so cheap.

THEN THE SELLERS OF SMALL WARES AND CLOTH TAPES, ETC. BEGIN, THE FLOWER SELLERS AND PIE SELLERS SINGING UNDER

4. SELLERS OF SMALL WARE: Cotton, tapes, laces,
Combs, scissors and braces,
Paint for your faces,
So fine, yet so cheap.

ALL COMBINE INDIVIDUAL VERSES, AND CLUSTER ROUND SCROOGE UNTIL HE DRIVES THEM AWAY WITH HIS STICK. CHILDREN GRADUALLY LEAVE THE STAGE. SCROOGE STANDS BEFORE HIS FRONT DOOR, FURTIVELY LOOKING UP AND DOWN AS HE PATS POCKETS FOR KEY. FINDS KEY AND IS ABOUT TO INSERT IT IN DOOR WHEN TWO JOLLY,

PROSPEROUS WOMEN ENTER CARRYING PAPERS AND LISTS. SCROOGE IMMEDIATELY PUTS AWAY HIS KEY AGAIN, AS IF TERRIFIED WOMEN WILL SEE INSIDE HIS HOUSE. WOMEN CONSULT THEIR LISTS AND CROSS TO SCROOGE

1. 1ST WOMAN: Mr Scrooge? … Mr Ebenezer Scrooge?

2. 2ND WOMAN: Of Scrooge and Marley …?

3. SCROOGE: Marley? … Marley is dead. Dead these seven years.

4. 1ST WOMAN: No matter. For I have no doubt his generosity is still represented by your good self.

5. SCROOGE: (AMAZED) MARLEY!! Generosity! … (LAUGHS LOUD AND LONG)

6. 2ND WOMAN: Come, Sir. How much do we put you down for?

7. SCROOGE: Put me down for? … I do not understand you, Madam.

8. 1ST WOMAN: Simply, Sir, in this festive season we collect for the poor and needy. Thousands are without food. As many without fire. While a multitude have no place to lay their heads. You are aware of this, Mr Scrooge?

9. SCROOGE: Constantly. Outside my front door!

10. 2ND WOMAN: That in this day and age people must hunt for crusts. Must sleep on the streets of London. They are poor, Mr Scrooge.

11. SCROOGE: (ASIDE) They are surplus population, Madam.

12. 1ST WOMAN: We constantly seek to alleviate distress …

13. 2ND WOMAN: Look for suggestions to help us …

14. SCROOGE: Suggestions, you say? … So … Are there no prisons, Madam?

15. 2ND WOMAN: There are, Sir.

16. SCROOGE: And no workhouses?

17. 2ND WOMAN: Indeed. Though I wish I could say there were not.

18. SCROOGE: And is there no treadmill? No poor law?

19. 1ST WOMAN: Ay. And both very busy.

20. SCROOGE: Then here, Madam, is my suggestion. That any with no place to lay their heads, or warm their hands, may

apply to any of those excellent institutions. And now ...

1. 1ST WOMAN: (TAKES UP PEN) Of course. You must be busy. It is that time of year. So, Mr Scrooge, what may I put you down for ...?

2. SCROOGE: Nothing, Madam! You may put me down as Nothing!

3. 1ST WOMAN: Ah, I see. You wish to be left anonymous?

4. SCROOGE: I wish to be left alone! ... (PAUSE) ... Good afternoon, ladies! ... (PAUSE) ... I say ... good afternoon!!

5. 2ND WOMAN: But Christmas Eve? Surely you will give something?

6. SCROOGE: Have I not given my wretched clerk, Bob Cratchit, the day off tomorrow?! That he may celebrate with his equally wretched family! Is that not enough?! A day's wages for no work!

7. 1ST WOMAN: But that is because it is Christmas tomorrow! Surely even you, Mr Scrooge, understand the message of Christmas?

8. SCROOGE: I do, Madam. And that message is Humbug!

9. 2ND WOMAN: Humbug, Sir?

10. SCROOGE: (WALKING UP TO HER) Humbug! Humbug! Humbug!! And now ... for the last time! Good afternoon!

THE TWO WOMEN GLANCE AT EACH OTHER SADLY, SHAKE THEIR HEADS IN SORROW AND MOVE OFF. SCROOGE SHAKES HIS FIST AFTER THEM, FURTIVELY LOOKS UP AND DOWN AGAIN, FUMBLES FOR HIS KEY. ABOUT TO PUT IT IN THE DOOR, TURNS TO SHAKE FIST AGAIN. AS HE DOES SO THE HEAD OF MARLEY'S GHOST APPEARS THROUGH HOLE IN DOOR. THE HEAD VANISHES JUST BEFORE SCROOGE TURNS BACK AND LOOKS AT DOOR. AGAIN SCROOGE TURNS AND SHAKES FIST, AGAIN HEAD APPEARS. SCROOGE TURNS BACK TO INSERT KEY. THIS TIME SCROOGE SEES HEAD – FALLS BACKWARDS. PICKS HIMSELF UP, RECOILS FROM DOOR IN HORROR.

11. SCROOGE: (TO AUDIENCE) Did I see? ... Well? ... Did I? ... Did I see Marley? ... (WAITS FOR AUDIENCE RESPONSE)

But Marley's dead. Dead these seven years ... I know it. I buried him! ... At a discount.

SCROOGE, VERY FRIGHTENED, APPROACHES DOOR AGAIN, EXTENDS KEY TOWARDS DOOR ... BECOMES BOLDER AND TURNS KEY IN DOOR. DOOR SWINGS OPEN. SCROOGE PEERS INSIDE. SEES NOTHING THAT FRIGHTENS HIM. SHAKES FIST ONCE AGAIN IN DIRECTION OF DEPARTING WOMEN.

1. SCROOGE: Christmas? ... The poor? ... The hungry? ... The homeless? ... (TURNS TO AUDIENCE) Humbug! I tell you! All humbug!

BLACKOUT

Exercises (3)

Adapt the above for radio. In your adaptation consider using either a narrator who speaks in the voice of Dickens, or a modern stand-up comedian/hip/rap style.

There is scope within this adaptation for unusual and innovative sound effects. Here are some examples of how the first few pages might go:

Example 1: using a narrator:

FX: BURIAL BELL TOLLING IN BACKGROUND

1. NARRATOR: Marley was dead. Dead as a door nail. There was no doubt about this whatever. The register was signed and Scrooge, his partner, had signed it. And Scrooge's name was good for anything he put his hand to. For Scrooge was a tight-fisted hand at the grindstone ...

FX: (UNDER, VARIOUS VOICES) Spare a penny, Mr Scrooge ... Mr Scrooge, Sir ... Please, Sir ... Bread, Sir ... For Christmas, Mr Scrooge ...

2. NARRATOR: (CONTINUES OVER VOICES) ... a squeezing, wrenching, grasping, scraping, covetous old sinner ... red eyes, thin lips ... grating voice ... Who knew no charity ... No kind thoughts ... No, not even at Christmas ...

And at this point we would go into the scene from the stage play with the two charitable women.

Example 2: in a school:

FX:	SOUND OF BOISTEROUS CLASS OF PRIMARY SCHOOL CHILDREN
1. TEACHER:	Now, children ... Quiet please ... Quiet ...!
FX:	CLASS GRADUALLY QUIETENS DOWN
2. TEACHER:	Today, we are going to learn about the story of Scrooge. Now ... can anyone tell me ... something about Scrooge?
3. CHILDREN:	Scrooge is cruel! Scrooge is mean! The meanest man We've ever seen! Hard as flint! Sharp as bone! But watch it, Scrooge YOU'RE ALL ALONE!!
FX:	SOUND OF WIND AND BLIZZARD. OVER THIS WE HEAR SINGER/TINY TIM AND BEGGAR CHILDREN.
4. SINGER/ TINY TIM:	Cold and hunger are our playmates, And to suffer is our task. Give a little, just a little. Little's all we ask ...
	BEGGAR CHILDREN SING TO THE TUNE OF 'ORANGES AND LEMONS'
5. CHILDREN:	Please buy our posies, Our bouquet and nosegays, Lilies, primroses, So fine, yet so cheap.
	AS THE FLOWER SELLERS REPEAT THIS QUIETLY, THE PIE SELLERS SING OVER THEM
6. PIE/MEAT SELLERS:	Please buy our meat, Sir, So tasty to eat, Sir, So juicy and sweet, Sir, So fine, yet so cheap.
	THEN THE SELLERS OF SMALL WARES AND CLOTH

TAPES, ETC., BEGIN, THE FLOWER SELLERS AND PIE SELLERS SINGING UNDER

1. SELLERS OF SMALL WARE: Cotton, tapes, laces,
Combs, scissors and braces,
Paint for your faces,
So fine, yet so cheap.

ALL COMBINE INDIVIDUAL VERSES UNTIL WE SUDDENLY HEAR.

2. SCROOGE: Away! ... Away with you, I say! ... Away or you'll feel this stick ... Leave an honest businessman alone ... Beggars! Parasites! ... Thieves ... Away, I say, A ... Ah! My apologies, Madam ...

3. 1ST WOMAN: Mr Scrooge ...? Mr Ebenezer Scrooge?

4. 2ND WOMAN: Of Scrooge and Marley ...?

ETC.

7 Radio talks and features

As drama becomes more and more expensive, talks, interviews and documentaries are gaining more and more ground on network radio. They have, however, always been the verbal staple of local radio.

They are often the best way to break into radio. Students/writers can ring a local radio station and ask what sort of material is required; can gain access to hospital radio and write/present items of local interest; can begin to run a radio station from the media department of a school or college.

The three areas occupied by talks, interviews and documentaries will be dealt with in the first part of this chapter, leaving the second part to be occupied by an examination of the 'feature'. Because of an overlap of definition among all of the categories in this section, and because talks, interviews and documentary material can all graduate towards a 'feature', and may become part of it, the chapter will incline to that form as the final artistic resting place of the other three catergories.

The 'local feature' will be dealt with at the end of the chapter in some length as this is often the way into radio.

The radio talk

A radio 'talk' is just that. Someone with a microphone, presenting information in a pleasant and easily understood fashion. Talks can be about anything, all that is required is that what is being discussed be presented in an informative, easy manner that generates simple but vivid mindvisible images to make the assimilation of the material immediate. And, as always, a thin film of humour tends to oil the wheels of intimacy between the microphone and the listener.

Radio talks have flourished since the beginning of broadcasting. The first talk was given on 23 December 1922; the second, 'How to Catch a Tiger', on 27 January – which gestated a Heath Robinson drawing.

By the 1930s a journalist, Collie Knox, was writing a weekly column of 'radio talks' for the *Daily Mail*. These were subsequently published in book form as *Collie Knox Calling*! A description of the giving of talks has been left by Collin Brooks, in his reminiscences *Tavern Talk* (1950). Brooks later sat on one of the radio 'Brains Trust' panels – panels notable for the intellects of their members. Prior to a 'Brains Trust' session, 'the protagonists, their entrepreneurs ... seconds and bottle holders' all dined together ... 'a very desirable prologue'. For those on the Forces Educational programmes, however, 'one walks in ... does the broadcast ... walks out'. Collins observes that this is because there is a hierarchical structure about the BBC, 'and rightly so'.

Collins relates there are many different kinds of talk, each with its own technique, then discusses his own first broadcast in 1925 or 1926, 'in the days of crystal sets ... on "The Editorial 'We'"', a piece of work that might bear repeating today, could it be disinterred. It was unscripted and unrehearsed and 'we didn't know, at least I didn't, if it was being heard by anybody at all'.

Collins broadcast as 'North Countryman', as chairman of 'Food Forum' and 'Taking Stock'; in 'Forces Educational', 'Great Victorians', 'Editors' Forum', 'Friday Forum' and 'Book Talks and Discussions'. An impressive body of work.

Talks, in those early days, seem to have been interesting, but bland. Controversy was not encouraged. Collins tells of the 'serious trouble' in which he found himself with his editor, Arthur Mann, for 'supporting Phillip Guedalla in his plea for controversial broadcasting'. Mr Mann, a future Governor of the BBC, declared such support to be 'unthinkable'.

Some day, Collins tells us, a young novelist will 'give us a kind of Zola ... [a] picture of the life of Portland Place and its bits of far-flung Empire at Bush House and elsewhere'. This was the Zola who refused to sign an appeal on behalf of Oscar Wilde; but who (except between the covers of a book) would seem as unlikely and unwelcome a visitor to Portland Place as became J. B. Priestley with his 'Postscript' series of talks.

In his informal history of the BBC, *The Biggest Aspidistra in the World*, Peter Black gives an account of what happened. Priestley's 'Postscripts' – possibly the most famous series of all radio talks – began in 1940, after the nine o'clock news, and with the country reeling under the initial effort of the Second World War. Priestley began with the heroism of the evacuation of Dunkirk, and his subject matter covered everything from the local defence volunteers, to how a pie shop in Bradford, together with its pies, survived the bombing raids. The talks seem to have been a mixture of the heroic and the 'wholesomely wholesome'. Priestley's voice, Black (1972) tells us, was 'as rich and unpretentious as a good Christmas pudding'.

Priestley became popular, an early 'media figure', recognised in shops and pubs as a sort of wartime guru. His gospel was that the country was like one of Bradford's rich gravy-filled pies – in which all deserved a share. That while it was all very well to cheer on RAF pilots – those pilots should not have to come back to the economic and social wilderness that their fathers inherited after the First World War, perhaps a reference to the post-First World War political promises of 'Homes Fit For Heroes' – which materialised, by the usual political chicanery, as tenements fit only for TB.

Then the broadcasts began to diversify further into social and political comment. Priestley advocated, among other suggestions for helping the war effort, that houses left by their owners who had fled to America ought to be requisitioned.

In 1941 Priestley began a further series of talks – even more sharply edged, speaking with what Black refers to as 'the voice of the people' against the 'faceless grey men'. Those who tried to 'confine the quality of life within a frame that matched their own narrow expectations of it'.

The pre-war governments had been Tory and, although the listening figures were as high as ever, the Tory newspapers turned on Priestley, asserting that nobody listened to him any more. Numeracy can be a difficult business.

Priestley had to go. He had an artistic voice that reached ordinary people and expressed a better vision of how the country should be run – the one thing, Black asserts, that the professional politician most resents and fears.

Priestley was stopped after six talks. He had one letter from the Ministry of Information and another from the BBC, each explaining that the other was responsible for his dismissal. Briggs (1941) writes that the minutes of the BBC's board of management recorded: 'Priestley series stopped on instruction of Minister', an example of Henry Adams's (1838–1918) observation that politics 'is the organisation of hatreds'.

It may seem bizarre that those who governed the BBC, together with those that governed the country, and in a time of war, combined to defend a raft of draft dodgers and vested interests.

Possibly there were good social, educational and family reasons why this happened.

By the end of the 1940s, near radio's apogee, there were twenty-six producers in the Talks Department, producing some eighty programmes a week.

Exercises (1)

Research and write a radio talk on why you think J. B. Priestley's 'Postscripts', although universally popular and uplifting in a time of national peril, were discontinued.

Radio talks, as can be gathered, are very much personal views of personal matters.

Interviews, documentaries and features are more collaborative efforts (either willingly or unwillingly) and, to differentiate between them, it might be profitable to consider briefly a single subject as it might be treated in these different formats as regards approach and structure.

As a subject which tends to attract high media interest, and is both topical and contentious, we could take as our differentiating example the subject of AIDS.

The radio interview

An interview is usually two people discussing an agreed subject; or variety of related subjects centred around a single area or under a clearly defined umbrella.

The test for a great work of art is said to be when there is no sign of the artist in the finished product. When, in looking at a painting or sculpture, or listening to a piece of radio or a piece of music, or viewing a play or film, all that strikes the onlooker is what is contained in the work itself. When no secondary considerations (techniques used, how much it's worth, how many times the artist/director has been married, etc.) intrude. Only then can a work be said to have fulfilled itself as art.

A great compliment was paid when, in an overheard conversation, a literary manager said to a writer: 'When I started reading this I hoped it would be good because it was by you – but six pages in I'd forgotten who had written it.'

Similarly, the test of a good interview is when the interviewer keeps completely in the background. When the interview is 'interviewee led' rather than 'interviewer led'.

In an AIDS interview the interviewer would want the listener to know how the disease was contracted. What the feelings of the interviewee are at the present time, and what message the interviewee would like to pass on to the listeners.

If interviewer led, the first question might come over as:

FX: PROGRAMME SIGNATURE MUSIC. FADES BACK TO

1. INT: Hi, everyone, and welcome to 'Fact and Fiction', your local show from the small station that takes on all the big questions. Today we're going to look at something where the myth and the truth often seem to have lost sight of each other – the subject of AIDS.

   So to learn what it's like, really like, both physically and socially, to have been struck by the disease, I've invited along to the studio X, who has generously offered to put both his/her time and experiences at our disposal ... Well, X. I believe you contracted AIDS through unprotected sex with a partner that you met in a night-club. Is this right?

2. INT/EE X: Yes, that's right.

But in the interviewee-led approach:

FX: PROGRAMME SIGNATURE MUSIC. FADES BACK TO

1. INT: Hi, everyone, and welcome to 'Fact and Fiction', your local show from the small station that takes on all the big questions. Today we're going to look at something where the myth and the truth often seem to have lost sight of each other – the subject of AIDS.

   So to learn what it's like, really like, both physically and socially, to have contracted the disease, I've invited along to the studio X, who has generously offered to put both his/her time and experiences at our disposal. X, I wonder if you'd like to tell us all how it happened?

2. INT/EE X: Yes, right ... I was in this club one evening ... I wasn't even going out that particular night ... Then some friends called ... invited me along ... so I just went ... you know, have a couple of drinks ... couple of

dances ... bit of a laugh ... Suddenly, standing there at the bar, I saw ...

Or, to stand the programme on its head:

FX: PROGRAMME SIGNATURE MUSIC. FADES BACK TO

1. INT/EE X: Yes, right ... I was in this club one evening ... I wasn't even going out that particular night ... Then some friends called ... invited me along ... so I just went ... you know, have a couple of drinks ... couple of dances ... bit of a laugh ... Suddenly, standing there at the bar, I saw ...

2. INT: Hi, everyone, and welcome to 'Fact and Fiction', your local show from the small station that takes on all the big questions. And those short sentences by X, my guest tonight, introduce to us a subject where the myth and the truth often seem to have lost sight of each other – AIDS.

In the latter two examples the interviewee immediately begins to live for the listener as a person who has social habits and emotional feelings similar to those of the listener. A rapport is established. The third example is even more immediate and engaging.

Exercises (2)

To practise interviewer/interviewee techniques, first find a partner with whom you will work. You will need a cassette recorder. One of you is an AIDS sufferer – the other is the radio interviewer at a local station. Sit down and agree an interview format. Who will begin? Is the interview to be completely 'free' – or are there certain areas which the interviewee wishes not to be touched upon? Is this area negotiable – is the excluded material seen as being necessary to the interview?

This interview should be aimed at lasting for about four or five minutes. It is surprising how much ground can be covered. This exercise is ideal for transmission from a college radio station.

The radio documentary

Documentaries can usually be classified as 'network'. They have more of a national approach and are generally the interview broadened, with the involvement of additional material and, at times, other people.

A documentary on AIDS would perhaps be built around a selection of people who have contracted the disease – but in a number of different ways. Drugs, sex, blood transfusions. Their attitudes to the fact of having the disease could be explored. Contributions could be canvassed from extreme pressure groups on both sides as to how much help should be given to sufferers. Plus intercuts with a selection of people who are researching/quantifying the disease; and with some thoughts on present and possible future methods of treatment. Plus, perhaps, a contribution from someone who is responsible for government thinking and policy. Documentaries usually involve heavy research.

The radio feature

> So scented the grim Feature, and upturned
> His nostril wide into the murky air,
> Sagacious of his quarry from so far.
>
> Milton, *Paradise Lost*, Bk IX

> Once broadcasting had got over its initial intoxication with its own existence, it started to wonder what it was for. It spent its first ten years happily cutting and adapting works created for other forms of art, entertainment and instruction. But slowly, obstinately, and with growing success, a group of writers and producers insisted on exploring the possibilities of the radio medium itself. Because what they produced fitted no known formula, and for that reason stood out from the run of programmes stemming from existing forms, they were grouped under the generic title of 'features programmes'.
>
> Laurence Gilliam (ed.), *BBC Features*

According to Black (1972), Lance Sieveking joined the BBC in 1925 as an actor and writer in education, and then switched to drama. Black felt it was Sieveking who wrote and produced the first true radio play, 'Kaleidoscope' – although this work now looks much more like the first feature.

It was produced, in 1928, from the first 'Dramatic Control Panel', especially built by Captain A. D. G. West, a BBC research engineer. This panel allowed the producer for the first time to work from more than one studio, listen to what was coming in, talk to the cast and cue with lights. The facility for cuts, mixes, fades, wipes and the ability to superimpose became a reality.

'Kaleidoscope' was 'A Rhythm, representing the life of man from Cradle to Grave'. It required over a hundred actors; sound-effects men; orchestras and musicians. The script went from a football game to someone singing 'Ich Liebe dich' ... musical boxes ... narration ... 'It's a long way to Tipperary' ... dance bands ... Beethoven's fourth and fifth symphonies ... lines from Ernest Dowson's 'Cynara' ('I called for madder music and for stronger wine' comes to mind) ... Chopin ... jazz ... Tennyson's 'The Lotus Eaters' ... a Negro spiritual ... and The Voice of Good.

It is difficult to accept this as a radio play as it falls into the category of what Sieveking himself defined as the radio 'feature', 'an arrangement of sounds which has a theme but no plot' (Black, 1972) Sieveking was attacked for works of this sort as a waste of public time and money, but was defended by J. C. W. Reith, the first director general of the BBC.

Reith, a moralist whose morals were carefully weighed against the exigencies of the day, steered the BBC through its first stormy years, and was strong on what could, or could not, be listened to by the nation.

An early example of Reith in action was when he had Eric Gill, the sculptor responsible for the statue of Ariel for the façade of Broadcasting House, alter the size of Ariel's reproductive organs, which Reith felt had been 'emphasised ... beyond necessity'.

In 1928 Sieveking set up the Programme Research Unit, with himself as head and E. A. Harding as one of the team. When he did this, he put the embryo Features Department on the rails.

In 1932 E. A. Harding, with Lawrence Gilliam, produced the first successful round-the-Empire Christmas Day broadcast. In 1933 he did a similar programme linking the countries of Europe on New Year's Eve – a programme in which he mentioned the proportion of the gross income which the Poles were spending on arms.

Next morning, the Polish Ambassador called at Broadcasting

House insisting that 'heads must roll'. Reith himself obligingly rolled over for the Ambassador, carpeted Harding and showed him the Black Spot – 'You're a very dangerous man, Harding, I think you'd better be up in the North where you can't do much damage.' Harding was transferred to be programmes director in the Northern Region.

Here, in Manchester, Harding met D. G. Bridson, a BBC staff writer from 1935–69, who worked mainly in Features and arrived at the BBC through 'that one-time apologist for Communism, Claud Cockburn, with whom I had been put in touch by that one-time apologist for Fascism, Ezra Pound'.

Harding imbued Bridson with the idea that since all broadcasting was propaganda, the people, and not just their spokesmen, had the right to use it. Harding felt that the BBC, because all that was spoken had to be read from scripts, only chose to use a 'southern upper-class accent' – the only sort of voice at that time allowed near a microphone. Harding thought it was time other voices were heard.

Bridson accepted the idea, and in his 1934 broadcast 'May Day in England' contrasted the old pastoral aspect of this holiday with May Day's new modern role as International Labour Day. A follow-up programme speaking of the three million people unemployed in Britain that year, and advocating social credit, was banned by Broadcasting House as 'seditious'.

Bridson redeemed himself, according to Black, by a feature on Coleridge – which threatened to bring down no more than the wrath of the literary establishment.

In 1937 Bridson was allowed to make 'Steel', in which he used 'every sound available to radio to convey the drama and excitement ... in a Sheffield steel works':

> Wan lights that glow in frosted windows
> Of dismal shops,
> And doors creak discreetly, as gurgling gutters
> Are choked with morning slops.
> Only the pipes of the shivering men are warm
> Huddling at a hundred tramway stops.

In 'Steel', by giving the working class of Britain a voice, Bridson began to put ordinary people on the air.

He was abetted in this by Lawrence Gilliam. Gilliam at this time was editing the *Radio Times*. Simultaneously with his editorial duties, Gilliam was assiduously, and under fictitious names, sending in letters to that same journal advocating more programmes like 'May Day in England'.

Gilliam, by such manoeuvres, moved from the *Radio Times* to become a features producer, began to build his kingdom, and the war years saw a huge rise in the output and flexibility of features.

Just as all wars advance quicker ways of dealing death, they also advance medicine and communications. People at home wanted coverage at first hand of the war. This meant broadcasting units going into Europe with the fighting forces. If this was to happen, recording equipment would have to become portable. The engineers put their minds to the problem and recording equipment shrank from what Black describes as 'fairly large kitchen mangles' and 'laundry vans', to something that could fit into 'the back of a saloon car or in an aircraft'. The first portable recorder was born. It weighed about 40 pounds and could be carried by one man. The gate to outside broadcasting was open.

Features were made a separate department in 1945 with Gilliam, known from his social habits as 'Lorenzo the Magnificent', at its head. He continued to pump out original work: 'Radio must initiate or die.'

Between 1949 and 1956, all the works submitted for the Italia Prize, radio's most prestigious international award, were products of Gilliam's Features Department (and between 1947 and 1955 all Italia prizes won for *drama* went to features).

Black refers to a memorandum that Gilliam apparently wrote describing his view of the Features Department. Gilliam's aim was to have about twenty people who ranged from poets to tough journalists so that whatever the subject was, and wherever it was, it could be handled by Features.

In 1950 Gilliam edited a book of sixteen features. The following list gives an indication of the variety and richness of the sort of work undertaken by the Features Department: 'A Year I Remember: 1900' by Compton Mackenzie; 'The Vermeer Forgeries' by Michael Wharton; 'The Last Days of Hitler' by H. R. Trevor Roper; 'The End of Mussolini' by D. G. Bridson; 'India At First Sight' by Louis MacNeice; 'The Peltzer Murder' by John Gough; 'Black House into White' by David Thompson; 'The Man from Belsen' by Leonard Cottrell; 'British Justice' by Jennifer Wayne; 'New Judgement: Cardinal Manning' by Christopher Sykes; 'The Brain at Work', by Nesta Pain;

'The Undefeated: Gladys Aylward' by Alan Burgess; 'From Anzio to Burgundy' by Wynford Vaughan Thomas; 'W. B. Yeats: A Dublin Portrait' by W. R. Rogers; 'The Battle that Beat Japan', by Chester Wilmot and David Woodward.

As a sample of the way the features were edited into book form, here are representative extracts from the first feature, 'A Year I Remember: 1900', which contained reminiscences by Compton Mackenzie.

Compton Mackenzie, at seventeen, had been 'dreaming for a year' under the influence of poets such as Baudelaire, Rimbaud and Verlaine. He hoped, by going without sleep, to end up like one of the 'nervous wrecks in the verse of Maurice Rollinat'. He eventually hoped to look like a skeletal consumptive mademoiselle found in one of the poems.

Understandably, before this occurred, Mackenzie suffered a severe nervous breakdown, and was sent to recuperate at a Hydro in Bournemouth that was run by an ex-Coldstream Guards' doctor, who had bought a row of houses and knocked them into one building, adding a Turkish bath.

Among the clientele were Major Nugent, a retired Irish Hussar, 'from one of the novels of Charles Lever'; Surgeon McMorris, who practised his golf putting along the Brussels carpet, hitting the ball from one woven rose to the next; and Colonel Sartorius who had shot the biggest bison ever killed in India – a horn spread of forty-seven inches. The Colonel would regale the young Mackenzie with tales of army life.

> Yes, I served with Baker Pasha. Colonel Valentine Pasha of the 10th Hussars. He kissed a gal in a railway carriage, poor chap, and the Queen insisted on his being cashiered. Pity. Very gallant fellah. He got back in the British Army later on.

And would speak of:

> Tuke, in his blue-serge suit, red knitted tie and brown boots – a fashionable combination in 1900. He was the only man I ever met who had eaten human flesh. 'Of course, it was eaten unintentionally,' he explained ... 'It happened when I was trekking in South Africa; a Kaffir baby died and my boy put it in the soup!'
>
> McMorris was enormously interested. 'What did you do?'
>
> 'I felt a bit sick when he told me ... and thrashed him with a sjambok.'

'What did it taste like?'
'Quite good. In fact, it was because I told my boy how good it was he started to brag about putting the baby into it.'

Then there the were more prosaic residents of the Hydro who Mackenzie mentions in passing, one being a native of Manchester:

> When the relief of Mafeking was announced ... the Manchester man declared he was going out to celebrate ... Two young fellows named Finnigan, and I, promised to let him in ... he fell through the glass roof into the Turkish bath. Next day he was invited to leave the Hydro – much to McMorris's satisfaction.
> 'In my opinion, Sir, the doctor behaved with great dignity. Told him to find the kind of hotel, Sir, where a fellow like him would feel more at home. Do you know what that Manchester bounder had to say to me last Sunday?'
> 'I wouldn't put anything past the fellow.'
> 'He had the impudence to ask me, when I was putting along the corridor ... whether I wasn't afraid of upsetting the religious folk in this one-eyed place ... I said Golf is *my* religion ... and kindly do not stand on that hole into which I am putting.'
> 'I'll bet that silenced him.'
> 'It shut him up, Sir, like a clam.'

And later, while Mackenzie was on his recuperative travels by railway:

> Coming from Glasgow to London ... a dark man with a heavy moustache and earnest glittering eyes began to stare at me so uncomfortably that I began to have visions of another train murder.
> 'I've been looking at you,' he said in a strong Lancashire accent.
> 'I know you have.'
> 'And I've been watching your soul. Fluttering and fluttering round the carriage and now it's fluttered out of the window. You're an atheist.'
> 'I'm not.'
> 'Oh, yes, you are. I've just come back from Dr Torrey's great revival meetings in Glasgow, and I know what an atheist looks like. They've a special sort of expression in their eyes.'
> 'I tell you I'm not an atheist.'
> 'I've got a brother just like you,' he continued, taking no notice. 'He's an atheist too and lives in Wigan.'
> The train steamed into Preston and pulled up.

'Where are we?' said the Lancashire man. 'Preston? I'll tell you what I'll do, lad. I'll send a telegram to this brother of mine to meet us at the next station. Then you'll see what I mean ...'.

When the stranger went off I debated with myself whether to escape to another carriage; but I didn't like to embarrass him by vanishing. He returned highly pleased with himself.

'We'll see Fred waiting on the platform,' he announced. But when the train approached Wigan it showed no sign of slowing down.

'Eh, we're not going to stop! Never mind, lad!' He pulled me across to the carriage window. 'There's Fred. There's atheist. Can you see him, lad?'

There, sure enough, in the murk of the January evening was a solitary figure gazing with a puzzled expression at the train thundering past.

'Did you notice that queer atheist look in his eyes?'

'Well, it was rather dark,' I replied, apologetically.

'When we get in I'll send Fred another telegram to say I'm sorry we missed him. He's got a queer temper, has Fred, him being an atheist.'

After that we talked agreeably about secular matters until we reached Crewe.

Then followed the great period of features which saw works such as Dylan Thomas's *Under Milk Wood,* Louis MacNeice's *The Dark Tower* and Barry Bermange's 'Inventions'.

The decline of the Features Department began in 1959. Television was beginning to bite and features were expensive. Gilliam was asked to reduce the number of his producers. In 1964 Features ceased to exist as a separate entity. The producers were invited to split between Drama, Talks, Current Affairs and Light Entertainment. Gilliam, the last of the barons, was dying of cancer and succumbed that year. But something of the old spirit remained.

The writer Bernard Kops recalls meeting Gilliam in a corridor in Broadcasting House. 'Hello, My Boy, what can I do for you?' was the greeting. Bernard Kops replied he would like to write a feature on Masada. Gilliam nodded, to be informed that the feature would probably be best written if the writer designate went to Masada personally to view things in situ. Gilliam thought for a moment, then recommended a certain type of portable recorder: '[I]t's bright green, I'm afraid, but fortunately no bigger than a large suitcase.' He then said 'Off you go!'

As Bernard Kops was walking away Gilliam called after him asking how long he could expect the feature to be. 'Not more than three hours' he was assured.

Gilliam gave a final nod, then urbanely strolled away.

Since that time features have gradually changed and become separated off from works of dramatic fiction, now generally regarded as being the effective presentation of documentary material. Features are seen to deal with fact, drama with fiction.

If this is the case, our earlier dialogue extract from *Under Milk Wood* can hardly be thought of nowadays as a feature – unless in a very rarefied sense. The sense that it perhaps presents a poetically realised factual account of a small Welsh town and its inhabitants.

Yet because of complexity of definition, and the enormous variety of subject matter and the myriad ways of handling it, features seem sometimes to encompass talks, drama, current affairs and even contemporary hard news.

Features, because of the scope they offer, might, in many ways, be thought to be the natural expression of radio. What radio does best. Where the medium of sound can be used in its most creative, artistic and original way. Where music can be used to complement narration; where both can supplement dialogue; and where all three can be enhanced and heightened by the sound effects. Where, it might be argued, all artistic aural experiences can be fused together as a single entity and radio as a pure, original art form, can perhaps be said to begin.

What sort of material could we choose to give in a feature? Let us look at the figure of Faust.

Faust, in life, seems to have been a wandering conjurer who lived in Germany in the late fifteenth/early sixteenth century, and is a perennial figure in art. Suppose we decided to trace the history of 'Faust in Art' for a radio programme – from where could we draw our material?

Faust has been the subject of plays by Marlowe and Goethe; of an opera by Gounod; of a symphony by Liszt. He is mentioned in numerous poems – serious and comic. Here are some lines written by James Smith in the volume *Wit Restored* in 1658. The form is a verse letter from Smith to a friend describing the lengths to which he has to go in order to avoid his creditors and get a dinner (or 'commons') on tick:

> To mend my commons, clad in jerkin,
> On Friday last I rode to Berkin,
> Where lowring heavens with welcome sauced us
> As when the fiends were sent for Faustus.

Beginning with this example for a feature on Faust and travelling forward, we would need a narrator, actors, historians and psychologists/sociologists for the verbal sections of the work. Musical contributions could consist of everything from a single performer to a full symphony orchestra. What would we have in the end? We would have what has come to be known as the radio 'feature'. A set of facts and fancies as to how Faust, and the legend surrounding him, have been presented throughout the ages.

Features can go anywhere, cover any topic and are only bound by a writer reaching the limits of her or his imagination and research powers. They can be narrated in the first person, or as a series of facts for which there is documentary back-up.

Here is an extract copied from the broadcast original script of 'Singing the Fishing' by Ewan MacColl and Charles Parker – MacColl worked with Harding and Bridson in the early days.

'Singing the Fishing' is a classic early feature that traced the fortunes of the herring fishing industry from before the turn of the twentieth century until after the Second World War. Before we look at the orginal script, here is an extract from (1967) pre-programming versus reality:

> 'We had to adjust our ideas about seagoing', said a report from their teacher. 'Living inland, our knowledge of nautical matters is mostly derived from tatty television films ... We expect a storm, and to be shipwrecked; it surprises us to find a captain who is not insane or a dipsomaniac, and a mate who is not in the pay of a rival firm or foreign power. The absence of a beautiful stowaway puzzled us too.'

This was the reaction of a class of ten-year-olds watching a film of fishing on the Grand Banks. Here is how the MacColl/Parker original script looked:

AS BROADCAST SCRIPT

'Singing the Fishing'

by Ewan MacColl and Charles Parker

---

1. ANNOUNCER:	This is the BBC Home Service from the Midlands we present Sam Larner of Winterton
2. TR Sam:	
Ins 1	Up jumped the herring the king of the sea,
(Sings) 19″	Said he to the Skipper look under your lea, Singing windy old weather boys, Stormy old weather boys, When the wind blows we'll all go together.
3.	BANJO INTRO BEGINS
4. ANNOUNCER:	and Ronnie Balls of Yarmouth in 'Singing the Fishing', a tribute to the fishing communities of East Anglia and of the Moray Firth whose livelihood has been the herring.
5. TR R.Balls: Ins 1a	If you fish for the herring they rule your life, they swim at night, you've got to be out there waiting for them to swim.
6. EWAN:	With our nets and our gear we're faring
7. TR R.Balls Ins 2 11″	'Cos it's a wonder to you see; you pick one of these little fish up! And that's vibrant with life brrrr like that.
7A. EWAN:	On the wild and wasteful ocean
8. TR R.Balls: Ins 3 9″	The numbers! You realise that that's only one of millions and millions and millions ... when the little people swim up properly they really do it.
9. EWAN:	It's there on the deep y'e harvest and reap our bread
10. TR R.Balls: Ins 5 7″	There's no lazy men when herring are about.

1. EWAN:	As we hunt the bonnie shoals of herring.
2. TR R.Balls: Ins 6	When you're doing well and catching fish they talk to them all the time 'Come on, spin up my darlings, come on' and they absolutely cajole them into the net!
3.	BANJO UP AND SEGUE WITH CONCERTINA BEHIND TR INSERT 7

To make the first nine pages of this feature required an announcer, fisherman, banjo, concertina, chorus, gulls, diesel engine, guitar, propeller tail shaft effects from fishing boat, fiddle and song, 'The Shoals of Herring'. Just one way of structuring the myriad of approaches that is offered by the feature.

So, in an AIDS feature we might begin by speculating on the origin of AIDS ... then the first cases ... friends of those who have died ... music that has been written ... charity concerts, plays and films that have been dedicated to heightening public awareness ... celebrities who have participated in AIDS support events ... poetry that has been written ... the latest medical thinking ... attitudes adopted in various countries ... religious views, and so on.

A final point – research. It is no use becoming interested in the building of the Pyramids, or the paintings of Rembrandt, on Monday, and then deciding you are going to write a feature about your new interest on Tuesday. Material for documentary features needs to be extensively researched, and well assimilated, before putting pen to paper. Time must be allowed for shape and structure to come together in the mind of the writer. Remember, the more research you undertake, the more material you will have to throw away – and the more you throw away the better your feature will be – because what is left will be the heart.

Anniversaries are always worth considering in any genre of spoken radio – especially in features. Famous artists, or battles, or national events are generally looked upon favourably as they provide an incentive as to why a particular piece of work might be commissioned, rather than why it should not. The eternal task of convincing a producer that the glass is half full rather than half empty.

Exercises (3)

Choose a famous historical/mythical character who has generated works across a broad artistic and historical spectrum; or choose a historical event. A character might be that of the Devil or that of Christ. An event could be the fall of Troy, the sinking of the *Titanic* or the destruction of Pompeii. Investigate sources for a proposed feature (historical, artistic) and write out a rough proposal as to how you would put your feature together.

The international feature

These are very rare undertakings, the last major excursion into the field being the making of the dramatic feature 'Australia'.

A dramatic feature is perhaps best described as a feature which has a substantial proportion of its material cast in play format; with perhaps the addition of a narrator to link the dramatic material to researched historical fact.

'Australia' began as a joint undertaking between the BBC and ABC (Australian Broadcasting Corporation). Later ABC withdrew because it considered the series might be regarded as an unqualified British statement.

The series was conceived to celebrate the bi-centenary, in 1988, of the first convict fleet to Australia – the personnel from which provided the first permanent European settlement in Australia.

A secondary thread was to examine the effect this invasion had on the original inhabitants of Australia, the Aborigines, and to examine their present situation.

Finally, to give a treatment of the land itself, that great bounteous continent of which Douglas Jerrold said, 'Earth is here so kind, just tickle her with a hoe and she laughs with a harvest.' Although, of course, there is the darker side of 'the interior'; that place of deserts and wastes, with extremes of climate that reduced those who tried to live there into relaxing by drinking 'Fitzroy Cocktails' ... one of the ingredients of which was boot polish. And to attempting to eat the Galah bird. According to Alan Moorehead in *Cooper's Creek*, his graphic account of the epic of Burke and Wills, the way to cook the Galah is to boil it in an old leather boot until the boot is tender. Then to throw away the bird and eat the boot.

To give an idea of the scope of the series, and the work involved, here are selections from the original proposal. The series was researched by Mike Walker and Shaun MacLoughlin, written by Mike Walker and produced by Shaun MacLoughlin.

'Australia'
13 x 60′ features for Radio 4

1988 is the bi-centenary of the first convict fleet and the first permanent European settlement in Australia.

Since then the story of Australia has been closely interwoven with the history of the British Isles. For about the first hundred years we unloaded most of our problems – most of our criminal population – there ... Very few Britons do not have at least a distant relative living in Australia.

Australia is both one of the last great unpopulated land masses in the world and one of the most open societies ... And for a country of only 16 million souls it is proving very influential in business, in sport, and especially in the arts.

The series also emphasises the effect of the British invasion on the original inhabitants, the Aborigines, and examines their recent renaissance.

The series ... takes the form of quotations from a multiplicity of original source material and hundreds of interviews with living Australians, together with the songs, the wild life and actuality of Australia to-day.

EPISODE 1 IN THE DREAMING

The Aborigines: Australia's original inhabitants

Aborigines go back some 100,000 years. This episode demonstrates some remarkable resemblances between the geology and natural history of the continent and the stories – the creation myths, for example – of the Aborigines.

It also looks at the earliest theories about, and expeditions to, Australia by Greeks, Portuguese, Dutch, British and other outsiders, but from an Aboriginal point of view.

EPISODE 2 THE MOST VALUABLE ACQUISITION

The settlement at Sydney Cove: Governor Phillip and the birth of modern Australia: 1788–92

The impact of the continent on the first settlers and convicts who sailed in badly equipped ships 11,000 miles, nearly half way around the world. Captain Arthur Phillip, at 48, had been on half pay and without a ship for five years; he seemed an unlikely candidate to put in charge of the operation. But in spite of lack of co-operation from the British authorities, a desperate lack of communication, disease, near starvation, internal dissension and threatening Aborigines, he was to make a success of the first settlement.

EPISODE 3 ANARCHY AND AFTER

The struggle between the Rum Corps and the governors: 1793–1808

... This episode examines the early history of the Irish in Australia and the first circumnavigation of the continent.

EPISODE 4 A NEW BEGINNING

Governor Macquarie and the growth of the colony: 1808–22

... This episode examines the Australian colonies in all their aspects: social, artistic and sporting, as well as political.

EPISODE 5 THE LAST OF BRITAIN

Convicts and settlers: the journey to Australia in the nineteenth century

The letters and memoirs of immigrants show the pressures and hopes which drove people to cross half the world in search of a new life.

The episode starts with Edward Gibbon Wakefield who (whilst in prison for abducting an heiress) put forward the idea of assisted passages for free settlers. It recounts the last impressions of England, the tribulations and entertainments of the voyage – that could take anything up to six months – and the first impressions of Australia, 'a land like nowhere else on earth ... thousands of miles of empty desert to tropical rain forests; its animals are from an earlier stage of evolution and the variety and voracity of its flies are equalled only by the appetite of its spiders'.

EPISODE 6 DID EVER MAN SEE SUCH COUNTRY?

The explorers: 1828–62

... The episode recounts the epic – and myth creating – adventures of Captain Charles Sturt who navigated the Murray Darling, of Edward John Eyre who traversed the vast and arid Nullarbor

Desert, and of Robert Burke who, having been the first to cross the continent from South to North, on the return journey missed his companions by twenty-four hours and starved to death at Cooper's Creek.

EPISODE 7 THE LUCK OF THE LAND

Rough homesteads and far, unfamiliar places

Portrays the life of the early shearers ... the gold rush of the 1850s that led to the phenomenal growth and wealth of Melbourne. It recounts the story of Eureka Stockade, in which fourteen diggers and five British soldiers died beneath the diggers' defiant standard, the flag of the Southern Cross which many hail as the first attempt to establish a Republic on Australian soil.

EPISODE 8 A BETTER LIFE

A national life and a national hero: 1850–89

The move away from the Bush to the beginnings of to-day's urban society. An eight-hour day, introduced decades before Europe ... The telegraph, and Australia becomes the richest country in the world. The career of Ned Kelly ... bushranger and local hero who took over whole towns in Victoria. Captured ... he faced death with a laconic bravery that typifies all the dubious virtues and decent vices Australia still fears to lose under the weight of respectability.

EPISODE 9 THE DREAMER WAKES

The Aborigines' struggle to survive: 1788–1988

What happened to the Aborigines once the Whites arrived, destroying a way of life that had survived for tens of thousands of years. But not all tragedy ... the resistance of historical figures like Pemulwuy who fought the British so successfully that they tried to wipe his name from recorded history ... Modern Aborigines tell of their struggle for civil rights and to give Australia their spiritual, ecological and artistic values.

EPISODE 10 HOME WITHIN OUR OWN SHORE

Federation and war: 1890–1916

The pressure and reasons that led to Federation in 1900 ... The First World War ... the struggle and sacrifice of Gallipoli. The reconstruction of the killing and the courage and the national myth that grew (or was created) from the heroic defeat.

EPISODE 11 INTO THE PACIFIC

The boom and bust of the twenties and thirties when thousands of Australians tramped the red dirt roads looking for work

The Second World War and career of Robert Menzies, 'British to his bootstraps'; and John Curtin, an 'Australian' Australian who led his country through the war. The Pacific ... and hell of New Guinea, along the Kokoda trail, where Australia really came of age.

EPISODE 12 THE NEW WAVE

The boom years

The Menzies years ... Vietnam ... the growth of middle Australia, the 'beer and barb' and political and social scandals of the fifties when the Labour Party split and Menzies tried to outlaw communism.

EPISODE 13 LUCKY COUNTRY

After the boom. Multiculturalism and the search for new values

The Whitlam years. This richest episode of all with a kaleidoscope of sounds and images, opinions and music, public quarrels and private deals ... The vitality and tensions of a young country facing its third century.

Exercises (4)

Think of what might provide material for an international feature. Write a short (1,500 word) proposal on why you feel the subject you have chosen holds enough interest and scope as does 'Australia'.

Local radio and the local feature

One of the nicest things about features is that the making of them is open to all. Features can be an interesting and rewarding exercise for all students/writers, in that only very basic recording and editing equipment is required.

The programmes can be local, need no travel or specialised knowledge, and provide a writer with a beginning of a career. Local radio is, for many people, the way into radio itself – 'A Day in a Local Police Station', 'The Outpatients' Department of the Local Hospital, 'Visiting the Old', 'The Rehearsal of a Play by Local Amateurs'.

All these aspects of community life, if sensitively and wittily compiled, can make excellent entertainment for all involved on both sides of the microphone.

To give experience in production, a group of students might conduct a social survey on the effect that bus deregulation has had on the lives of people living in an outlying area or village; and then reshape the results to form a programme. By participating as producers a whole new aspect of radio would be understood.

Local radio also produces tapes of features of local interest – listening to which can prove extremely educational in all senses of the word, presenting multifaceted aspects of the lives and people, past and present, of an area. These tapes can be copied for educational uses; and so schools and colleges can build up a library of the sort of material that makes good local features, and from them can learn how that material has been assembled and co-ordinated. This in turn may give students ideas for assembling programmes of their own, for units of course or examination work. A student writer could ring a local station and enquire what material is available and thereby gain some idea of what material might be acceptable. A credit in local radio has eventually led to openings at network level.

An idea for a novel feature might be to produce an account of a famous local incident from the past as if it were taking place at the present moment; say a first balloon ascent. So we could have the announcer at the news desk bringing us up to date with events at the scene of the launch, and then commenting on the weather, and then the other local headlines, and then some of the latest discoveries that made it possible for men to ascend in balloons. Then return to the outside broadcaster, who has the latest developments from the field in which the balloon is moored, which has now just broken away/caught fire/suddenly been released with the mayor and all the civic dignitaries in the basket.

Translating events out of their own time is an interesting convention which really seems to work.

'Liverpool Characters' was a mini-series of four local features run by Radio Merseyside. It included interviews with 'characters' who had had jobs that had long since vanished. Programmes included 'Roll Out the Barrel' (memories of a pre-war itinerant pub piano player); 'Down There on a Visit' (a pre-war Irish District Nurse/Health Visitor in one of the worst slum areas of Liverpool); and 'Da Doo Ron Ron!' (a teddy-boy who still affected that way of life and the clothing of the 1950s and 1960s.

In these interviews the interviewer asked questions and recorded the answers given by the people concerned. The interviewer edited out the questions and formed the answers given by the interviewees into monologues. The interview was then broadcast, read by a professional actor or member of the station staff.

Here is the interview with the Health Visitor. The Matron of Guy's Hospital, writing in the *Guy's Hospital Nursing Guide* in 1923, states, 'the object of District Nursing may be said to be "Nursing the patients and nursing the homes"' – a precept echoed in the following.

'Down There on a Visit'

> When I first came to Liverpool I came right off the boat and went straight to work at Walton Hospital. Long hours – unbelievable by today's standards. Half a day off a week if you were lucky – none at all if there was work to catch up on.
>
> I got used to that. One thing I never got used to was the noise. I was a country girl who had never been to a town before – not even Dublin. I never did get used to the noise – even now it makes me uneasy. Those days, the trams going past the hospital would keep me awake half the night.
>
> But, of course, trams were what we used to travel about on. And all the drivers knew us. When our finals were coming up we'd all go down to St Ann's by tram to make a novena to the Blessed Virgin. Waves of us in our capes and head-dresses. 'Exams coming up again girls?' the driver would shout as he roared the tram round the curves until we screamed.
>
> You could go anywhere in your nurse's uniform in Liverpool in those days. Anywhere at all without a moment's fear.
>
> After my finals I did midwifery and became a District Health Visitor. Mainly down Scotland Road, Stanley Road, Reading Street. Reading Street was unbelievable – landings of tenements, more people than the Galway Races, and crammed on top of one another

like the Black Hole of Calcutta. It was heartbreaking. I had one old lady, a diabetic. She lived in one room with a chair, a bed and a huge kitchen range. She'd light the fire herself every morning, the ashes were everywhere. She had to go along the landing to the toilet. There was one window in her room which looked out on to a brick wall about a foot away that was covered in soot. They were all coal fires, you see …

One of the rarest sights would be a mother pushing a pram with twins. There would be that many people want to look at them on the road she would hardly be able to get the pram along. For what woman, in those days, could feed two, and one was always stronger than the other. The mother could hardly feed, anyway, and National Health food they were giving them those days was bad … something was wrong with it, anyway. I think it was eventually withdrawn.

Gastro-enteritis was rife. The only way of sterilising anything was on the stove in a pan of boiling water … or put our instruments in the oven on a tray. Often the people had no money for the gas … Unofficially, we were allowed a few coppers for this …

I never, in the whole of my career, saw a man change a nappy. Some of them weren't bad souls … but with others, those who had work, it would be pay night on the docks and then the pub, where it would all go on drink or playing dice. The poor women would be trying to put a meal together on nothing for a family of maybe six or seven. Fried cow's udder … anything that was cheap … anything at all … I even had cases of rickets when I started.

The units were very tightly knit. Gran was always no more than a few doors away and one of the family. Otherwise, there was only the Parish Priest to turn to for help. No social workers. The Parish Priest was often a good man but those women had problems a man like that couldn't begin to understand – couldn't begin to deal with. Besides, some parishes offered a cash prize for the biggest family. What could you do? Only once I came across a case of illegitimacy. At least a case where the girl who'd had her baby stayed in the district. Her family were wonderful. She couldn't have done it otherwise. She would have been out on the street. No money. No help. There were no back-up services then. She would have been forgotten. Forced to move quietly away to God knows what. The codes down there were very strict … No one ever really got to know anything … but our uniform was always respected …

All the houses were furnished the same. A table. Two or three straight hard-backed chairs and an old low sofa. These are not the poorest people I'm talking about ...

You became inured after a time, but some things got through no matter how hard you tried. One poor girl had had ten kiddies. You couldn't get pregnant mothers into hospital, though, unless there were complications. All straight births were at home. So she'd had ten at home and it was killing her. This time she was in danger of losing the baby and so we got her in. The surgeon, I'll never forget him, said, 'Ethics or not, I'll make sure she has no more.' And he did.

I had an interest in a family then. I used to visit them quite often. The eldest girl was twelve. She'd never been anywhere – anywhere in her life.

Then there was this parish outing and she was invited on it. Her mother, I don't know how, found her sixpence spending money.

I was round that day – and the outing was due home about tea-time. So we all waited, mother, children, to see what she'd bought with her sixpence. She came in and handed her mother a parcel. It was a brass gong. She'd spent everything on a gift for her mother. Her mother looked at the gong, and the roomful of children, and at the battered bits of furniture. 'Now we'll be able to ring for dinner,' she said. For the first time for a long time I went home and cried that night ...

There's a special place in heaven for all mothers, especially those who brought up families down there ...

The above recalls the remark quoted in the programme 'New Judgement: Cardinal Manning', by Christopher Sykes, in Gilliam's *BBC Features*. Manning, a harsh authoritarian in old age, who inspired dread and was known as 'The Marble Arch', would always rise in the middle of the night to bail out a drunkard, or attend the poor or sick in the East End. 'Give all yourself to London', he wrote. 'No one knows the depths of suffering of the women save the doctor and the priest.'

The Health Visitor feature, dealing with an immediately recognisable and sympathetic character, sits well on local radio; identifying an area and a philosophy. Providing a nugget of local history and giving the local writer a chance to find a voice. Contact your local station. Discuss possible ideas which may be open to submissions.

In the 'Liverpool Characters' series, a decision was taken not to describe the people involved, unless the description was necessary to lend something to the subject of the broadcast.

In the teddy-boy broadcast, for instance, his midnight-blue suit, string tie, brothel-creeper shoes, thickly Vaselined hair, and fists with 'kill' and 'cure' tattoos on the knuckles were mentioned, as it was felt these things gave a more rounded view of his lifestyle and aspirations.

The decision was reached because radio is the one arm of the media which gives people a chance to build up their own pictures of the subjects. In some ways, we will never see the great Dickens characters for ourselves. The drawings of Cruikshank, of Hablot Browne and others have done that work for us. We have a unified Dickens gallery – Fagin will always be the Fagin of Cruikshank – the Fagin of the thieves' kitchen and the condemned cell; no one who has seen these illustrations will ever picture him in any other way.

Exercises (5)

1. At the time of her interview the Health Visitor lived in a council house in the suburbs of Liverpool with patio doors looking on to a garden. The interview was carried out in the early 1970s – the Health Visitor was seventy-six at the time. As a radio piece of about 1,200 words, describe how you think the Health Visitor looked, was dressed, how the room was furnished and how she behaved.
2. Choose a famous/colourful local figure that you know personally or about whom you have heard. Try to establish contact with a view to carrying out an interview on the same lines. Take along a cassette and tape the interview. Write up the interview for broadcasting on local/college radio. (About 750 words will produce five minutes' broadcasting time.)
3. Compose an interview for local radio between yourself and any great figure from the past in which you question him or her closely about their lives and actions.

Local features for the disabled

Local radio can also play a great part in helping the disabled reach a wider public and each other on matters as diverse as, say, cooking and holidays – two of many areas where disabled groups may be able to pass on tips or hard information to help those in similar situations. A major network programme that most people will have heard of and which serves its group well and topically is, of course, Radio 4's 'In Touch'.

Professional broadcasters at all levels are always interested in sharp, well-informed, interesting ideas from voluntary groups that can be turned into informative and lively additions to a station's output.

By phoning your local station, either BBC or commercial, you will be able to find out who produces the sort of programme in which you are interested, and perhaps how to go about, through this contact, advertising your own group.

Remember, local radio is just that. Matters of local interest for local people. Find out what is required in the way of material as well as trying to think up interesting ideas of your own.

Is there anywhere that doesn't have radio where radio might prove a community boon? The beginnings of radio in hospital are instructive. Philip Inman, sometime administrator of Charing Cross Hospital in the 1920s and 30s, writes of walking the wards with the Matron, and asking what she thought was 'the greatest force contributive to the happiness of patients since you entered the hospital world?' She touched a pair of headphones over a bed.

In his biography *Oil and Wine*, Inman explains how individual headsets for patients were made possible.

The *Daily News* of 23 December 1925 carried an article by its Managing Director, Mr John Hugh Jones. The gist of this article was that, in talking to Philip Inman the previous year, Mr Jones had discovered that wireless had not been introduced to hospitals because it required a communal loudspeaker that was 'a bigger nuisance than blessing'. During that conversation, 'the idea of equipping every hospital bed in London with head-phones was first conceived'.

Jones went to see Reith at Savoy Hill for his support, and 'thanks to the generosity of *Daily News* readers and the superhuman efforts of John Hugh Jones, within a few months thirty-four thousand pounds was subscribed and 15,781 beds in 122 hospitals were equipped with earphones ... lighthouses and lightships ... and I believe some of the Borstal institutions were also provided with apparatus'.

As can be surmised from the variety of programmes mentioned in this section, each feature tends to dictate its own approach by virtue of what material is available, how difficult it is to bring that material together, and the final shape that the writer/producer decides upon for the completed work. The process of making features can therefore be both endless and endlessly fascinating.

To sum up. The making of features, and listening to features, fulfils an important part in the growth of both the individual and the nation. Features impose a shape upon, interpret and reinterpret people and events, and re-focus them on the present-day world around us. They are a way of structuring the past to serve as a lesson for the present. Drama releases and stimulates the imagination and should instruct us morally – a well-made feature should help us to attempt to pass on that morality to the world in which we move as individuals.

And then we have poetry and poets – which simply defy analysis.

8 Verse ... and worse

Poetry presents the thing in order to convey the feeling. It should be precise about the thing and reticent about the feeling, for as soon as the mind connects and responds to the thing the feeling shows in the words ... If the poet presents directly feelings that overwhelm him, and keeps nothing back ... he stirs us superficially.

Wei Tai (11th century)
Trans. A. C. Graham

liars by profession

David Hume

Poets – excepting those in paid lackeydom to the State – have always excited unease. Seen as no respecters of the four cornerstones of civilisation – marriage, mortgage, teabags and television – poets are understood to enjoy a life of total revolt and unceasing pleasure. Free love, free drinks, free verse – and all without any sort of visible employment or source of identifiable income.

They have drawn upon themselves and their writings contempt and contumely from almost all circles. The mathematician Isaac Newton (1642–1727) referred to poetry as a 'kind of ingenious nonsense'. They have had more vituperation poured over their collective heads than any other species of writer. At the same time, the few great practitioners of the art have received unqualified universal praise.

Shakespeare is a good case of the opposing views that can be taken of poets and their work. Tolstoy assesses Shakespeare's output as 'A heap of dung', echoing Voltaire's 'A great dunghill' – while neither George II ('a bombast fellow') nor George III claimed to be able to read him, and Pepys regarded him as a bore.

Against this is Carlyle's likening of him to a 'celestial Lightship', while Frank Harris showed how far idolatry can go by saying that although, unlike his friend Oscar Wilde, he knew nothing about homosexuality, if Shakespeare asked him he 'would have to submit'. Harris's own lasting contribution to Shakespeare scholarship has to be his remark that Macbeth was 'Hamlet in a kilt'.

Shakespeare was a cautious practitioner who put any subversive remarks he had to make into the mouths of his fools, eccentrics and mad people – differing only from today's cautious practitioners in that these latter are too frightened to make any subversive remarks at all.

In general, Shakespeare seems simply another of those who tacitly agree to take the money and keep their mouths shut on what they really know is going on all around. He is great rambling garden, whose very weeds can be carefully cultivated to sprout easy careers and reputations. Some of the poetry, the 'verbal music', is among the most beautiful ever written:

> Why didst thou promise such a beauteous day,
> And make me travel forth alone without my cloak,
> To let base clouds o'ertake me in my way,
> Hiding thy brav'ry in their rotten smoke?
> 'Tis not enough that through the clouds thou break
> To dry the rain on my storm-beaten face
> For no man well of such a salve can speak
> That heals the wound, and cures not the disgrace ...
>
> Shakespeare; Sonnets, 34

If the true unspoken wish of the bourgeoisie is the death of the artist (suitably drink sodden and disease ridden), the path to Parnassus is well strewn with the corpses of versifiers; a species that deliberately seems to bite off more than it can chew for the sole pleasure of spitting it back into the face of society.

As a caricature portrait of a poet's usual surroundings and approach to life, Oliver Goldsmith (1728–74) left a short sketch that seems to cover the main points – one full of readily understood and mindvisible concepts. Goldsmith sets up Scroggen's lodgings across the way from the Red Lion, among 'the drabs and bloods of Drury Lane', then

> There, in a lonely room, from bailiffs snug,
> The muse found Scroggen stretched beneath a rug:
> A window, patched with paper, lent a ray,

That dimly shew'd the state in which he lay;
The sanded floor that grits beneath the tread;
The humid wall with paltry pictures spread ...

Goldsmith

Goldsmith on poet Scroggen, and writing from experience. Boswell (1740–95), in his *Life of Johnson*, tells how Johnson (1709–84) had once to go to Goldsmith's lodging to rescue Goldsmith from his landlady, who had arrested him for 'rent owing'.

'Scroggen' would read well on radio because it has structure, and is strong in controlled and accurate imagery – 'stretched beneath a rug', 'a window, patched with paper', 'sanded floor'. As recognisable and relevant now as in the eighteenth century, and therefore immediately available to listeners. The extract also has an oral cast to the writing, inasmuch as it is written in iambic pentameters – a perceived natural mode of ordinary speech. This allows the overall flow and thrust of a piece to be immediately grasped:

'Today/ I went /to see/ a foot/ball match.'
'She asked/ if he/ would go/ with her/ to town.'
'The mot/orways/ are full/ of lun/atics.'
'Men call/ us birds/ because/ we pick/ up worms.'

More difficult to assimilate and readily understand in the one hearing that radio allows, would be the lines written by Byron (1788–1824) on another poet, Coleridge (1772–1834):

Shall gentle Coleridge pass unnoticed here?
To turgid ode and tumid stanza dear?
Though themes of innocence amuse him best,
Yet still obscurity's a welcome guest.
If inspiration should her aid refuse
To him who takes a pixy for a muse,
Yet none in lofty numbers can surpass
The bard who soars to elegise an ass;
So well the subject suits his noble mind,
He brays, the laureat of the long-ear'd kind.

Byron

This, on radio, would not really work. 'To turgid ode and tumid stanza dear?' gives immediate problems as regards mindvisibility or anything else. There is little in the extract that gives simple ideas or concepts. The word 'pixy' gives an image; to take a 'pixy for a muse' keeps the sense, but means taking a pixie dressed in the clothing of one of the Greek muses, and by that time the extract has moved on, and the listener is floundering with 'The bard who soars to elegise an ass'.

While Goldsmith has chosen to expose the universal concept of the 'struggling artist', Byron is launching one of his many personal attacks. Attacks which need an understanding of four things: Byron himself; his life and the times in which he lived; the classical tradition; and the personality of the subject of the poem – in this case, Coleridge.

To understand Byron himself needs no more than the anecdote concerning his answer to his tutor as to why Byron was keeping a bear in his rooms at Cambridge – that he was considering entering it for a fellowship. His times can be understood, as can ours, by the fact that Byron claims he awoke next morning and found himself famous (after the publication of 'Childe Harold', 1812) and, like many others before, then and since, began to believe his publicity. The classical tradition is the history of English life and education – male orientated and dominated, with envy and ignorance well to the fore, and the chastity belts, and chained books and minds, just out of sight inside the porter's lodge. The target at which Byron is aiming, Coleridge, can be judged from the attention he has received from many hands and pens. These range from Hazlitt's (1778–1830) assertion that Coleridge swam on empty bladders in a sea without shore or soundings; to Virginia Woolf's (1882–1941) assessment which begins, 'Coleridge the innumerable, the mutable, the atmospheric'; to T. S. Eliot's (1888–1965) observation that, 'Coleridge was one of those unhappy persons … of whom one might say, that if they had not been poets, they might have made something of their lives, might even have had a career.'

A similar case is John Wilmot, the second Earl of Rochester (1647–80), and John Dryden (1631–1700) discussing a third poet, Thomas Shadwell (1642?–92).

Dryden, in his poem 'Mac Flecknoe', has Richard Flecknoe (?–1678), an Irish poet, discussing who will inherit his crown of dullness. He fixes on a son attributed to him by Dryden, the poet Shadwell, who then becomes 'Mac'(son of) Flecknoe, and thus gives the piece its title. Dryden, speaking through the mouth of Flecknoe, writes:

Shadwell alone my perfect image bears,
Mature in dulness from his tender years;
Shadwell alone of all my Sons is he
Who stands confirmed in full stupidity.
The rest to some faint meaning make pretence,
But Shadwell never deviates into sense.

Dryden

Clever, and understandable, but paints no real radio pictures, as the lines consist primarily of abstractions with no common visual concepts and simple ideas.

Rochester, friend, then enemy, of Dryden, and cautious admirer of Shadwell, writes:

Of all our modern wits, none seem to me
Once to have touched upon true comedy
But hasty Shadwell and slow Wycherley.
Shadwell's unfinished works do yet impart
Great proofs of force of nature, none of art:
With just, bold strokes he dashes here and there,
Showing great mastery, with little care,
And scorns to varnish his good touches o'er
To make the fools and women praise 'em more.

Rochester

And in Rochester, although we seem to gain a clearer picture of Shadwell's abilities, there are still not the absolute mindvisible images that we find in the Goldsmith; although the painting images, 'bold strokes', 'varnish', give us something of the visible platform that radio requires.

What is in Rochester's writing is a sense of honesty. And Rochester is correct. Shadwell's work is all over the place, but in his plays there is a great sense of truth and humanity and the understanding of life – far more than in Dryden.

For over three hundred years Shadwell's reputation has been destroyed by the attack mounted by Dryden in 'Mac Flecknoe'. The ferocity of Dryden's attack has received much comment, but not the reason it was launched.

Dryden and Shadwell were two literary friends who then became enemies – with the attendant vaporings and hysteria this produces. But Dryden's attack is at once deeper and subtler than usual.

Dryden, on the surface, mentally and technically, was afraid of no other writer – mocking Milton that Milton would have written *Paradise Lost* again in rhyming couplets – if he could. But Dryden was afraid of Shadwell – for Shadwell's writing has the ring of truth – which can neither be studied for, nor bought. Shadwell knew and understood ordinary people and what moves them – the pleasures, vices, and general attrition of daily living. George Saintsbury (1845–1933) states: 'He [Shadwell] had a much greater command of comic incident and situation, and a much sharper eye for a play, than Dryden himself ... much more direct power of dramatic observation of actual life.'

Academically, however, it is probably safer to be wrong endorsing Dryden, than to attempt an individual judgement on the texts.

In this extract from a radio script adapted from Shadwell's *The Virtuoso*, Sir Nicholas Gimcrack, 'The Virtuoso' of the title, had decided to learn to swim:

SCENE 8	OUTSIDE SIR NICHOLAS'S LABORATORY
1. LADY GIMCRACK:	The door to my husband's laboratory. He is inside learning to swim.
2. BRUCE:	To swim? What water is inside the house, Madam?
3. LADY G:	Water, Sir? Sir Nicholas does not swim in water.
4. LONGVIL:	Then where, Madam?
5. LADY G:	Why on the table in his laboratory. His method? He has a frog in a bowl of liquid on the floor. His Swimming Master, and Sir Formal Trifle wait by. The frog has a thread tied round its middle. Sir Nicholas lies belly down on the table holding the thread in his mouth to support the frog. Then, as the frog strikes out – so does my husband copy it.
6. LONGVIL:	I wonder the University have not snapped at him.
7. LADY G:	They refused him, Sir. They envied him ...

Fast, mindvisible writing. Add to this ability the fact that Shadwell was accepted by Rochester and his circle of 'court wits'. And named by Rochester as being so – and it becomes apparent how Dryden's spite was engaged as this circle was one to which Dryden fruitlessly craved entry.

Rochester's own work has very visual radiophonic lines. It has been quietly unavailable for the past three hundred years, except to those who have been understood to have the high moral rectitude and scholarly equanimity necessary to appreciate verses such as the following:

1. NELL [GWYN]: When to the King I bid good morrow
With tongue in mouth and hand on tarse,*
Portsmouth may rend her cunt for sorrow,
And Mazarin may kiss mine arse.

2. PORTSMOUTH: When England's monarch's on my belly
With prick in cunt, though double crammed,
Fart of mine arse for small whore Nelly,
And great whore Mazarin be damned.

Rochester

Rochester's longer satires, too, often have a very narrative radio cast. In his masterpiece, 'A Letter From Artemisia in the Town to Chloe in the Country', he describes a country wife arriving in London, getting rid of her husband, then proceeding to visit a friend. After catching up on gossip, and airing her opinions in a non-stop commentary,

Here forced to cease
Through want of breath, not will to hold her peace,
She to the window runs, where she had spied
Her much esteemed dear friend, the monkey, tied.
With forty smiles, as many antic bows,
As if't been the mistress of the house,
The dirty, chattering monster she embraced,
And made it this fine tender speech at last:
'Kiss me, thou curious miniature of man!
How odd thou art! How pretty! How japan!
Oh, I could live and die with thee!' Then on
For half an hour in compliment she run ...

Rochester

Rochester, deeply loved and hated by many men and women, received a telling epitaph in having his wit referred to as 'a torch ...

---

* Penis; Nell Gwyn, Louise de Keroualle, Duchess of Portsmouth and Hortense Mancini, Duchess Mazarin, were all mistreses of Charles II, and simultaneously competing for pole position on the royal circuit.

to light himself to hell'. Which only just fails as brilliant radio – the listener being unable to conjure the mindvisible image of a flaming bundle of wit being held above someone's head. On the page it is outstanding.

Peter Eckersley seems to have been the first person to broadcast verse. In his book *The Power Behind the Microphone*, he relates some of the impromptu doggerel he was prone to recite over the air:

> Four and twenty B valves, standing on a shelf,
> Ash [bridge] couldn't find one so I had to go myself.
> When the circuit opened, the phones began to sing,
> Don't you think that I was right to smash the beastly thing?
>
> Eckersley

Radio as a medium was celebrated in poetry in 1925. Leslie Baily, describing the new high-powered transmitter 5xx being opened at Daventry in his *Scrapbook of the 20s*, tells how it was advertised as the most powerful transmitter in the world and that it would reach 23 million listeners – for the first time bringing the spoken word to those outside the major cities. Part of this spoken word was to be a poem by Alfred Noyes, written especially to be broadcast on the opening night:

> You shall hear their lightest tone
> Stealing through your walls of stone ...
> 'Til your loneliest valleys hear
> The far cathedral's whispered prayer ...
> Daventry calling ... Daventry calling ...
> Daventry calling ... Dark and still.
> The tree of memory stands like a sentry ...
> Over the graves on the silent hill ...
>
> Noyes

Daventry's aerials were above Borough Hill on the site of a prehistoric military camp.

Punch approached the new innovation in its own fashion:

> Gaunt poles that rise into the upper air,
> High o'er my clumps of holly and genista,
> How my whole soul revolts to see thee there,
> Bisecting what was once a high-class vista.
> Not – oh, believe me – not from whim or choice
> Would I maintain an object so appalling,

> But lo! From thy slim apex comes the Voice
> That nightly tells me 'This is London calling' ...
>
> 'Algol', *Punch*, 1926
> Quoted in Briggs (1941), quoting Hibberd

While the apparatus itself, that bakelite Pandora's box, received a nod from a Teutonic muse in Bertolt Brecht's poem 'To My Small Radio Receiver', a work written as Brecht was fleeing Germany in 1940:

> You little box I carried when I fled,
> Your inner light protected carefully,
> Through house, and street, and train, and ship, and shed,
> That my still distant foe might speak to me ...

But the true prophet of radio poetry was George Orwell. Towards the end of the Second World War, Orwell was involved in a literary programme broadcast in India for the BBC; a programme in which 'a good deal of verse' was transmitted. In his essay 'Poetry and the Microphone', Orwell reviews the programme itself and examines the possibilities for poetry on the radio.

He begins by detailing the thinking behind the programme, and makes the point that those involved were essentially broadcasting to Indian university students, a hostile audience unapproachable by 'anything that could be described as British propaganda'. At a time when there was no television, he states that it was known in advance that they could not hope for more than a few thousand listeners at most – and so 'could afford to be a bit more "highbrow" than is generally possible on the air'.

Orwell and his colleagues decided that the programme would adopt the format of a monthly literary magazine, with each 'issue' being devoted to a single theme. One theme was war, to which W. H. Auden (1907–73) contributed 'September 1941'.

(Of more interest, perhaps, is Auden's vignette of Reith in a poem entitled 'A Happy New Year':

> Soon I saw Mosley, the descendant of Pitt,
>   Standing a boxer a small port wine.
> Rothermere and Beaverbrook were eating bananas,
>   Sir Owen Seaman was teaching some swine
>   To sneer at a char with a washing line,

And standing aloof like a blasted tree
Was the gaunt Director of the B.B.C.

Auden

The above poem is interesting, in that, although full of simple mindvisible concepts, because of lack of immediate causal continuity, it does not work absolutely as radio.

Orwell (1943) tells us that in the studio there would be a general discussion by the 'editorial staff' of the magazine, and then a poem would be read – preferably by the author. Orwell felt this gave the poet a new relationship with his or her work.

This point of view is echoed by Alec Reid, editor/producer of Radio 4's 'Time For Verse' for fifteen years. Alec Reid, in interview, feels that poets are better at reading their own work than actors, because even some of the best actors, when faced with reading a poem, ask primarily not 'What is this about?' but 'Who am I supposed to be?' If they cannot obtain an answer they sometimes fall back on technique, 'inflect each word differently, and the line of the poem is lost'.

Another interesting point, made by Orwell in describing his programme's format, was that the poems often had music before and after. Orwell thought this helped to isolate and insulate the poem from the rest of the programme.

Orwell continues that he felt the programmes were of no great value in themselves, but aroused the possibilities of radio as a means of popularising poetry. And that reading poetry over the radio guarantees the right audience and does away with stage fright and embarrassment suffered by some readers at what Orwell describes as 'that grisly thing, a "poetry reading"'. His view was that poetry read in the studio is going out to people to whom poetry means something, and that broadcasting is the only way that the poet can be brought into a situation where 'reading verse aloud seems a natural un-embarrassing thing'.

In a fit of Orwellian gloom, he adds that he sees little hope for poetry on radio, quoting Arnold Bennett's (1867–1931) remark that 'in English-speaking countries, the word "poetry" would disperse a crowd quicker than a fire hose'. Orwell feels that poetry on the radio is disliked because it is associated with unintelligibility and intellectual pretentiousness. He speaks of T. S. Eliot's suggestion that poetry might be brought back into the consciousness of ordinary people through the medium of the music hall, and adds that perhaps

Eliot's 'Sweeney Agonistes' 'would in fact be conceivable as a music-hall turn'.

Orwell says he believes that radio could be a more hopeful medium for poetry, but then, falling into his four legs good, two legs bad mode, thinks there is little chance of this happening. This is because people are unable to imagine the radio being used for the dissemination of anything except tripe. 'Roaring dictators or genteel throaty voices ... the muse in striped trousers.' He adds that it is harder to capture five minutes on the air in which to broadcast a poem, than twelve hours in which to disseminate 'lying propaganda, tinned music, stale jokes, faked "discussions" or what-have-you'. A view endorsing Eckersley, who wrote in 1941:

> Self satisfaction oozes between salacious jokes, hardly tolerable in a music hall, while views are given in prosy essays read in the high-pitched whine of emasculated liberalism. Issues are dodged which even a commercial press has no fear to expose. The B.B.C. stands, either remote or dictatorial or pawky and condescending, oblivious of opportunity, hopeless in its timidity.

Reith, eschewing for a moment the BBC timidity of which Eckersley spoke, ruined Eckersley's career by forcing him to resign when Eckersley was cited in a divorce case. As an obituary upon himself, Eckersley suggested, 'He had ideas, we blocked them.'

The issue of the 'BBC accent', which engaged, and seemed to enrage, both Eckersley and Orwell, has rolled on down the years. But Buckingham Palace was never the only Job Creation Scheme for those tottering around upon, or near the top of, the termite mound.

This 'BBC' accent must not be confused with the 'Oxford' accent, which is thought to have developed from the affected and artificial locutions and vocal peculiarities used by Swinburne when he was, as he was as often as possible, raving drunk.

Ford Madox Ford tells how his grandfather, Madox Brown, would provide Swinburne, and other poets and dipsomaniacs, with labels containing the address of Brown's house in Fitzrovia. When they were found stumbling about the streets they could be brought back quickly by cab drivers or the police. Swinburne was inevitably carried up to the top floor and put into a bathtub from which he could not roll out and injure himself.

Orwell's overall feeling seems to have been that though the

loudspeaker is the enemy of the creative writer, there are still possibilities in radio to bring back poetry to the common people through the power of the microphone. People might seem on the surface to object to poetry, but that if rhyme and metre were really disliked, neither songs nor radio verse nor 'dirty limericks' would be popular.

And so it has proved for, with all Orwell's fears, poetry has always been given a place in the schedules. In 1950 a committee was formed to organise a series of poetry readings for the Third Programme, and since then there has seldom been a week when some sort of programme reviewing, requesting or reciting verse has not been broadcast. The contents range from the present rhyming-dictionary bland, to Kenneth Rexroth's 1950s feature 'Beat Poetry – and After', which generated the question of the moment – whether Allen Ginsberg's line, 'America go fuck yourself with your Atom bomb', could be broadcast. Eventually, after being passed ever upwards across the slippery rungs of the ladder of bladder, the Director General gave the green light. We do not know whether this decision was made on literary merit. The broadcaster D. G. Bridson observed that a man who was later arrested on Brighton Promenade for declaiming the same line in public might well have called the Director General in his defence.

Here are two samples of the sort of music-hall recitation/verse that Orwell probably felt worked well on radio:

Marriot Edgar 'King 'Arold at 'Astings'

I'll tell of the Battle of 'Astings,
As 'appened in days long gone by,
When Duke William became King of England
And 'Arold got shot in the eye.

It were this way – one day in October,
The Duke, who were always a toff,
'Avin' no battles on at the moment,
'Ad given the lads a day off.

They'd all taken boats to go fishin',
When some chap said in Conqueror's ear,
'Let's go and put breeze up the Saxons,'
Said William, ''Ere, that's an idea.'

Then, turnin' around to his soldiers,
'E lifted 'is big Norman voice,
Shoutin' ''Ands up who's comin' to England'
(That were swank, as they 'adn't no choice.)

They started away about tea-time,
The sea was so calm and so still,
And at quarter to ten the next mornin'
They arrived at a place called Bex'ill.

King 'Arold came up as they landed,
'Is face full of venom and 'ate;
'E said, 'If you've come for t'regatta,
You've got 'ere just six weeks too late.'

At that William rose, cool but 'aughty,
And said, 'Give us none of your cheek.
You'd best 'ave your throne reupholstered,
I'll be wantin' to use it next week.'

When 'Arold 'eard this 'ere defiance,
With rage 'e turned purple and blue,
And shouted some rude words in Saxon,
To which William answered, 'And you!'

'Twere a beautiful day for a battle,
The Normans set off with a will,
And when both sides was duly assembled
They tossed for the top of the 'ill.

King 'Arold 'e won the advantage,
On the 'ill-top 'e took up 'is stand,
With 'is knaves and 'is cads all round 'im,
On 'is horse, with 'is 'awk in 'is 'and.

The Normans 'ad nowt in their favour,
Their chance of a vict'ry seemed small,
For the slope of the field were against 'em,
And the wind in their faces an' all.

The kick-off were sharp at two-thirty;
As soon as the whistle 'ad went,
Both sides started bangin' each other,
Till the swine-'erds could 'ear 'em in Kent.

The Saxons 'ad best line of forwards,
Well armed, both with buckler and sword,
But the Normans 'ad best combination,
And when 'alf-time came neither 'ad scored.

So the Duke called 'is cohorts together,
And said, 'Let's pretend that we're beat;
Once we get Saxons down on the level
We'll cut off their means of retreat.'

So they ran, and the Saxons ran after,
Just exactly as William 'ad planned,
Leavin' 'Arold alone on the 'ill-top,
On 'is 'orse, with 'is 'awk in 'is 'and.

When Conqueror saw what 'ad 'appened,
A bow and an arrer 'e drew,
'E went right up to 'Arold an' shot 'im;
'E were off-side – but what could they do?

The Normans turned round in a fury,
And gave back both parry and thrust,
Till the fight were all over bar shoutin'
And you couldn't see Saxons for dust.

And after the battle were over,
They found 'Arold so stately and grand,
Sittin' there with an eye full of arrer,
On 'is 'orse, with 'is 'awk in 'is 'and.

J. Milton Hayes 'The Green Eye of the Little Yellow God'

There's a one-eyed yellow idol to the north of Khatmandu,
There's a little marble cross beneath the town,
And a broken-hearted woman guards the grave of 'Mad Carew',
While the Yellow God forever gazes down.

He was known as 'Mad Carew' by the subs at Khatmandu
He was hotter than they felt inclined to tell;
But for all his foolish pranks, he was worshipped in the ranks
And the Colonel's daughter smiled on him as well.

He had loved her all along, with the passion of the strong,
And the fact that she loved him was plain to all.

She was nearly twenty-one, and arrangements had begun
To celebrate her birthday with a ball.

He wrote to ask what present she would like from 'Mad Carew',
They met next day as he dismissed a squad,
And jestingly she answered him that nothing else would do
But the green eye of the little Yellow God.

On the night before the dance, 'Mad Carew' seemed in a trance,
And they chafed him as they puffed on their cigars;
But for once he failed to smile, and he sat alone a while;
Then went out into the night beneath the stars.

He returned before the dawn, with his shirt and tunic torn,
And a gash across his temple dripping red;
He was patched up right away, and slept throughout the day
While the Colonel's daughter watched beside his bed.

He woke at last and asked if they could send his tunic through;
She brought it, and he thanked her with a nod;
He bade her search the pocket saying, 'That's from "Mad
  Carew"',
And she found the little green eye of the God.

She upbraided poor Carew in the way that women do,
Though both her eyes were hot and strangely wet;
But she wouldn't take the stone and 'Mad Carew' was left alone
With the jewel that he'd chanced his life to get.

When the ball was at its height, on that still and tropic night,
She thought of him and hastened to his room;
As she crossed the Barrack Square, she could hear the dreamy air
Of a waltz tune softly stealing through the gloom.

His door was opened wide, silver moonlight shone inside,
The floor was wet and slippery where she trod.
An ugly wavy knife, from 'Mad Carew' had stole his life
'Twas the 'Vengeance of the Little Yellow God'.

There's a one-eyed yellow idol to the north of Khatmandu,
There's a little marble cross beneath the town;
There's a broken-hearted woman guards the grave of 'Mad
  Carew',
And the Yellow God forever gazes down.

Exercises (1)

Read the two music-hall recitations again carefully and decide which, if either, you think works for radio. Which tells a story and produces the pictures and mindvisible sequences necessary for a good narrative. Record and test this assumption. Then find a narrative poem/music-hall ballad/recitation you think would work well on radio and test this.

And now the limerick.

The easiest radio verse to write is probably the limerick. The construction of the limerick is fixed, which allows the student to concentrate on content rather than form. Limericks also tend to produce very visual verse and to be amusing. The best also tell a story.

Limericks have a rhyming scansion: A/A/B/B/A:

A There was a young lady of Riga
A Who went for a ride on a tiger
B They returned from the ride
B With the lady inside
A And a smile on the face of the tiger

The limerick is a form of facetious jingle, of which the first instance occurs in *Anecdotes and Adventures of Fifteen Young Ladies* and *The History of Sixteen Wonderful Old Women*. The form was later popularised by Edward Lear (1812–88) in his *Book of Nonsense*.

An example of Lear's writing:

There was an old person of Anerley
Whose manners were strange and un-mannerly
He rushed down The Strand
With a pig in each hand
But returned in the evening to Anerley

Lear's limericks have often been criticised for the last line being merely a repetition of the first. It has been offered in his defence that his limericks were composed for young children, who would probably find a repeated last line easier to understand:

So, though at the Lim'ricks of Lear
We may feel a temptation to sneer
We should never forget

That we owe him a debt
As a diligent, keen pioneer

The origin of the modern limerick is said to have been at convivial Victorian parties where impromptu verses were composed by each guest in turn followed by a chorus containing the words 'Will you come up to Limerick?', at which the next guest had to make up his or her particular effort.

In his *Complete Limerick Book*, Langford Reed attempts a history of the form. He mentions the limerick used by Dickens in *Our Mutual Friend*, beginning 'There was an old man of Tobago', which he claims was acknowledged by Lear as the rhyme which served as a model for the verses in The *Book of Nonsense*. Then he takes us back to the time of Charles II, and gives two limericks which he considers were in circulation at that time, one of which was:

There was an old woman of Leeds
Who spent all her time in good deeds
She worked for the poor
Till her fingers were sore
This pious old woman of Leeds

He considers the limerick originally to have been religious – if only from the fact that clergymen are responsible for 'perpetrating more limericks than all the other professions put together'.

Reed discusses Latin and French limericks and suggests that the limerick may have originated in France, and from there moved to Ireland – France's 'nearest Catholic neighbour'. His deduction is based upon Boswell finding a French limerick in 1716, and assuming that the limerick is French in origin. Reed speculates that it eventually came to the town of Limerick in Ireland through the returned veterans of the Irish Brigade, which was attached to the French Army for a period of nearly one hundred years from 1691. The Brigade was raised as a result of the treaty of Limerick in 1691. This treaty brought peace between England and Ireland and released 20,000 trained Irish soldiers for service as mercenaries – mainly to France. It was these men and their descendants, Reed feels, who brought back the verse form.

The great limerick boom occurred a little after the turn of the twentieth century, around 1907–8. Very large prizes were offered for limerick 'last lines' and a craze began similar to that occasioned by the beginning of the present-day lottery – contestants regarding the construction and analysis of their efforts as a profession going on a mystical experience. The limerick had its own journals and 'professors' who, for a fee, offered to supply last lines almost certain to win prizes.

All competitions, it seems, were run generally on the lines laid down by Mr Lincoln Springfield's journal, the *London Opinion*. Competitors would forward a postal order for sixpence, and a last line for a limerick of which the first four lines had been provided – the prize being all the monies received less 5 per cent for expenses. So the newspapers were able to run circulation-enhancing weekly competitions with no loss to themselves.

In a Post Office revenue speech made in the House of Commons, it was stated that in the last six months of 1907 the public bought 11,400,000 postal orders for limerick competitions.

There were court cases over the stealing of last lines – a railway clerk from Walthamstow suing for £79 7*s* on the grounds that the sum of £158 4*s* had been awarded by a popular weekly journal to a competitor with the same last line as himself, and so he was entitled to half. The defence argued that every care had been taken examining the entries and the plaintiff's effort could not be traced. The plaintiff lost on the grounds that the editor's decision was final.

Many limerick competitions were allied to advertising. Some of the prizes, for the time, were notable. The 'Limerick Contest King' was Mr Samuda, a well-known tobacco baron. Mr Samuda ran a limerick competition to advertise his cigarettes in which the winner was assured of £3 a week for life. The entry fee was a coupon proving that the competitor had purchased half a crown's worth of Mr Samuda's cigarettes. In view of the death-dealing properties of his product, the £3 paying-out period may not have unduly stretched Mr Samuda's resources.

The four lines offered in this competition were:

> That the Traylee's the best cigarette
> Is a 'tip' that we cannot forget
> And in buying, I'll mention
> There's a three pounds a week pension
> – – – ? – – – ? – – – ?

Part of the judging panel were the editors of the *Strand Magazine*, publishers of the Sherlock Holmes stories. It is not mentioned if they felt betrayed by Mr Samuda supporting cigarettes rather than cocaine – Holmes's own preferred relaxant. The winning last line was sent in by Mr Rhodes, of Romilly Road, Cardiff: 'Two good "lines" – one you give, one you get'.

In future competitions Mr Samuda went on to offer the triple award of 'a freehold house (a pretty well-kept country villa standing in its own grounds, and decorated and furnished by Waring & Gillow), a horse and trap, and an income of £2 a week for life'.

The magnificence of this prize prompted Langford Reed to wonder that the Poet Laureate was not tempted to emerge from seclusion to 'enter the lists himself, however great the risk of offending Calliope'. And while the muse of epic song might be offended, it may not have offended the Laureate's bank manager. But in the face of the talent against which he must have been pitted, and the fact that his work would be judged in the light of having to make sense, and impress and entertain ordinary people, the Laureate (whose position Ford Madox Ford defined for American friends as 'preposterous ... eminent ... obsolescent, harmless and ridiculous') may not have thought it worth his while.

A later, straight prize of £1,000 excited Mr Reed so much that he wrote to Mr Samuda directly, humbly hoping to gain a 'few hints'. Mr Reed relates that Mr Samuda did not reply, 'presumably due to the modesty which is said to surround great benefactors'. Mr Reed added sadly that Mr Samuda 'did not even send a box of his well-known cigars'.

On this note he turns to practical advice, and tells us that the essential constituents of a good limerick are: (1) a good last line, (2) ingenuity of rhyme and (3) plot.

He states that every limerick should be a short story in miniature which appeals to the ear rather than the eye. Radio, in fact. The first line sets up the story, the second develops it, third and fourth give the outcome of the adventure, and the fifth line rounds off the ending.

Part of Reed's closing advice was that, in entering competitions, never enclose more than one entry per envelope; and that in considering your last line you should decide what is the likeliest thing that could happen and then put the direct opposite. Finally, should you win a prize, send in all subsequent entries under an assumed name.

Famous classic limericks include:

There was an old party of Lyme
Who married three wives at a time
When asked 'Why the third?'
He replied 'One's absurd,
And bigamy, Sir, is a crime!'

There was a young lady named Bright
Whose speed was much faster than light
She set out one day
In a relative way
And returned home the previous night

An epicure, dining at Crewe
Found quite a large mouse in his stew
Said the waiter 'Don't shout,
And wave it about
Or the rest will be wanting one, too!'

The 'pelican' limerick shows how language can be manipulated amusingly and cleverly:

A wonderful bird is the pelican
His beak can hold more than his belly-can
He can hold in his beak
Enough for a week
But I'm darned if I know how the hell-he-can

Then there's the limerick which plays upon pronunciation:

There was a young fellow of Gloucester
Whose wife ran away with a coucester
He traced her to Leicester
And tried to arreicester
But in spite of his efforts he loucester

Exercises (2)

Four limericks to complete:

1	A	A student came out of a pub
	A	And said 'I'll go on to to a club
	B	That one over there
	B	Looks exceedingly rare
	A	– – – ? – – – ? – – – ?

Here the last rhyming word could be ... rub, shrub, dub, nub, hub, grub, and so on ... A last line could run,

'But first I'll adjourn for some grub'

2	A	Said a student of radio writing
	A	For me there's no 'Camera!' or 'Lighting!'
	B	– – – ? – – – ? – – – ?
	B	– – – ? – – – ? – – – ?
	A	But this just makes life more exciting

This is a completely open choice of rhymes for the second and third lines. A middle couplet might be

It's all in my head
Where I see it in red

3	A	A student whose grant had long passed
	A	– – – ? – – – ? – – – ?
	B	Just a mildewed old spud,
	B	And some cheese turned to wood,
	A	– – – ? – – – ? – – – ?

In this last example the words offered for the second line might be ... aghast, classed, last, massed, fast, passed, repast, vast.

If the writer then chooses, say, the words 'aghast' and 'repast', the eventual outcome of the verse could be something like:

A student whose grant was long past
Looked into the larder, aghast.
Just a mildewed old spud,
And some cheese turned to wood,
Was her breakfast, lunch, dinner repast.

4	A radio writer named Mellish ...
	– – – ? – – – ? – – – ?
	– – – ? – – – ? – – – ?

– – – ? – – – ? – – – ?
– – – ? – – – ? – – – ?

Other lines for this limerick might produce something to the effect of:

A radio writer named Mellish
Concocted a Lim'rick with relish
The duty producer
Said 'This will not do, Sir!
As your rhyming and timing are hellish!'

Construct four original radio limericks:

- One connected with the name of a country; for example, 'There was a young lady from France ...'.
- One connected with a profession/sport; for example, 'A boxer deciding to fight ...' or 'A lawyer consid'ring a case ...'.
- One connected with a food; for example, 'A lass who ate nothing but beef ...'.
- One connected with the name of a town; for example, 'There was a young person from Poole ...'.

First write them out. Then record, then listen. Then analyse whether or not they work as radio and if you think they fulfil Langford Reed's essential criteria of (1) a good last line, (2) ingenuity of rhyme and (3) plot.

The radio poem

The object of this section of the chapter will be to attempt to identify what type of poetry will, or will not, work as radio.

Here is a selection of poems. Two poems on spring, then one poem on summer, autumn and winter. Read the two spring poems carefully; try to decide whether one, both or neither works as radio. Record and test your assumption. Then read the poem on summer. Will it work for radio? If you think it will, then look through the anthologies for a poem on summer you feel will *not* work for radio. If you think the poem below won't work for radio, then find a poem on summer that you think *will* produce mindvisible pictures for radio. Do the same for the poems on autumn and winter.

Two poems on spring:

A. C. Swinburne (1837–1909) From 'Atalanta in Calydon'

When the hounds of spring are on winter's traces,
The mother of months in meadow or plain
Fills the shadows and windy places
With lisp of leaves and ripple of rain;
And the brown bright nightingale amorous
Is half assuaged for Itylus
For the Thracian ships and the foreign faces,
The tongueless vigil, and all the pain.

J. L. Uhland (1787–1862) 'Frühlingsglaube'
('Spring's Re-affirmation')

The gentle breezes wake and play
Flutt'ring, whisp'ring, night and day,
Busy and far they range.
New sights and scents. New colours; sounds.
Accept each spring new life resounds.
All things, all things, must change.

The world enhanced each passing dawn,
At earth's rebirth one should not mourn.
Life's neither new nor strange.
In deep, green valleys, flowers cascading;
Their efflorescence all pervading.
All things, all things, must change!

A poem on summer:

'Equinoctial'

Falcon falling,
Curlew calling,
Gold leaves, trees; golden sky.
Hesitating,
Evening's waiting,
Goodbye Summer, Summer Goodbye.

Pale moon rising,
Mist disguising,
From the church a sombre bell
Tolls our sorrow,
That tomorrow,
Farewell Summer, Summer Farewell.

Small breeze hustling,
Hedgehog rustling,
Starts the early morning dew.
Lay now quiet
'Til flowers run riot
Adieu Summer, Summer Adieu.

A poem on autumn:

Keats from 'To Autumn'

Season of mists and mellow fruitfulness!
Close bosom-friend of the maturing sun;
Conspiring with him how to load and bless
With fruit the vines that round the thatch-eaves run;
To bend with apples the moss'd cottage-trees,
And fill all fruit with ripeness to the core;
To swell the gourd, and plump the hazel shells
With a sweet kernel; to set budding more,
And still more, later flowers for the bees,
Until they think warm days will never cease,
For Summer has o'er-brimm'd their clammy cells ...

A poem on winter:

Elizabeth Daryush 'November Sun'

His face is pale and shrunk, his shining hair
Is prison-shorn;
Trailing his dark cloak, up the short dark stair
He creeps each morn.

Looks out to his lost throne, to the noon-height
Once his, then turns;
Back to his alien dungeon, where all night
Unseen he burns.

Now carry out the same test with each of two poems on love and death.

Two poems on love:

Anna Wickham (1883–?) 'The Fired Pot'

In our town people live in rows,
The only irregular thing in the street is the steeple;
And where that points to, God only knows,

And not the poor disciplined people.
And I have watched women growing old,
Passionate about pins, and pence, and soap.
Till the heart within my wedded breast grew cold,
And I lost hope.
But a young soldier came to our town,
He spoke his mind most candidly.
He asked me quickly to lie down,
And that was very good for me.
For though I gave him no embrace –
Remembering my duty –
He altered the expression of my face
And gave me back my beauty.

Akua Lezli Hope 'My Muse Relentless'

my muse is on me relentless
he is the shover
he pushes and pushes me
and twists my body
with demanding caresses
my juice is not enough
nor is my sweat nor my fear nor my longing
my muse is upon me and won't let me rest
we are coupled and gasping
he is the elephant in the sky
he is the grey whale
I see the many teeth in his mouth
his full lips are parted
he does not bite but thrusts
me in another direction
turns me around and then around
applies me to his largesse
and wipes me with his generosity
he is what I asked for
he does not kiss but clutches me
I think I want to sleep
his tongue is in my ear
he fills my nostrils
his scent is stronger than incense
I cannot shout him out
he flicks his tongue across my nipples

I can only sing him in
my muse is upon me
he is what I asked for
but he doesn't always visit
I have learned to make do in his absence
I keep a good kitchen
I have appliances
my muse is upon me
he is bigger than I thought
he drives me through pleasure and discomfort
he stretches me
I am dazed
he wakes me
my head reels with this insistence
I want to scream but others are listening
his silence drives the passion deeper
my mouth is open
my ears stuffed with the roar of his many voices
he is here
he is here
I try to accommodate him
I wrap my thighs around him
arch my back and type

Two poems on death:

Emily Dickinson (1830–86)

I died for beauty – but was scarce
Adjusted in the Tomb
When One who died for Truth, was lain
In an adjoining Room –

He questioned softly 'Why I failed?'
'For Beauty' I replied
'And I – for Truth – Themselves are One –
We Brethren are', He said

And so, as Kinsmen, met at Night –
We talked between the Rooms –
Until the Moss had reached our lips –
And covered up – our names –

Frances Cornford (1886–?) 'The Watch'

I wakened on my hot, hard bed,
Upon the pillow lay my head;
Beneath the pillow I could hear
My little watch was ticking clear.
I thought the throbbing of it went
Like my continual discontent.
I thought it said in every tick:
I am so sick, so sick, so sick;
O death, come quick, come
quick, come quick,
Come quick, come quick, come
quick, come quick.

Exercises (3)

Write a radio poem yourself on one of the four seasons. Then a poem on love, then a poem on death. Try and build each poem on simple ideas and concepts. Record, listen; what do you see as you hear it from the cassette? Then write a rap poem on a sporting or musical theme. Record, listen, check for good mindvisible images and strong aural and oral felicity.

Football Rap

Switched the radio, heard 'Three–Two'
Us in red, them in blue.
Black now sweeping down the right
White now marking silver tight
Grey now poaching fast and quick
Brown sent off for dangerous kick
Grass green turf, blinding lights
Roars, applause, fast tackles, fights.
Amber's dribbling was a dream
In the Rainbow Rappers football team.

Write one final poem on the days of the week, Sunday to Saturday, applied to a common theme – food, work, journeys, love, death, sport, and so on.

In Love, A Week Is A Long Time

I fell in love on Sunday,
And lay in bed all Monday.
Made my proposal Tuesday,
Wednesday was 'no news' day.
Thursday morn her answer brought,
Friday long, a gun I sought.
Saturday, I shot the cat,
And got blind drunk; and that was that.

9 The radio advertisement

Repetition is Reputation

Anon.

Even when the manufacture of radio sets achieved the status of an industry, in 1920, newspaper publishers slumbered in fancied security. Even while that industry ... multiplied its sales three hundred fold they refused to heed the alarm clock. Not until five million families gathered round the loud speaker did the publishers yawn, stretch and ask themselves what it was all about ... The answer was entertainment, news and advertising. It was all about their own field – about and above it.

Silas Bent, *Ballyhoo*, 1927

The Conservatives quickly pushed the wretched maggot of commercialism into the body politic of broadcasting; and that was that.

Reith, quoted by Scupham, *Broadcasting in the Community*

The climber wants to plant his flag on the highest mountain, the astronaut to do the same on the furthest planet, but the product salesman merely wants to plant his feet on your living room carpet, either physically or metaphorically. Physically by knocking on your door, metaphorically by extolling the virtue of what he is selling through an aspect of the media. Radio, newspapers, television.

Television is the salesman's dream. A chance to bombard the potential buyer with pictures, colour, music, jingles, actors, facts, figures and fancies.

Newspapers are more limited in format and range, but offer a chance to target, in a definite and controlled fashion, known social groups who read certain newspapers.

Radio offers something else again. Radio is with us always. In the bedroom as we get up. Alongside us in our baths, in most rooms of the house, in the car, as we walk through the streets, in airport lounges, department stores. We need not stop what we are doing to concentrate as with television, because we can take in its message while doing most, if not all, of our everyday tasks.

It is something that will surround and cocoon us twenty-four hours a day if that is what we wish. From here to eternity. A famous early science-fiction story developed a plot where all the radio waves broadcast since the inception of broadcasting were eventually reflected back to Earth so people had to listen again to the programmes of the 1920s and 1930s. What a bonus for the advertisers.

It seems to have been dimly understood from almost the beginning that the world might eventually be profitably enfolded within the blanket of radio. And with the broadcasting of the American presidential election results in 1920, by station KDKA in Pittsburgh, the advertisers realised that if people would listen to election results – they would listen to anything.

Briggs (1941) observes: 'The first commercial went on the air on 28th August, 1922 – ten minutes of station WEAF's radio time sold to a real-estate developer', and with this the die was cast.

Yet the fact that the floodgates were open to the financial and political mass manipulation of humanity in general seemed to be not yet fully understood by those best placed to take advantage of this opportunity – the politicians. Herbert Hoover, at the first American Radio Conference in that same year of 1922, stated that it was 'inconceivable that we should allow so great accessibility for service ... to be drowned in advertising chatter'.

Within a year of this 'inconceivable' notion some 500 licences had been issued for stations in America, and by 1923 the Tower of Babel had been rebuilt as the listeners' earphones were assaulted from all sides by shouting, counter-shouting and deliberate jamming; a situation described by E. S. Turner in his entertaining and informative book *The Shocking History of Advertising* (1953).

What could the listener do? No licence fee had been paid – to whom could complaint be made? In the end, those themselves who were causing the air-jam grew tired, and asked the government to intervene. In 1927 a Federal Radio Commission was finally set up to enforce order and decency.

The arguments began.

From the religious came inquiries as to whether salesmen should be allowed to use a form of selling that could possibly be wafting right up through the ether to the gates of Heaven. They argued that this would not only disturb the rest of the Almighty and his Host of Angels; but also souls who, having thought to have finally escaped the Earth and all its blandishments and temptations, now found themselves doomed to eternal pitching from bodiless salesmen. The opposing camp argued that whoever met the cost of the programmes should be allowed to canvass whomever they pleased – in this world or out of it.

And it was this latter line that the manufacturers pursued. Some pushed their products to the point of overkill; others contented themselves to the briefest mention of who they were and what they were selling, interested only in simply generating goodwill – an essential method of pitching for those who peddle such items as cars and other expensive knick-knacks which are purchased in terms of years rather than days.

Inevitably, the seamier side of radio advertising followed as rapidly as ideas were formed for setting it in motion. In the late 1920s, John R. Brinkley, the 'goat gland specialist', used his radio station in Kansas to persuade people to pay $750 for his 'rejuvenating' treatment. Having caught his hares, or goats, Brinkley then went on to offer an over-the-air free prescription service to any listeners who would send in symptoms – making his profit by directing sufferers to a chain of chemists he himself owned.

Doctors began to lose patients, and therefore money, and seeing their status as a club for supermen threatened, began to attack Brinkley and his 'goat gland' operation. Brinkley retaliated by producing many prominent figures from the worlds of oil and politics to testify that they had had their money's worth from the operation, but his station was eventually closed.

Brinkley himself then turned to politics, and after various shenanigans, during which he announced that he was intending to stand for governor, ended up crossing the Rio Grande to Mexico, where he continued defiantly broadcasting from a new station – the first 'pirate' radio station of all.

A clean-up campaign was suggested to stop rogue broadcasters and limit blanket advertising. At this point the 'Oregon Wildcat' surfaced. The 'Wildcat' bought nightly advertising himself to attack chain store advertisers over the air. However, the 'Wildcat's' own language was so 'indecent, obscene and profane' that he himself was banned and the chain stores marched on.

Turner quotes Llewellyn White, in *American Radio*, who, in a piece that in tone and content might have been written on behalf of the very people and processes it attacks, commented: 'Like the beleaguered Czechs of Ancient Bohemia, the broadcasters cried out for succour. Like the Hapsburgs, the advertising men who came to the rescue remained to rule. And, like many a philosophical Slav, the broadcasters accepted the conqueror's tongue.'

The Wall Street crash occurred and suddenly goods now 'had' to be sold. The selling became more aggressive, with machine-gun-like delivery.

Some networks actually began to limit the number of words that could be delivered each minute. The answer to this was to hire deep, plummy, slow-voiced actors whose delivery and method seemed to contain all the wisdom of Central Casting, the Actors' Guild and the Holy Ghost.

Commercials became dramatised. Girls sobbed over the men they had lost through the wrong face cream; young men bewailed the fact that passion had been put beyond their grasp through the number and fieriness of their pimples.

Then came making a joke of the whole thing, including, eventually, sending up the product itself. A fashion which has continued, deliberately or unwittingly, to the present day.

Eventually sponsors began to look for new forms to keep the masses tuned in and turned on, and came up with 'light entertainment'. 'Soaps' came into being, and life as we know it today began. The most famous of the earlier shows was 'Amos 'n' Andy', sponsored by Pepsodent.

Some advertisers mixed music and enlightenment. Tanner (1968) speaks of 'The Maxwell House Showboat' introduced by 'Let's Have Another Cup of Coffee', where a talk on ancient superstitions went a long way 'to dispelling the particular supersitution that coffee keeps people awake'.

Then came amateur talent shows, quizzes, give-away and take-away and take-back programmes – all of which did well. For they came free, while cinemas and theatre tickets cost money. These programmes quickly developed into a national frenzy, and now the American radio industry was in the hands of the advertisers, and the advertisers were concerned with only one thing – money. This meant bigger and bigger audiences, and this meant giving people what they wanted.

In vain were the ghosts and works of Shakespeare and Beethoven invoked – what was required were popular programmes which kept firmly away from anything leading towards thought or controversy.

Commercial broadcasting began to take on its final aspect – intervals of lurid but easily assimilated entertainment to occupy the time between bouts of salesmanship, with the 'soap opera' firmly established in the vanguard.

Taking a lead from serials running in books and magazines, any radio soap was kept going as long as it had a sufficient audience to attract a sponsor. Charles Andrews wrote 2,600 scripts for the show 'Just Plain Bill' in ten years.

At the end of the 1930s came the 'singing commercial'. A two-man team sang of the virtues of Pepsi-Cola and a new form was born. In 1941 this commercial was played 296,426 times over 469 stations. Repetition is reputation. Things have steadily progressed in all directions since then – even in Britain.

Advertising in British broadcasting

How did Britain escape the descent into advertising in the early days of radio? Most believe that it was Reith who kept the advertiser at bay, others that it was the fact that 'advertising' was not the sort of thing of which the 1920s' British public approved. Eckersley, as usual, has his own viewpoint: 'Commercial Broadcasting ... would have been instituted in Britain had it not been for wave length shortage.'

After the First World War the Marconi company broadcast the amateur service in which Eckersley was involved, and soon many requests were made to set up broadcasting stations. Requests which included big stores and newspapers – these requests were denied.

Eventually, however, the decision was taken to allow radio manufacturers to form a single broadcasting company – the British Broadcasting Company (later Corporation).

The question of advertising was again considered and rejected. That was in 1922. In 1923 the question arose once more in the Sykes Committee on Broadcasting, but found fierce opposition from the newspaper proprietors. Lord Riddell, their spokesman, was of the opinion that, 'If traders wish to advertise they should confine themselves to the existing methods'; that is, newspapers. American newspaper owners dealt with this matter by simply buying into radio. In 1927, in America, nearly one hundred daily papers owned or leased broadcasting facilities.

Contrary, however, to accepted belief, sponsored broadcasts did take place in Britain in the early days – Harrod's in 1923, and a fashion talk by Selfridge's from the Eiffel Tower in 1925.

There was, as now, unlimited covert advertising in the self aggrandisement of the broadcasters themselves. Plus allowing their favourite artists and politicians to hawk, in the wheelbarrows of their ineptitude, their shoddy wares and lives from studio to studio.

In 1930, a Captain Plugge founded his International Broadcasting Company and began to transmit programmes in English from Radio Normandie, taking in advertising.

Then came the advent of the 'pirate' radio station proper, the most famous being Radio Luxembourg, which opened in 1933 and enlivened many a long evening for schoolboys struggling with homework, while their sisters struggled on couches. 'Luxie' eventually overtook the audience figures for the BBC's Home Service.

In 1936 came one of the best pieces of advertising on radio, when it managed to advertise itself as being able to do what the newspapers could not. The Crystal Palace burned down after the evening papers were already on the streets and before the morning papers appeared, and Richard Dimbleby broadcast a report from the scene of the fire to a background of shouts and flames. Radio finally demonstrated its true flexibility.

In America there was already Floyd Gibbons, romantic, handsome, rugged; with a white patch covering an eye he lost at Belleau Wood in the First World War.

Gibbons was always 'on location', and pioneered on-the-spot broadcasting with a speed of 217 words per minute from fire, flood and earthquake, and, in 1932, from the battlefields of Manchuria.

The controversy over 'commercial' advertising still flourished, and in 1949 yet another Committee on Broadcasting was set up. Many big firms advanced the proposition that it was essential for British advertisers to get into radio if export markets were to be developed. These firms, which included Lever Brothers and Rowntree, did not necessarily want to see the BBC displaced – they would settle for a separate commercial network.

In reply, the BBC pleaded that 'it would be the lower forms of mass appetite which would more and more be catered for in programmes'. Tolstoy once observed that the greatest art was that which is most popular. But this view had little interest for those who saw their task as instructing everyone else in what was acceptable as regards information and entertainment.

The Committee, delivering its report in 1951, turned down the idea that broadcasting should become financially dependent on sponsoring. As for broadcasts from abroad, the Committee thought that 'the choice may lie between jamming them and making bargains to keep them under control'. An advertisement in itself for official probity and high-mindedness.

In 1972 came the Independent Broadcasting Authority, empowered to license a number of independent radio stations. At the present time there are about fifty, though there have been closures and mergers.

Due to the proliferation of television, twenty-four hour viewing is now available to those who wish it. So where, in the night, the sleepless might have once sat alongside a radio, now there is the choice of sound and vision. But while even the most alert must close their eyes from time to time and lose vision – the sound goes on, even subconsciously, and the brain, sleeping or waking, can be reached by microphone.

To lessen the impact of having to pay for the broadcasting licence in one sum, the BBC decided to inaugurate a budget scheme whereby the cost of the licence could be spread over four quarterly payments. There would be a selection of advertisements for the scheme for each of the networks – Radios 1, 2, 3, 4 and 5 – with some crossing the gaps between various networks and having multiple exposure.

In the case of Radio 4, options were considered as to the type of programme a listener to that station might elect to listen to – and an advert be written to use this choice.

The following was commissioned by BBC Corporate Promotions for Radio 4 as one of a series to advertise the Quarterly Licence Scheme:

SCENE 1 HOLMES'S ROOMS

FX: MELANCHOLY VIOLIN MUSIC. FADES DOWN ...

1. WATSON: (READS SLOWLY) 0–2–7–2 7–6–9 1–0–0. (REPEATS MORE CONFIDENTLY) 0272 769 100 ... But what on earth does it mean, Holmes?

1. HOLMES: (PUFFS ON PIPE) 'Peace' ... Watson ... 'Security'!

2. WATSON: Ah! Then it's 'Her' number? ... Irene Adler's? The only woman you've ever loved?

3. HOLMES: 'Peace', I said, Doctor.

4. WATSON: Hmmm ...

PAUSE

5. HOLMES: Watson ... (PAUSE) ... Watson, old chap. You know I've got one?

6. WATSON: (CHOKES) Really, Holmes ...!

7. HOLMES: Of course, I only put it on at night ... (PAUSE) ... When you've gone to bed.

8. WATSON: Holmes. Should you be telling me this?

9. HOLMES: (DREAMILY) For years, Watson, I didn't care. The cocaine – that hat and cape. Then I thought, what if they send round the van ...?

10. WATSON: (HEAVILY) What indeed, Holmes ...!

11. HOLMES: And so I finally acquired ... A broadcasting licence!

12. WATSON: What! – But a licence now costs ...! And you never accept payment for a case ...! Then the recession ... While yesterday! That begging musician outside Waterloo Station! ... One of your better disguises ... I admit ... but ... (PAUSE) Holmes, old fellow! Can you afford it?

13. HOLMES: I can now Watson! – With the BBC Licence Budget Scheme. Direct debit 'now', security 'ever after!'

14. WATSON: But how does one ...? Ah ... I see ... (READS) 0–2–7–2 7–4–9 1–0–0 ... (AFTER PAUSE. COUGHS) Astonishing! ... My dear Holmes!

15. HOLMES: (QUIETLY) Elementary, my dear Watson!

16. ANNOUNCER: 'SOLVE' YOUR 'TV LICENCE' WORRIES BY THE DIRECT DEBIT BUDGET SCHEME. FOUR QUARTERLY INSTALMENTS OF ONLY —. RING 0272 769 100 FOR FULL DETAILS.

17. HOLMES: That, my dear Watson is 0–2–7–2 7–6–9 1–0–0.

ENDS

Radio 4 is generally known to have listeners of a certain age, education and finance. Holmes and Watson would need no explaining to a Radio 4 audience, would be familiar from long usage, and would appear generally as popular, safe, trustworthy icons of life as we know it. If your money or bank account number isn't going to be safe and well looked after in the hands of Holmes and Watson, well ...

Using the same thinking the following was written for Radio 3's Quarterly Direct Debit Campaign:

'Radio 3 (After A. E. Housman)'

In summertime on Bredon
The channels came in clear;
Through both the shires we viewed them
As sharp as Ludlow beer
Yet we'd a hidden fear.

For, though of Sunday morning
My love and I would lie
And watch the coloured pictures
We'd keep the shades drawn by
Lest any should espy.

For, Oh! we had a secret,
Those summer days about,
As unlike death and hangings,
Our licence had run out,
And we were wracked with doubt.

So we went down to Bristol
To where an office sits;
That's open morn 'til even,
To calm a ploughman's wits,
And cure a sweetheart's fits.

'Tis known as direct debit,
And buys uncommon ease ...
So Shropshire lads! – With lasses
That you would put at ease
Just ring this number, please

And the number to ring is ... I repeat, ... Using this scheme you will be debited for four quarterly amounts of £ ...

This was devised and written for an audience considered highly literate and literature informed, who listen to the most elitist radio channel ever funded from a public purse. But a station that has generated such good stories as the orchestral broadcast which suddenly stopped with the words:

> We apologise for this interruption, but have just been informed a nuclear missile is heading towards Britain and will strike in three minutes. Until then, here is a recording of Artur Schnabel playing the Schubert Impromptu in G flat major, Opus 90, number 3. Unfortunately, this recording was available only in mono ...

Writing radio commercials is writing to pack as much information into as tight a format as possible and to bring one particular piece of information, the name of the product or firm, firmly to the forefront of the mind and memory of the listener.

If you are contracted by an advertiser to engage the attention, and hopefully the pocket, of the consumer, you will do so in the same way you would engage the attention of someone at a party you would like to impress and attract. By being short, witty, entertaining. By sizing up the person concerned and making a valid judgement as to what approach will serve you best. For instance, if X comes along and says sell lots of product Y for me – the first thing to try to identify is the potential set of customers.

And if X's product is necklaces, then you look at the giraffe market, and leave armadillos alone.

Once you identify the customer, and the sort of money he/she has available, and the social habits involved, you identify the approach that is needed.

Exercises (1)

Four preliminary exercises to practise condensing as much information as possible into as short a time as possible in the most memorable way. Try for a maximum of thirty seconds for each advert.

1 Write 'An Advertisement Advertising Oneself'. Make a potential employer 'buy' you.

2 'A Public/Corporate Service Announcement.' Advice to the elderly regarding cold weather. Save the atmosphere. Reduce pollution. Help fight crime. Use a song which you feel is apt to introduce each of the foregoing.

3 'An Advertisement for a Product.' A new aftershave, perfume, drink, brand of food.

4 An advertisement using 'sound' alone (i.e. non-verbal) except for the name of the product. For an advert in this last category using 'sound alone' we might hear something like:

FX:	SHIP'S SIREN, THE SOUND OF A MARKETPLACE IN AN EASTERN COUNTRY, THE SOUND OF MEXICAN MUSIC, THE TRUMPETING OF AN ELEPHANT, HONKING OF TAXI HORNS, A DANCE BAND, THEN SHIP'S SIREN AGAIN.
	PAUSE
1. NARRATOR:	Magic Carpet Holidays! ... Just close your eyes and you're there!

Exercises (2)

1 The possibility has arisen of designing a series of radio advertisements to run over a period of time; each different, but all having certain characteristics in common. This characteristic might be a theme which is pursued in order to push the product, or characters who might build up a following among a target audience for the product. This product could be a new car, or new drink that is being tried in the marketplace.

Try using pairs of famous characters and some of their leading characteristics to put across a message for example, Holmes and Watson, Romeo and Juliet, Samson and Delilah – or any other pair. In these adverts famous lines such as 'Elementary, my dear Watson' would be used at critical points in the advert. As when Holmes deduces that the only choice for A Great Detective and everyone else is the product that is being pushed.

'Romeo, Romeo, wherefore art thou Romeo?' could be used to point up the fact that Romeo is someone who prefers the product in question to the charms of Juliet.

Samson, in his advert, will be only too happy for Delilah to cut off his hair as long as she will promise to give him whatever it is the sponsors are advocating.

When you attempt this option remember that in using a famous pair of characters you must try to choose two that are universally recognisable and not two just confined to a small area and age range. The sellers of a new food/drink would wish to attract as wide a range of ages and tastes as possible – which must be reflected in the advertising connected with the product.

2 Walk through town. Pick any shop. Not a well-known store or supermarket but a private establishment. One that does not look too prosperous. Spend some time examining and thinking about what it sells and what in advertising terms it has going for it. At whom the product is aimed. Then write a letter to the owner accepting the job of marketing his shop through advertising and describe how you would lay out your campaign, given limited funds.

Appendix Getting started

Consult yourself, and if you find
A powerful Impulse urge your Mind
Impartial judge within your Breast
What Subject you can manage best;
Whether your Genius most inclines
To Satire, Praise, or hum'rous Lines;
To Elegies in mournful Tone,
Or Prologue sent from Hand unknown.
Then rising with Aurora's Light,
The Muse invok'd, sit down to write;
Blot out, correct, insert, refine,
Enlarge, diminish, interline;
Be mindful, when Invention fails,
To scratch your head, and bite your Nails.

Swift

Having worked through the exercises and examples in this book, you should, by now, have gauged your particular strengths and weaknesses, and made a decision as to which of the various radio writing forms interests you. You may now wish to begin a short story, play, adaptation, documentary or collection of radio poems.

When you begin you may have an enormous amount of ideas, though little technique to mould and manipulate them into a successful script. Conversely, you may have a fair idea about the techniques required, but be lost for an idea with which to begin. But first you have to make a start.

Getting started

Genius may be thought to flourish in attics and cellars but those who are said to 'have starved' are often found to know far more about starving than writing. There is no formula for success, but there are suggestions for producing work. Children may scream, milkmen knock, bailiffs pound, but if you can get a roof over your head, a supply of food and a routine – you have a beginning.

You have made the decision about the subject area for your first piece of radio. Writing it will cost considerable time and effort so it should be something you really want to say. For what you expend in time and creative energy can never be reclaimed. And, as it is as hard and draining to write a bad piece as a good piece, it is as well to aim for the latter.

All writers have different methods of realising their intentions on paper; most agree some sort of schedule is necessary. Perhaps, for a beginner, two or three hours of a morning, afternoon or evening.

Balzac (1799–1850), in a letter to Madame de Hanska, speaks of his belief in the incomprehensibility of God. Balzac's own life was equally incomprehensible. Balzac, C. P. Snow tells us, would set his alarm clock for midnight, don a spotless white monk's robe and begin to write until early morning, when he would stop and bathe. Then on until one o'clock in the afternoon correcting proofs. Then an egg; and more proof reading. Incessantly drinking strong black coffee.

Snow points out that this could mean 'a working day, a real working day, pen close to paper, of about thirteen hours'. But given the structure of most people's lives (and bearing in mind Balzac's relatively early death), a short session some time prior to midnight might be safer.

In time, stamina builds up, but at first the intense effort required to steer between the contrary winds of uncertain technique and racing imagination will all too often lead to mouth ulcers, aching limbs, itchy eyes.

Having chosen your best time, try to stick to it. And try, initially, to write for three hours in one solid block. Half an hour here, there and everywhere, destroys both concentration and continuity.

Finally, once you do begin a piece of work, bring it to some sort of conclusion. A thousand writers have desk drawers full of half-completed plays, adaptations, talks, stories, which were 'going to be finished off next week – but ...'. An unfinished project is an un-sellable project – now and forever. It holds you back and gives the rest of the field a headstart. You can be sure that while you are shoving the uncompleted labour of three months into the back of a drawer, someone else is shoving their completed play into an envelope and sending it to a producer.

As to the mechanical means with which you write. The best and fastest processor you can afford. If you are serious about writing, you will require serious equipment.

The only real long-term critic is time, but in the short term a writer's success depends very much on the paying public. What the public is interested in at any given time. This means a look at some of the current dramatic material that seems to have a waiting audience.

In what follows you will find a list of possible ideas and plot scenarios that may be useful. There are also hints as to how to find a title, and what sort of music, if any, should be considered. How to time a piece of writing. Where and to whom it should be sent. Subjects are divided into three catergories: contemporary issues/things in vogue, personal interests, hobbies and pursuits, and the subjective/psychological play.

Contemporary issues/things in vogue

These are events and issues which have now, to a greater or lesser extent, become part of our daily lives – but which still have enough novelty to make them of dramatic interest. Physical fitness, sports and sporting events. Social, religious and ethnic concerns. The environment. Modern technology. Present political issues.

They would primarily be the concern of what might be termed the 'investigative dramatist', who bases work in and around present-day themes and events. A great opportunity to present to an audience of perhaps hundreds of thousands facts and figures, or points of view, about which that audience may not have previously thought or had access to. To look at this category in more detail.

Physical fitness, sports and sporting events

Marathons, sponsored walks, jogging, aerobics, rock climbing, pot-holing, hang gliding, windsurfing, skateboarding, snowboarding, and so on. Leading to the greater media interest in local/national/world soccer competitions, the Olympic Games, chess tournaments, grand prix racing, the turf, international yachting, the climbing of great mountains – and the now endemically popular snooker and darts tournaments.

Events on a world scale have their darker side, with soccer hooliganism, the stealing/doping of valuable racehorses and the ever-pervading threat of terrorist intervention.

Ideas, serious and comical, in this sub-section might include something on the lines of:

- The athlete in a small country which is a dictatorship. This athlete has a good chance of an Olympic gold which will be good propaganda for the regime, but will not give his best because of a case of injustice in which he has an interest. The double-edged game that ensues as each side manoeuvres for victory.

In a lighter vein, on the smaller, local scene:

- The two lifetime rivals in a love/hate relationship finally fall out, seemingly irreparably, over the same person/business deal. They decide to settle the issue by slogging it out in a two-person gruelling running marathon – one of the rules is that to stop running for any reason means instant disqualification. Within sight of the finishing line one collapses. Does the other stop to help or ignore and win?
- The chess champion playing to retain his world title against his only serious contender, much older than him, and who has a daughter, also a fine player, whom the younger man loves. The two men are drawing with one game left to play. The younger man knows the older man is now too old and tired, and that this will be his last chance for a world title. The younger man also knows that if he deliberately throws the game his opponent and his opponent's daughter will both know and never forgive him. What does he do?
- The captain of the macho local pub darts team who, a week before the league final, tells his colleagues that he intends to include a woman in the side. His battle for his survival and sanity for the next seven days. The final itself.

Social, religious and ethnic concerns

Street festivals and carnivals. The rights of sexual and ethnic minorities. Gambling, drink, drugs. The changing role of the Church in the modern world. The participation of the general public in issues of law and order – such as the 'Neighbourhood Watch' schemes. Or in those of a more caring nature, 'Age Concern' groups, accident support schemes.

This section gives scope to follow and explore modern social, sexual and inter-racial movements as society adjusts, or fails to adjust, to the spirit of the age. Examples of plays or issues that might be explored dramatically in this category could be:

- The harrowing and possibly ultimately destructive result of having a compulsive drunk or gambler within the immediate family.
- The pressures to look good by fitting into a standard weight/shape pattern which can lead into the twilight world of anorexia nervosa and slim-at-all-costs syndromes.
- The young black who manages to get a job in a shop and the immediate barriers and hostility that might have to be overcome on both sides of the counter.
- The woman who, for years, has struggled with depression and tranquillisers. Her finding out about allergies and her battle to get herself taken seriously, tested and try to kick the pills.
- This is the first generation, the parents of whom are going to live prolonged lives. The trials of trying to cope with a senile/very old parent for whom there is no local care place available. The tensions of having an elderly, confused relative within the framework of an ordinary mum, dad and two-kids family.
- The young policewoman's first day on the beat in an inner-city area. Going into a shop she walks into an armed robbery and is taken hostage. The subsequent events.
- The introduction of a woman deacon into a church situation where the old order is very much in evidence.

In a lighter mood:

- The person organising the 'Neighbourhood Watch' scheme has been burgled three times. He/she suspects it is his/her partner. What could be the reason for the partner's behaviour?
- The local church fete where, due to strong punch and excitement, the first prize is awarded to the wrong child in the 'beautiful baby' competition. The minister's subsequent treat-

ment at the hands of the four enraged parents to whom this result means so much.

The environment

A very high-profile issue in media and politics. Pollution, radiation leaks, infringement of green belts/siting of new roads/housing complexes/air terminals.

Examples of plays in this section could be:

- The poisoning of a stretch of river and the dangers faced by an investigator trying to track down the particular source of pollution when up against powerful business or political interests.
- The villagers of all classes and attitudes who band together to fight for, or against, the siting of a proposed video/chip shop.
- The mother who puts career and reputation in jeopardy by protesting outside a nuclear base, being arrested and electing for trial by jury to put forward her beliefs about the potential horrors of a nuclear strike.

Modern technology

The computer/internet explosion. 'The hacker' and the potential information that can fall under his or her hand. Manned spaceflight and the exploration of the planets. The implications for the future as machines do more of the work and man is gradually edged out of the labour market.

Ideas for plays in this section might include:

- The pensioner in an all-electric flat who, due to computer error, receives a quarterly gas bill for half a million pounds. His Kafka-like fight against the machine.
- What is much worse, a slightly confused pensioner who receives a bill that is too much to be probable, but unfortunately not large enough to be impossible.
- The man who sees the only job he is fitted to do taken away from him by the machine. His reactions? Perhaps set against those of a ribbon-weaver in the seventeenth century. A chance to run two similar attitudes, from different centuries, side by side.
- Life in a Martian frontier-town when man begins to mine and explore the planets.

- Cats and dogs given human translators. Suddenly they can communicate and we can understand them.
- The rights of robots. Robots programmed to think. What rights, if any, do they have?

Political issues

Perhaps more a question of bias in relation to issues already raised in this section. There are, though, the obvious questions of nuclear power, unemployment, the police, and attitudes and investigations into the structure of society in general. Plays in this section could include:

- A single parent trying to bring up a child in an inner-city bedsit in the face of DHSS indifference/inability to help, vandalism, racketeer landlord, and so on.
- The parent, in an area of high unemployment, forced to leave the family each week and travel to work elsewhere. The strains this can impose on a relationship.
- The reporter given sensitive information about a nuclear/germ warfare issue. The decisions, professional, moral and domestic, that must be considered before deciding whether to expose the information or bury it.

A final note. Daily newspapers can provide a constant update for the types of play that come within this first section overall, and can provide, or spark off, original treatments for ideas within this whole category. But with events of major significance, such as war or violent death, it is advisable to wait until all the evidence is in before putting pen to paper. If a writer is too close it may be offensive to those who still feel personally involved. If it is left too long then people may have lost interest. So the dramatist must strike a fine balance.

Personal interests, hobbies and pursuits

> He learned the art of riding, fencing, gunnery,
> And how to scale a fortress or a nunnery.
>
> Byron

This is a field where everyone should have something to offer. Stamp collecting, bee keeping, ceramics, train spotting, vintage cars, home brewing, walking, riding, cycling, swimming, astronomy, astrology, the occult; as many possibilities as there are hobbies, interests and manias. Samples of plays within this section might include such ideas as:

- The great stamp collector is found murdered. No money or valuables have been removed. Then a detective, also a stamp expert, notices that a rare stamp is missing from the dead collector's albums. The hunt is on.
- The person who buys a pack of tarot cards and begins to give readings. What starts as a joke soon becomes both serious and dangerous as fact begins to match up with the predictions.
- The abbey has fallen on hard times. Brother Barnabas has dabbled for years in home-brew to give the monks small cheer with their evening repast. At compline he falls senseless from his stall. A vision? A coronary? No. Just the effects of a new liquor he has distilled. A financial adviser and set of ad-men make their appearance and the abbey is saved – or is it?

The aforegoing categories, 'Contemporary issues' and 'Personal interests' are, in many ways, objective issues brought under a subjective hammer, but there is another, third, category of play – to many people the most natural first play of all.

The subjective/psychological work

'Fool' said my muse to me, 'Look in thy heart and write'
Sir Phillip Sydney

The subjective/psychological work is the result of experience rather than imagination. It is set in an area where the writer has total familiarity and control – because it is the writer writing about him- or herself. Write from experience and you will write honestly and cogently. Your greatest wish, dramatically, may be to send up a meeting of a group of anarchists, or that of the local Young Conservative club, but unless you have the vocabulary and syntax required for either of these groups you will simply send up yourself. This can be tested by a very simple experiment:

Set yourself the task of writing a couple of pages from a work/social situation totally outside your experience. Follow this with a page or two from a situation with which you are totally familiar. Then show your efforts to someone whose judgement you trust, and ask them for an honest opinion of both pieces of work.

Exercises (1)

1 The son/daughter of the house, aged ten, is suddenly found to be missing and has not been seen by anybody since early morning. It is now evening. Write the conversations you think might ensue between the parents living in:

- a detached country house in its own extensive grounds;
- a semi-detached house in a fashionable London suburb;
- a terraced house in a prosperous working-class area;
- a tower-block flat in a deprived inner-city area.

Write the first scene from a radio play from each of the above situations.

1 Write the first page of a story or documentary from each of the above situations.

2 Do the same for a situation whereby the sets of parents of the above families announce to their children that there is to be a divorce.

3 Do the same whereby the daughter/son of any two of the above-mentioned families announces that they hope to join the army/police as a private/constable.

As writers grow in maturity they gain the experience and social mobility to deal with backgrounds outside their own – but this takes time. Often quite a long time.

The need for patience and perseverance must be understood quite early. A writer without patience is like a sailor without a compass. He/she is not going to get there.

What sort of play should a writer attempt as a beginner to perhaps bring the best out in him/herself? In any of our minds there are moments we tend to re-live – no matter how long ago they occurred. Memories of past events that we regularly take out to re-polish and re-live. They may be of times of great happiness, of great sadness, of pride, of humiliation. Things that can come to us unbidden at any time and which we will carry in our hearts until we die. Any of these memories should make a good play for the following reasons:

- The memories concerned in such a play would be set in reality as people know and understand it.
- The psychology, thinking, plot and characters in such a play will come over as true to life because of the writer's direct involvement with those things. The writer, to a great extent, will be inventing nothing as regards time, people and place.
- If the incident in question is of constant and abiding interest to the writer it can probably be assumed that, handled properly, it will be of interest to others. To handle such a play properly will require revealing something of yourself, perhaps a great deal – but this is part of the price that has to be paid to construct a truthful work of art.

  Some primitive tribes will not be photographed for fear the camera (photographer) would steal their 'soul' or 'identities', seeing this soul or identity as their essence. So, should a writer be prepared to allow people into his/her 'identity', his/her 'soul', they are usually more or less guaranteed an audience. *Faust* always plays to full houses.

Titles

> You are the titles and you catch the eye.
>
> Rostand

Catching the eye is what it's all about. For that is what often persuades the casual browser looking through the listings. Sometimes a title comes to a writer and he or she writes a play around it. Sometimes a writer has an idea for a play and the title comes with the idea. Sometimes a title will occur in the middle of a play, sometimes at its end, and sometimes not at all. Script readers are well used to receiving work with UNTITLED written across the top. In the long run the director and writer may have to put their heads together to sort something out.

It is important to find the right title because, as mentioned earlier, they can be very effective publicity. If you get it wrong, though, people may just look at the title, mutter 'bore-ing' and move on.

A good way to find a title if you are really stuck is to read through a favourite poet, or poetry anthology, or a book of biblical or Shakespearean quotations. Within these compilations there is usually something to be found that will come near to aptly summing up what you feel your work to be about.

Exercises (2)

Think up alternative titles for the following plays in the form of clichés or well-known expressions, or use famous titles of other pieces of writing, painting or music; for example, *Othello* – 'Death In Venice'.

- *Othello*
- *Macbeth*
- *Dr Faustus*
- *The Importance of Being Ernest*
- *The Playboy of the Western World*
- *St Joan*
- *Peter Pan*
- *Pygmalion*
- *Tom Thumb*
- *Antony and Cleopatra*

Find an alternative title for 'Bed, Bored and Banjaxed'.

Music

> I like Wagner's music better than anybody's. It is so loud that one can talk the whole time without other people hearing what one says.
>
> Oscar Wilde

> I got into music 'cause I couldn't get into athletics.
>
> Jackson Browne

Think carefully about the use of music within radio. Suggesting a popular piece to be used within, say, a play may often have the reverse of the writer's desired effect. Instead of the listener concentrating on the dialogue, he or she may begin to sing or hum along with what is going on musically in the background, and perhaps miss information vital to the understanding, smooth running and resolution of the play.

The same sort of reasoning applies to the use of instrumentalists. A dreamy nocturne may seem just the thing to set off a romantic scene; or a furious rhapsody to capture the storm. But the listener all too often imagines him/herself as soloist, acting out the part of the great virtuoso – 'The last pupil of the last pupil of Liszt'. And, again, you've lost your audience.

Your writing may easily suffer as a result of making the background music too attractive. Disco and bland classical are the best types of music to use to keep the writing, rather than the musical accompaniment, central to the listener's mind.

Music and songs written especially for a play are another matter. A song adds enormously to the production costs in radio – especially if it needs to be played by a group. The Musicians' Union has very fixed rates and the band must be paid those rates. Although the band may be willing to do the song for nothing, this is impossible. They must be paid. A song would need to be very much a part of the absolute warp and woof of the play before a producer would consider giving up so much of his or her budget.

Can you imagine a scene in 'Bed, Bored and Banjaxed' that might take a song?

Language

On the stage, in film and to a lesser extent in television, writers are allowed to say what they want in whatever way they want. This is an attitude that can be understood. Once art is prescribed, it becomes predictable.

In the theatre, however, you pay your money and take your choice; while a television programme with language that might offend is usually screened quite late in the evening and usually carries a warning proviso before it begins.

Radio is different. The audience for an afternoon play or short story, two natural slots for new writers, may run from granny doing her knitting to young Billy taking a half-day off school. There is no fixed watershed on radio, and besides, a writer should always be able to make any point through hesitation, deviation and exclamation! And 'four letter' words take on a curious linguistic 'value' on radio. Given the mindvisability of basic concept words, as we hear a thing, we see the thing – think about hearing the word 'shit' on the radio. This can cause both embarrassment and distaste across a whole range of listeners – although this might artistically be the effect the writer wants.

There is the classic question asked by a producer of a young writer who was arguing for the retention of a number of four letter words in a script that was to go forward as an afternoon play on Radio 4. 'What would your mother say,' asked the producer, 'if she turned the radio on to listen to this play of yours, and heard all this realism you keep telling me about?'

Sound effects

> Producers deplored the attention that their ingenuities received, but the public was and is fascinated by sound effects. A cartoon of the time showed a producer shouting at the effects man: 'I said a warm, wet wind from *the south*!'
>
> Peter Black, *The Biggest Aspidistra in the World*

Sound effects really fall within the province of the director, but there is one category that perhaps should be mentioned here – those which could be termed 'psychological' sound effects. That is, effects that do not actually reflect an action going on at the time (a tap being run when a character suggests a cup of tea, or a gun going off when somebody is shot) but rather a hint of things to come, or a possible future answer to a present state of uncertainty.

Here, we can reconsider an earlier example. A man and woman sit in their house, their child is late home, they are becoming seriously worried. They exchange views, discuss the fact that the child has to pass across an unlit common to reach home.

As they speak we cut, under their voices, to the common and perhaps hear an owl hoot. This would be a standard sound effect. Also, we could have the sound of laboured breathing and perhaps footsteps dragging through fallen leaves.

Psychologically, this will trigger off in a listener's mind a number of possible causes. But also it would certainly cause deep disquiet for the listener as to the safety of the child; so the sound effect in this case would not reflect a direct action but psychologically jolt the listener on to his or her toes and, in a way, command attention and further commitment to the play.

Exercises (3)

Imagine three scenes where psychological sound effects could be used.

Timing and editing

> If you don't know a sailor's religion I'll tell you it and this is my religion: a clear conscience, a sharp knife and ready to cut at a minute's notice.
>
> Capt. William Morris Barnes, *Rolling Home*

There is only one way of timing a script, especially a play, and that is by reading it aloud with somebody else, and allowing time for action, sound effects and music. Then the whole should be brought under the stop watch.

To read a work through by oneself will give some rough idea, but in the heat of the moment, it is difficult to allow the natural pauses and adjustments that occur when two people are speaking against each other.

If anything, it is advisable that your work be slightly overlong upon submission. Cuts are usual, and material coming out of a piece never did any harm. The opposite case – having to put in a couple of pages of waffle to plug a time gap – is another matter. Padding is padding.

One of the greatest difficulties that writers have is agreeing to any cuts suggested by the producer/director. Writers often feel as if they are being asked to take out their own teeth without Novocain. The onlooker always sees more of the game. A good producer/script reader knows professionally where overwriting and repetition occur in a script, and how the listener will react. Cuts suggested by experts are usually correct. Many a writer has been saved from making a fool of him- or herself by the insistence of the producer/script editor. A television cameraman being interviewed about filming 'stars' and 'personalities' observed, 'If we don't like them we take the shots they suggest.'

Though a good original script is one half of the battle, a good script editor is very much the other.

Your work goes forward

Your piece is now written and as presentable as you can make it. If your work is intended for the BBC you will send it to the Script Unit at London, or one of the regional centres. These are Belfast, Birmingham, Bristol, Cardiff, Edinburgh, Manchester and Glasgow.

It is probably better for a new writer to send a script to the regional centre nearest his or her home – especially if a work is of local interest. A regional producer may be better qualified to understand and appreciate regional characteristics that occur in the script. It also cuts down on postage and travel expenses should a writer be invited to meet a producer to talk about a particular script. The BBC also has to take a fixed amount from the regions and this may help, whereas all is grist to the mill that comes to London.

When the script arrives it will be seen by a 'reader/researcher' and then perhaps by a producer. There will either be a standard rejection or a report. A report will indicate whether the reader considers the script has enough in it to possibly reach production standards. 'Readers' are sometimes producers in their own right, and may write for radio. The reader will signify in his or her report what he or she sees as both the strengths and weaknesses of a particular script, and return the script to the producer.

The producer, if interested, may read the script, and either reject it or ask the writer for one, or a series, of 're-writes'. These 're-writes' are reworkings of the script to iron out deficiencies in form and content. For an unknown writer these re-writes will be done 'on spec'. That is, no guarantee will be given as to the eventual fate of the play, no matter how much work is put in by the writer.

When the producer finally considers the script/proposal a viable proposition, he or she will present it to those in charge of commissioning. There it will be bought or rejected – which is where originality of storyline and treatment will figure heavily.

If it is bought, the writer's job is now over – except possibly as a script consultant during production. If rejected, try and find out why, then begin again.

Afterword To writers

> The desire for notoriety and recognition sterilizes the seeds from which greatness must spring. A place in the stars is more important than a place in the sun
>
> Reith, *Broadcast Over Britain*
> Quoted in Asa Briggs, *The Birth of Broadcasting*

> At the moment when one writes, one is what one is, and the damage of a lifetime … cannot be repaired at the moment of composition.
>
> T. S. Eliot, quoted in Greene, *Collected Essays*

> Capablanca was sitting in a chess café when a stranger came over and sat opposite him.
>
> 'You don't know me,' said the stranger. 'But I can beat you.'
>
> 'If you could beat me,' said Capablanca. 'I would know you.'
>
> Anon.

Writing, ideally, is perhaps something to come to late – but not too late. There is nothing sadder than to see a young writer become the victim of the sort of reviews that inflict lethal damage to the ego without offering a scrap of advice as to technique.

Schopenhauer believed there were ten great fallacies to which all human beings were subject – one of these being 'that the insane are very unhappy'. Here are four reviews of a type sometimes found in the pages of the critical papers and magazines:

> Until I read this I thought Dickens was dead!

> O Milton! Thou should be living at this hour!

> Dare one speculate, ask, hope, believe, that the ghost of Jane Austen, beloved of so many of our Hampstead, Highgate, Islington and Arts Council literati, has come to life once more in these quiet but tellingly acerbically observed pages?

> I was sitting in Maurice's, that's *the* Maurice's, of course, with a glass of Nouvelle Beaujolais and THAT book of poems (*Licking Pavlov's Dogs*!!) in front of me, daring myself to open it. Suddenly, at a nearby table, I noticed Vespasian Tosser, his Pegasus Trainers carefully unlaced, his still yet unravished review copies laying beside his glass of absinthe. I watched through narrowed eyes as he rolled a rather, to me, sloppy joint, and then lit it and casually gazed around. He saw me, immediately grasped what I was about to essay, and threw up his hands in ecstasy as he pointed at the poems. Then he blew me a kiss! Me! Noticed by Vespasian Tosser! I can only say one word – 'Gobsmacked'!!!

Reviews like these are referred to by Graham Greene as a 'dead hand' on a writer's shoulder. Greene also invites the casual reader to wonder what words the critics who write such reviews would have left 'if ever they came to discuss literature'.

Writing is a trade – and the only way to learn a trade is to serve an apprenticeship. Progress should be slow, at the pace the writer desires, and should be dictated by intuition and growing ability rather than by a financial prompt book held by an agent or reviewer.

At twenty-one, if you write that 'classic' best-selling novel about university life, then you will be expected, shortly afterwards, to write a sequel. You will be reduced to writing the novel about writing the first novel; a rushed and stretched effort that will gain only 'lukewarm' reviews. You will then be faced with the impossible task of writing a third work to redeem your reputation. You may not have a famous father, or strong Oxbridge connections, and at this stage you will vanish from sight. Filleted by fame.

Henry Wotton (1568–1639) wrote:

> Who envies none whom chance doth raise,
> Or vice; who never understood
> How deepest wounds are given by praise;
> Nor rules of state, but rules of good.

Far better you work away at what you want to say, until you reach the level of technique which allows you to express yourself in the way that suits you. If what you write has any worth, it may lie submerged for a time, but will eventually surface when the present *wankfest* has passed.

In writing there are no categorically right answers, as there are to simple mathematical questions. Your writing may go to a buyer who may judge it subjectively, and who will usually be a slave to market trends. That is, what you write may go to someone who may not like what you say because it conflicts with already ingrained views morally, or as to what the market is seeking at that time.

You will come up against this, and more. But go on. Do not be afraid. Do not lose your sense of humour. There are no producers buried in Westminster Abbey or Pére Lachaise. No statues anywhere on Earth to publishers' readers.

And it's never too late to start. Hugo wrote *Les Misérables* when he was sixty. There is no retirement age for writers. The more experience, the better the writing.

And if you believe you have an individual voice – develop it. Don't get side-tracked.

'Satrapy'

What a misfortune for you who are made
For beautiful and great accomplishments
This unfair destiny of yours should always
Deny you still encouragement and success;
That vulgar habits should ever hinder you,
Meanness prevent you, and indifferences.
And how dreadful the day when you surrender
(The day you let yourself go and you surrender),
And you go off wayfaring to Susa,
You go to the great King Artaxerxes,
Who very kindly puts you in his court,
Offers you satrapies and the rest of it.
And you accept them with despair,
The very things which you don't want at all.
Your soul seeks other things, and cries for them;
The praises of the crowd and of the Sophists,
The difficult and inestimable applause,
The Assembly, and the Theatre, and the Crowns.
How will you get all this from Artaxerxes?
How will you find these things in your satrapy?
What will your life be like without all these?

C. P. Cavafy
Trans. John Mavrogordato

Switch on your computer. Now is the time.

Select bibliography

Auden, W. H., *The English Auden* (Faber, 1977).

Bailey, Leslie, *Scrapbook for the Twenties* (Frederick Muller Limited, 1959).

Barrie, J. M., *The Admirable Crichton* (Hodder & Stoughton, 1939).

Bent, Silas, *Ballyhoo* (Boni & Liveright, 1927).

Black, Peter, *The Biggest Aspidistra in the World* (BBC, 1972).

Blake, William, *William Blake* (The Penguin Poets, Penguin Books, 1958).

Brecht, Bertolt, *Poems* (Suhrkamp, Frankfurt am Main, 1976).

Bridson, D. G., *Prospero and Ariel* (Gollancz, 1971).

Briggs, A., *The History of Broadcasting in the United Kingdom*, Vol. 1 (Oxford University Press, 1941).

Brooks, Collin, *Tavern Talk* (James Barrie, 1950).

Brough, J. (trans.), *Poems from the Sanskrit* (Penguin Classics, 1977).

Brown, Hilton (ed.), *Late Night Specials.* Short stories broadcast by the BBC (Vallancey Press, 1946).

—— (ed.) *Twice Told Tales.* Short stories Broadcast by the BBC (Vallancey Press, 1946).

Cain, John, *Seventy Years of Broadcasting* (BBC, 1992).

Cavafy, C. P., *Poems* (trans. John Mavrogordato) (Hogarth Press, 1971).

Charnley, Mitchell V., *News by Radio* (Macmillan Company, 1948).

Coleridge, Samuel Taylor, *The Poems of Samuel Taylor Coleridge* (Oxford University Press, 1961).

Conan Doyle, A., *Complete Sherlock Holmes* (Chancellor Press, 1985).

Crisell, Andrew, *Understanding Radio* (Methuen, 1986).

Curran, J. and Seaton, J., *Power Without Responsibility* (4th edn, Routledge, 1991).

Dickens, C., *David Copperfield* (Waverley Press, n.d.).

Dyer, Gillian, *Advertising as Communication* (Routledge, 1990).

Eckersley, P. P., *The Power Behind the Microphone* (Jonathan Cape, 1941).

Eliot, T. S., *Selected Prose* (ed. John Hayward) (Penguin, in association with Faber & Faber, 1953).

Fest, Joachim C., *The Face of the Third Reich* (trans. Michael Bullock) (Penguin, 1972).

Fiedler, L. A., *Waiting for the End* (Pelican Books, 1964).

Fielding, H. (ed. Richard W. Bevis), *The Historical Register for the Year 1736* (J. Roberts, 1737; Oxford University Press, 1970).

—— *Pasquin* (*Works*, ed. George Saintsbury) (J. M. Dent & Co., 1893).

Ford, Ford Madox, *Memories and Impressions* (The Bodley Head, 1971).

Fulop-Miller, Rene, *Leaders, Dreamers, and Rebels* (trans. Eden and Cedar Paul) (George Harrap & Co., Ltd, 1935).

Gay, John, Pope, Alexander and Arbuthnot, John, *Three Hours After Marriage* (Bernard Lintot, 1717).

Gielgud, Val, *The Right Way to Radio Playwriting* (Right Way Books, Andrew George Elliot, n.d.).

—— *British Radio Drama 1922–1956* (Harrap, 1957).

Gilliam, L. (ed.) *BBC Features* (Evans Brothers Limited, by arrangement with the BBC, 1950).

Goldsmith, O., *The Citizen of the World* (Taylor & Hessey, 1809).
Gorky, M. (trans. Ivy Litvinov), *Literary Portraits* (Foreign Languages Publishing House, n.d.).
Graham, A. C. (trans.), *Poems of the Late T'ang* (Penguin Classics, Penguin Books, 1965).
Grant, Michael, *Nero* (Weidenfeld & Nicolson, 1970; Corgi Books, 1973).
Greene, Graham, *Lord Rochester's Monkey* (Futura Publications, Ltd, 1976).
—— *Collected Essays* (Penguin, 1978).
Hyde, F. A. and Fifth, W. G. S., 'Wireless and Sich-Like' in *Seven Modern Plays* (Thomas Nelson & Sons Ltd, 1935).
Hope, A. L., 'My Muse Relentless', reprinted from *Sisterfire*, ed. Charlotte Watson Sherman, published in Great Britain by (The Women's Press, 1995).
Hume, David, *A Treatise of Human Nature* (2 Vols, Everyman, Dent, 1951).
Inman, Philip, *Oil and Wine* (Chapman & Hall, 1935).
Jim, 'Uncle', 'A Wireless "Leg-Pull"' in *Hello Boys! The Wireless Uncles' Annual* (Cecil Palmer, 1924).
Johnstone, Charles, *Chrysal or The Adventures of a Guinea* (London, 1760–65).
Keats, J., *The Poems of John Keats* (J. M. Dent & Sons, 1913).
Knox, Collie, *'Collie Knox Calling'* (Chapman & Hall, 1937).
Kobal, J., *People Will Talk* (Aurum Press, 1986).
Lewis, Peter, *Radio Drama* (Longman, 1981).
Locke, John, *An Essay Concerning Human Understanding* (2 Vols, Everyman, Dent, 1961).
MacDonald, Angus, *The Sinking of the 'City of Cairo'* (Original Mss, n.d.).
McLuhan, Marshall, *Understanding Media* (Sphere Books, 1969).
Moorehead, Alan, *Cooper's Creek* (Hamish Hamilton, 1963).
Ogilvie, Vivian, *Our Times* (Batsford, 1953).
Orwell, G., *Charles Dickens* (Copyright George Orwell, 1940).
—— *Nineteen Eighty-Four* (Copyright George Orwell, 1949).
—— 'Poetry and the Microphone' (Copyright George Orwell, 1943). Reproduced by permission of A. M. Heath & Co. Ltd on behalf of Bill Hamilton as the literary executor of the Estate of the Late Sonia Brownell Orwell and Martin Secker & Warburg Ltd.
Pearson, Hesketh, *The Life of Oscar Wilde* (Penguin Biography, 1960).
Quennell, Peter, *Byron* (Book Club Associates, by arrangement with William Collins Sons & Co., Ltd, 1974).
Radio Advertising Bureau, The, *The Radio Advertising Hall of Fame* (The Radio Advertising Bureau, London, 2000).
Reed, L., *The Complete Limerick Book* (Jarrolds, 1924).
Robinson, John, *Learning Over the Air* (BBC, 1982).
Salmon, C., 'Broadcasting, Speech and Writing', in *The Mint* (ed. Geoffrey Grigson) (Routledge and Sons Ltd, 1946).
Scannell, P. and Cardiff, D., *A Social History of British Broadcasting*: Volume I, *1922–1939* (Basil Blackwell, 1991).
Schopenhauer, A., *Essays and Aphorisms* (trans. R. J. Hollingdale) (Penguin Classics, 1970).
Scupham, J., *Broadcasting and the Community* (C. A. Watts & Co., 1967).
Shadwell, T., The Virtuoso in *Collected Plays*, ed. George Saintsbury (Printed by T. N. for Henry Herringman, 1676).
Smollet, Tobias, *The History and Adventures of an Atom* (London, 1769).
Snow, C. P., *The Realists* (Macmillan, 1978).
Swift, Jonathan, *A Modest Proposal* (*The Portable Swift*, ed. Carl Van Doren) (Viking Press, 1948).

Swinburne, C. A., *Swinburne* (The Penguin Poets, Penguin Books, 1961).
Talbot, Ethel, *Listening-In* (Thomas Nelson & Sons, Ltd, n.d.).
Tanner, Louise, *All the Things We Were* (Doubleday & Company, Inc. 1968).
Tolstoy, Leo, *War and Peace* (trans. Louise and Aylmer Maude) (Oxford University Press, 1941).
Turner, E. S., *The Shocking History of Advertising* (Ballantine Books, 1953).
Uhland, Ludwig, *Works* (ed. Hermann Fischer) (Wissenschaftlichte Buchgesellschaft, 1977).
Various of the BBC Aunties, *Hullo Girls! The Wireless Aunties' Annual* (Cecil Palmer, 1924).
Webb, G., *The Inside Story of Dick Barton* (Convoy Publications, 1950).
Wilmot, John, *The Complete Poems* (ed. David M. Vieth) (Yale University Press, 1968).
Wilson, Edmund, *The Wound and the Bow* (University Paperbacks, Methuen, 1961).

Index